Philippe Legrain is chief econom̶ ̶ ̶ ̶ ̶ ̶ ̶ ̶ ̶ ̶
previously special adviser to the d̶i̶r̶e̶c̶t̶o̶r̶ ̶g̶
Trade Organisation, Mike Moore. Before that, he was t̶r̶a̶d̶e̶ ̶a̶n̶d̶
economics correspondent for *The Economist*. He has also written
for the *Financial Times*, the *Wall Street Journal Europe*, the *Guardian*,
the *Independent*, *Prospect*, *Foreign Policy*, *New Statesman*, the *Ecologist*
and other publications. He has a first-class honours degree in
economics and a masters in politics of the world economy, both
from the London School of Economics. Philippe is 29 and lives in
London.

www.philippelegrain.com

'In this wonderfully lucid and intelligent book, Philippe Legrain
takes on the many mistakes of the anti-globalisers. Globalisation,
he argues, is neither a label for Americanisation, nor an excuse
for worldwide corporate domination. It does not eliminate local
cultures. Still less does it make governments irrelevant. It
is a chance for mutual enrichment, not a route to global
impoverishment'

Martin Wolf

'One of those rare books that grabs the conventional wisdom
and turns it on its head. With brio and verve, and the unique
insight of the insider, Philippe Legrain examines the bogeyman
of globalisation close up – and decides the scaremongers have
got it wrong. The result is an accessible, passionately argued case
for the defence: anyone who cares about our world and its future
should read it'

Jonathan Freedland,
author of *Bring Home the Revolution*

OPEN WORLD:
The Truth About Globalisation

Philippe Legrain

[handwritten signature] — 2007

ABACUS

An *Abacus* Book

First published in Great Britain by Abacus in 2002
Reprinted 2002
This edition published in 2003

A CIP catalogue record for this book is
available from the British Library.

ISBN 0 349 11529 X

Typeset in Swift by M Rules
Printed and bound in Great Britain by
Clays Ltd, St Ives plc

Abacus
An Imprint of
Time Warner Books UK
Brettenham House
Lancaster Place
London WC2E 7EN

www.TimeWarnerBooks.co.uk

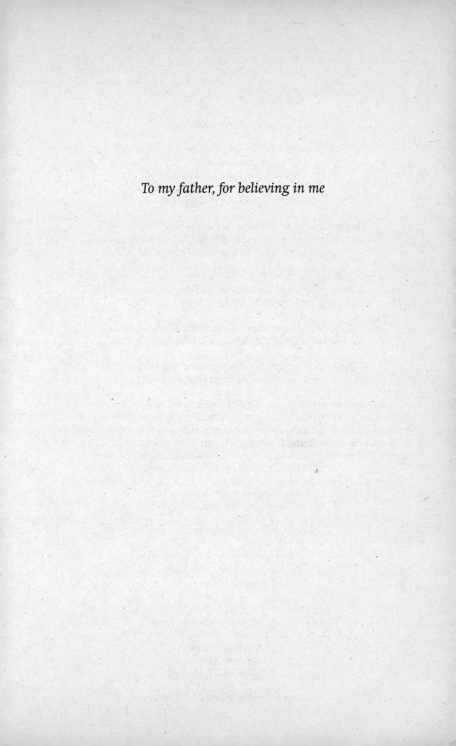

To my father, for believing in me

Contents

Acknowledgements

It is impossible to name everyone who helped me in some way with *Open World*, so I shall mention only a few. Many people encouraged me to write a book, Jeremy Haneman, in particular. But Jonathan Freedland deserves special thanks: his advice finally convinced me to try. He also introduced me to Jonny Geller, his (and now my) agent, who helped make my idea a reality. His assistance has been invaluable, as was that of Doug Kean, his assistant at Curtis Brown. I also have to thank Tim Whiting, my editor at Abacus, for taking a gamble on a first-time author and for all his help since then.

I owe a huge debt to Simon Long, who was kind enough to read through the manuscript and suggest some very welcome improvements. He was also a great editor when I worked at *The Economist*. Unfortunately, he's also a Tottenham fan, but then nobody's perfect.

I did nearly all the research for this book myself. But Jo Malvisi was also a life-saver. Thanks, too to all those who helped with my round-the-world research trip. Martin Wolf, for providing me with so many useful contacts, and for all the stimulating conversations we have had. Andreas Kluth and Dominic Ziegler, who helped me in Hong Kong. Carmen and Sydney Lock for their kind hospitality. Soogil Young in Seoul for providing me with many good contacts. Ken Janssens in New York. Carlos Salas Porras and his wife Maruca for helping me in Ciudad Juárez. Gideon Lichfield for doing the same in Mexico City (as well as for being such a good friend). Joseph Mutti, for helping me discover the real Cuba. Peter Collins, for his invaluable assistance in Brazil. I also want to thank Chris Helzer and Bette Kovach for going beyond the call of duty to help me.

So many people have helped me out in journalism. Anthony Robinson and Andrew Gowers gave me a break at the *Financial Times*. Alan Riding of the *New York Times* has always been there to provide advice. I have countless people to thank at *The Economist*, where I spent some of the happiest years of my life. Thanks, among many others, to Edward Lucas for recommending me, Bill Emmott for taking a chance by hiring me, Clive Crook for inspiring me, Pam Woodall for supporting me, John Peet for putting up with me, and Richard Cookson, Iain Carson and Tim Laxton for being good mates. Thanks too to David Goodhart at *Prospect*. At the WTO, Mike Moore tolerated my faults and spurred me on to greater things.

Finally, I want to thank my friends and family. Lots of love to my mum and dad, and my brother and sister. Special thanks to Peter and Marion Doyle for their love and support, but also to, among others, Adham Nicola, Allison Gallienne, Chris Foges, Colin Iles, Dusch Atkinson, Harry Rich, Hugo Macgregor, Linda Pearson, Martyn Fitzgerald and Paul Bates.

OPEN WORLD

Free to Choose

What kind of globalisation do we want?

Beijing, 12 July 2001. Fireworks light up the skies. Crowds of revellers pile into Tiananmen Square to celebrate the news from Moscow. Students dance the conga; old men whoop with joy. 'We've Won' flashes in big red characters on Chinese state television. Chen Wena, a national volleyball player, captures the mood of patriotic joy. 'It's our turn,' she says. 'This is our time.'

Awarding the 2008 Olympics to Beijing was richly symbolic. In 1993, when the Chinese capital lost out by two votes to Sydney in the contest to hold the 2000 Games, the country's ageing Communist leaders and the public at large were deeply upset. Many Chinese felt they had been slapped in the face by the Western world. But now, as the Communist Party prepared to celebrate its eightieth anniversary, China's pride was assuaged. Here, finally, was recognition of how far China had come.

Many people outside China cheered the Olympic decision too. The Games are now big business. Its corporate sponsors, which include Coca-Cola, Visa, McDonald's and Kodak, are licking their lips at the prospect of pitching their wares to 1,300 million Chinese consumers. Even in Taiwan, which China considers a renegade province and periodically threatens to recapture by force, many were pleased. Beijing is thought to be less likely to behave aggressively towards Taiwan while it is trying to curry favour with international opinion in the run-up to the Games.

Some optimists go further. They see the Olympics as an important part of encouraging political reform in China. The hope is that Beijing may become more tolerant of diversity and dissent, and more open to demands for greater democracy, religious freedom and autonomy for Tibet. But others strongly disagree. Many human-rights campaigners are fuming. 'This will put the stamp of international approval for Beijing's human-rights abuses and will encourage China to escalate its repression,' said Kalon T. C. Tethong, a spokesman for the Tibetan government in exile.

What globalisation is

All this fuss over a sporting event is a microcosm of a much broader debate about the defining issue of our time: globalisation. This ugly word is shorthand for how our lives are becoming increasingly intertwined with those of distant people and places around the world – economically, politically and culturally. These links are not always new, but they are more pervasive than ever before.

Globalisation is all-embracing, and yet profoundly misunderstood – two reasons why so many people fear it. Is globalisation eroding our identity, national or otherwise? Are global brands colonising the world economy (and our minds)? Are we losing control of our lives to heartless mega-corporations and faceless markets? Many people think so – and there is an element of truth to all these worries. But for the most part, the answer, as we shall see, is a reassuring no.

The ties that bind us together are first the economic ones of trade, investment and migration. As goods, money and people move around the world, they bring far-off places closer together.

We drive German cars, listen to Japanese hi-fis, eat French food, drink Colombian coffee, wear Italian clothes, buy Chinese toys, chat on Finnish mobile phones, work on computers made in Taiwan and use American software. Americans work for German car companies, Germans for US investment banks, Britons for South Korean electronics firms. Mexican hands pick Californian fruit, Asian brains power Silicon Valley start-ups, Pakistanis tend British pharmacies, Algerians run French groceries. International businessmen, bankers, consultants and lawyers criss-cross the globe, tying our jobs and pensions to far-flung markets through a web of exports and investments.

The links are also political: the unique experiment in governments working together that is the European Union (EU); the binding together of Canada, the United States and Mexico, their poor southern neighbour, through the North American Free-Trade Agreement (NAFTA); the growing framework of international rules on trade, the environment, human rights, war and much else; and the swelling ranks of cross-border pressure groups that are fomenting the beginning of a global politics – newish campaign groups like Friends of the Earth and Amnesty International, as well as long-established bodies like the Catholic Church and the international labour movement. US soldiers patrol Kosovo, the US navy protects the Taiwan Straits, US planes fly over the Persian Gulf. UN peacekeepers are dotted around the globe. The Irish Republican Army (IRA) trains Colombian terrorists; Spain tried to extradite Augusto Pinochet, Chile's former dictator, from Britain for human-rights abuses.

Last, but not least, come the cultural ties: the mixing of cultures through migration; the rapid spread of news, ideas and fashions through trade, travel and the media; and the growth of global brands – Coca-Cola, McDonald's, Disney – that serve as common reference points. Whites are no longer a majority in California. By 2050, a third of Americans are set to have Asian or Hispanic roots. Islam is the second most popular religion in France: one in thirteen Frenchmen worship Allah. Robin Cook, the then foreign secretary, famously declared that Britain's national dish was chicken tikka masala. Many of us have foreign colleagues, as well as foreign friends from school, university or holidays. We chat on the Internet to 'buddies' who might be on the other side of the world, or across the street. Westerners snort Colombian cocaine, suffer from diseases of African origin like Aids, fret about Islamic terrorists and worry about global warming. At the same time, American films, music, food and clothes spread with no respect for national borders. Western ideas about human rights permeate traditional societies in the Third World. Virtually all countries compete in the Olympic Games and most in football's World Cup.

A hundred years ago, football was a British working-class pursuit. Even twenty years ago, it was still a predominantly European and South American working-class sport. Now it's a huge global business. David Beckham is a global brand. Japan and South Korea played host to the 2002 World Cup. Arsenal is managed by a Frenchman; its squad at the time of writing includes six Frenchmen, two Dutchmen, two Brazilians, a Swede, a Dane, a Ukrainian, a Latvian, a Greek, a Nigerian, a Cameroonian, a Congolese and a Japanese player. Thai schoolboys sporting Liverpool tops (Steven Gerrard is a local favourite) play the beautiful game around Wat Saket, Bangkok's Temple of the Golden Mount. Such cultural mixing is of the essence of twenty-first-century globalisation.

All this globalisation is driven partly by cheaper, easier and faster transport and communications: airplanes, radio, television, telephones, the Internet (and before that railways, steamships and the telegraph). In 1850 it took nearly a year to sail – or send a message – around the world. Now, you can fly around the globe in a day or so and send an email anywhere almost instantly. Sending a forty-page document from Chile to Kenya costs $50 by courier, $10 by fax and less than 10 cents by email.[1] Until recently, foreign holidays were a preserve of the rich; now the poor in rich countries expect them. A telephone was once a luxury; now Internet cafés have sprung up in Third World shanty towns.

Yet globalisation involves more than technological change. It is also a political choice. It involves consciously opening national borders to foreign influences. The explosion in cross-border links is as much a result of government decisions to remove restrictions on trade, foreign investment and capital flows as it is of better transport and communications. Where governments choose to impede it, international traffic is stunted. In the first decade of the twentieth century, America welcomed as many as a million and a half immigrants a year. In the final decade, with both the world's and America's population several times what they were then, half as many foreigners a year were allowed in to the US – and most countries have much tighter immigration controls. After the First World War and then the Great Depression convinced them to turn inwards, governments put a stop to the first great wave of globalisation that had begun in the nineteenth century. Imports to America, which had bought nearly two-fifths of the world's exports in 1929, fell by 70 per cent between 1929 and 1932. International lending fell by over 90 per cent between 1927 and 1933.

If governments wanted to, they could put globalisation into reverse again. So when people like Thomas Friedman, a journalist for the *New York Times* and author of *The Lexus and the Olive Tree*, tell you 'globalisation isn't a choice. It's a reality,' they are very much mistaken. We have opened our borders to international trade over the past fifty years; we can close them again. The Internet cannot be uninvented, but access to foreign websites can be restricted – just ask the Chinese government. For all the talk about the technological inevitability of globalisation, North Korea is doing a good job at shutting itself off from the rest of the world.

The limits of globalisation

Globalisation is blurring the borders between nation states. Yet it is neither uniform nor universal. Talk of a 'borderless world' or the 'end of the nation state', the titles of two books by Kenichi

Ohmae, a Japanese management guru, is nonsense. Some parts of the economy (most manufacturing) are more open than others (steel, clothing, farming and many services). Some economies are more international than others: Britain's is over twice as open as America's, but three and a half times less open than Ireland's.[2] Few countries are genuinely global traders: most trade primarily with a handful of others, typically their regional neighbours. All EU countries do over half their trade with other EU members. Even though the world economy is more globalised than ever, it is not as globalised at it seems, as we will discuss in chapter three.

Three-quarters of what Britons buy in the shops is made domestically; nine-tenths is from within the EU. Most people in Britain work for British companies: the biggest employer by far is the quintessentially British National Health Service. Most pension-fund money is invested in Britain. The same is true in other European countries. Although many decisions about our future are now taken at a European and some at a global level, most of the big ones are still taken nationally. Finance ministers like Britain's Gordon Brown or Germany's Hans Eichel still set their respective budgets (although the European Commission tries to meddle); governments still decide how much to spend on schools, hospitals, transport and so on; pensions, unemployment benefits and welfare spending in general are all still set at a national level. Moreover, most Britons have mainly British friends, live within ten miles of where they were born, and are obsessed by *Big Brother*, *Pop Idol*, *EastEnders*, Posh and Becks, and Premiership football – all reassuringly (or depressingly) parochial.

A similar story can be told of the US. Nearly nine-tenths of what Americans consume is produced within the fifty states. Nearly nine in ten Americans work for US companies. Their savings are mainly invested on Wall Street. The US government is free to cut taxes, trim welfare or spend more on schools. Only one in ten Americans has a passport. Notwithstanding the so-called 'World Series', Americans' sporting obsessions – American football, baseball and basketball – are primarily domestic, as is their taste in TV and movies. Television news is overwhelmingly about America or Americans abroad (in Afghanistan, for instance), as indeed are quality newspapers like the *Washington Post*. American TV is overwhelmingly produced at home; few foreign films break Hollywood's stranglehold.

If anyone tells you geography doesn't matter anymore, just think how different your life would be had you been born in an African village. Or consider how Chinese immigrants in the US lead different lives to those of their comrades in China. Whereas a majority of Americans use the Internet, half the world has never made a phone call.

More importantly, we will never live in a truly global world, where geography and local culture do not matter. Globalisation is a process, not a destination. For a start, people are sedentary. Moving about will always take time and money. Most of what we consume cannot be traded. Since many services have to be provided on the spot, much of the economy is set to remain local: nurses, nannies, hairdressers, gardeners, shop assistants, fitness instructors, cleaners and therapists cannot ply their trade from the other side of the globe. These services are the fastest-growing area of rich-country economies.

National borders are not about to disappear. Even if the remaining trade barriers are abolished, differences in accounting, tax and regulatory standards will still form more subtle barriers. Despite NAFTA, neighbouring US states trade twelve times more with each other than they do with a neighbouring Canadian one. Language, custom and culture also set countries apart. Most risks we face are still local too: however worried we might feel about dying at the hands of Osama Bin Laden, we are far more likely to be hit by a car while crossing the road. Even more importantly, democracy remains rooted in local communities and nation states – as does our identity. As long as that stays true, nation states – and the borders that they imply – are not going to disappear.

What globalisation is not

Globalisation is not shorthand for the way the world is today, let alone everything you dislike about it. Yet it has become a convenient scapegoat for all manner of real and perceived ills that have little or nothing to do with it. For instance, globalisation cannot possibly be to blame for the wretched poverty of many African subsistence farmers. They don't trade, so they can't be harmed by it. Nor is globalisation responsible for every perceived vice of capitalism. John Kay, a British business writer, summed it up perfectly: 'Once, privatisation was used as an umbrella term by opponents of market-oriented reforms. Today, globalisation has a similar interpretation. Globalisation is things that people hostile to the modern market economy dislike.'[3]

Globalisation is not the same thing as privatisation and deregulation. They can be mutually reinforcing, but they need not go together. Deregulation or privatisation need not imply globalisation. For instance, America deregulated its airline market in 1978. US airlines are free to set their fares competitively; they can decide whether or not to ply routes; new companies can enter the market. Yet foreign companies are still not allowed to buy American carriers or fly American domestic routes. The US airline industry has been deregulated, but not opened up to international competition. Or consider Europe. British Airways, Air France and Germany's Lufthansa have all been privatised, but do not face American competition on routes within Europe. Conversely, globalisation need not imply deregulation or privatisation. American drugs companies, such as Merck or Pfizer, face vigorous competition from foreign pharmaceuticals companies such as Britain's GlaxoSmithKline or Switzerland's Novartis, yet the American market remains tightly regulated by the Food and Drug Administration (FDA). Britain's Post Office, now ridiculously rebranded as Consignia, faces competition from foreign courier companies like Germany's DHL and America's Federal Express, but is still state-owned.

Clearly, privatisation can encourage globalisation if a foreign firm takes over a domestic one, as can deregulation if it allows in foreign competition. Clearly too, if a government wants to increase competition, it may have to deregulate as well as lower its trade barriers. Also, if you believe in free markets, you are likely to support both, although not necessarily: intelligent free-marketeers realise that markets can fail and regulation is sometimes needed. Globalisation is not the same as, and need not imply, an end to state intervention.

Many writers seem unclear about what globalisation is. In *The Lexus and the Olive Tree*,[4] Thomas Friedman argues that globalisation is a 'system' that replaced the 'Cold War system'. He thinks it began around 1989. He is right that the end of the Cold War has transformed international politics and that the death of the Soviet Union helped to discredit government intervention – and hence encouraged globalisation – in the 1990s. But he is wrong to describe globalisation as a 'system' that began in 1989. Much of the world economy was already quite closely integrated through trade and finance before 1989. There has not been a step change since then. The rolling back of government began in the early 1980s with Deng Xiaoping in China, Margaret Thatcher in Britain and Ronald Reagan in America. Economically, the 1980s and 1990s have far more in common than Friedman claims. Similarly, the spread of American culture precedes 1989. Hollywood, Coca-Cola, Levi jeans and Big Macs had long colonised commercial culture. To talk of 1989 as the beginning of globalisation is very misleading. Moreover, globalisation is not a 'system': it is a process of integration and internationalisation, one that was happening during the Cold War and has continued since. If the Cold War system dominated international politics from 1945 to 1989, then its successor is American hegemony, not globalisation. America is now the only 'hyperpower'.

Others seem just as confused. Ulrich Beck, a German sociologist, says globalisation denotes 'the *processes* through which sovereign national states are criss-crossed and undermined by transnational actors with varying prospects of power, orientation,

identities and networks'.[5] Ugh. Anthony Giddens, a British sociologist and Third Way guru, uses it as a catchphrase for all manner of
contemporary change: the 'communications revolution', the
'weightless economy', the 'post-1989 world', and even the 'growing
equality between women and men'.[6] And while you're at it, why
not New Labour too?

A force for good

Globalisation has the potential to do immense good. Just look at
the amazing leap in American and European living standards since
the Second World War. Or see how the Japanese went from rags
to riches in a generation. Compare it with the protectionist nightmare of the Great Depression in the 1930s, when the US slammed
the door on the world with the Smoot-Hawley tariff and the
Europeans retaliated with beggar-thy-neighbour policies: such folly
soon made beggars of us all. Study after study confirms it: freer
trade makes us richer. Foreign competition keeps companies on
their toes; new technologies spread faster; countries specialise
in what they do best and buy the rest for less from abroad. Think
how much better American cars have become since the Japanese
muscled in on Motown's monopoly. Marvel at the new opportunities of the American-led revolution in computing and the Internet:
I researched and wrote this book (almost) single-handed on a
Dell laptop linked to the world through a broadband Internet
connection. Ten years ago, I would have struggled to do so alone
and so quickly. Cast your eyes along the shelves at Wal-Mart, Tesco,
Carrefour or Aldi and see how many of the cornucopia of products
that enrich our lives are sourced cheaply from abroad.

Politically, consider what an incredible achievement the EU is.
War in western Europe is unthinkable. Fifteen countries share a
single market; twelve a single currency. For a Londoner, going to
Barcelona for the weekend is almost as easy as going to Brighton.
EU governments strive to work together rather than against each

other. They enhance their power by sharing it, rather than squan-
der it through destructive rivalry. Look east at the bevy of countries
at the gates of the EU. By and large, they are peaceful democracies
with pretty liberal economies. Not bad, for countries that until
recently were Soviet puppet states and many of which were before
that nasty despotisms. Thank the EU, in part: the lure of joining
the European club has helped curb any wayward instincts. Soon
many will be EU members: Poles will travel as freely as the
Portuguese, Estonia's booming high-tech economy will plug into
Europe as Ireland's has, people in western Europe will not need to
fret about war or terror on their eastern doorstep. Europe will be
whole and free: the wounds of communism and the Second World
War will finally heal.

NAFTA too is an impressive project. Mexico and the US had been
at loggerheads for as long as anyone can remember. Not surprisingly, since in 1848 the US forced Mexico to cede it huge swathes of
territory – Texas, California, Arizona, Utah and parts of Colorado,
New Mexico and Wyoming – after defeating it in a war. Until the
1980s, Mexico was a fiercely nationalistic, protectionist country
that shied away from co-operation with the US. They were, as
author and journalist Alan Riding memorably put it, 'distant
neighbours'. Now they are drawing closer together, with NAFTA the
cement that binds them. Mexico is becoming more of a liberal
democracy: seventy-one years of one-party rule ended in 2000.
Trade between them is much freer, and the border, despite
American immigration controls, is blurring. Bilateral bodies have
sprung up to tackle shared problems such as migration, border
control and water shortages, as well as drug trafficking. As Latinos
in the US grow in number and start to flex their political muscle,
the US will be drawn ever closer to Mexico. Here too the scars of
war will finally fade.

For all their failings – and they are many – international bodies
like the UN, the World Bank and the World Trade Organisation
(WTO) also do a lot of good. Years of plodding negotiation at the
WTO (and its predecessor, the General Agreement on Tariffs and

Trade (GATT)) have dismantled many of the barriers that stifled world trade in the 1930s – the average import duty on manufactures has been slashed from over 40 per cent to less than 4 per cent – and built a framework of rules to support it. Our open world rests on this mammoth achievement. The World Bank is a parent that supports countries' development: its long-term loans are the main source of investment for many of the world's poorest countries. The UN's peacekeeping missions, to mention but one of its many roles, are a step forward from what the rapidly ineffectual League of Nations achieved in the inter-war years. International treaties are eliminating ozone-destroying CFCs, have made a start at combating climate change and have limited the spread of chemical weapons, among other things. These examples, however flawed, of governments working together are still better than going it alone or turning one's back on the world.

Culturally too, globalisation enriches our lives. I have to declare a bias: I am a hybrid, born and bred in Britain, of a French father and an Estonian-American mother. I speak English, French, Spanish and a smattering of Estonian, Portuguese and Russian. But my home is London, I root for Arsenal and England in football, and I'm immensely proud to be British. Confused? Perhaps. But, *pace* Norman Tebbit, certainly much the richer for it. As, indeed, is anyone who can take holidays in Spain or Florida, have sushi or spaghetti for dinner, drink Coke or Chilean wine, watch a Hollywood blockbuster or an Almodovar, listen to bhangra or rap, practise yoga or kick-boxing, read *Vanity Fair* or *The Economist*, have friends from around the world. Remember: we could not always enjoy the best the world has to offer.

These benefits of globalisation are not just for the rich. Poor countries have everything to gain too. Just look at China. Once, it was the richest and most scientifically advanced country in the world. It developed gunpowder and the printing press long before Europe did. But its imperial rulers stamped on change and closed the country off from the rest of the world. (In 1867 Grand Secretary Wo Jen, a top imperial bureaucrat, sent a memo to the emperor warning against setting up a college to teach astronomy and mathematics that would 'make the people proselytes of foreignism' and result 'in the collapse of uprightedness and the spread of wickedness'.) By the nineteenth century, China was so weak and backward that it humiliatingly had to concede trading posts to Europe's colonial powers. An Englishman 'assisted' in administering Chinese customs revenue. In practice, he was the master of the Chinese economy.

China eventually sought salvation from the Communist Party. In the three decades after they took full control in 1949, Chairman Mao and his cronies tried to catch up with the West by pursuing socialism along national lines. But their Great Leap Forward (and other follies) led to a dead-end. Rather than catching up with the West, China fell behind its neighbours – Japan, South Korea, Taiwan, Singapore and Hong Kong – that had chosen to develop in a very different way: by exporting to the West. So, soon after Mao died in 1976, China changed tack. His successor, Deng Xiaoping, sought to ape East Asia's export-led success.

The transformation of China since 1978 is nothing short of astounding. Skyscrapers have sprouted from rice paddies. Teenagers worship Madonna, not Mao. Supermarkets are stocked full of foreign consumer goods. China's urban population has doubled in twenty years as peasants flock to work in new bustling cities. The economy has grown in leaps and bounds: by an average of over 10 per cent a year in the 1980s and 1990s. In just twenty years, China's economy has grown eight times bigger. The average Chinese – over one in five of the world's population – has become six times richer. Between 1990 and 1998, the number of Chinese living on less than a dollar a day fell by 150 million. That is the fastest fall in poverty the world has ever seen.

The source of this success is not a secret. China has grown richer by freeing its economy and opening up to the rest of the world. It has embraced international trade and foreign investment. The value of its exports has climbed on average by 15 per cent a year for twenty years, while imports have grown by an annual 13 per cent.

In 1970, China's combined exports and imports were equivalent to 4 per cent of its national income. That had risen to 50 per cent by 2000. China's share of world trade has almost sextupled from 0.6 per cent in 1977 to 3.5 per cent in 2000. At least one-third of the suitcases and handbags sold elsewhere in the world are Chinese-made, along with a quarter of the world's toys and one-eighth of the world's footwear and clothing. To crown its success, China joined the WTO on 1 January 2002, thereby committing itself to open up more and giving it a say in writing world-trade rules.

China's achievements – and those of Japan, South Korea, Taiwan and other Asian tiger economies – are an example to the rest of the developing world, where billions of people are scrambling to build a better future. Freer markets and infusions of foreign investment and technology, combined with forward-looking government policies, can work their magic elsewhere too. India's one billion people could yet emulate China's success. We all have a stake in their future. Not only because we are all human, but also because if the poor get richer, we in the rich countries will gain new markets for our products. But if the poor stay poor, we must not only live with our consciences but also in fear of the hatred that envy and despair breed.

Fears and misconceptions

The benefits of globalisation are clear. It makes countries richer and individuals freer. But what about its downsides?

Genoa, 20 July 2001. The leaders of the Group of Eight (G8) rich countries (and Russia) gather behind a wall of steel. Beyond the pale, a mob runs riot. Tens of thousands of demonstrators fight running battles with 20,000 armed police. The protesters hurl cobblestones and Molotov cocktails. The police respond with water cannon, teargas and clubs. And, fatally, with bullets. A twenty-year-old Italian policeman is trapped in his jeep, under assault from masked assailants. One of them, aged twenty-three, also Italian, is about to throw a heavy fire-extinguisher at him. The terrified cop shoots and kills the protester. The anti-globalisation movement has its first martyr: Carlo Giuliani.

The global protest movement first hit the big time in Seattle. It was November 1999 and the governments that make up the WTO were meeting to try to launch a new push to free world trade. There to report on the event for *The Economist*, I was steeling myself for many tedious hours of hanging round the official conference centre. But I ended up spending most of my time in the streets. They were full of American college kids sporting Japanese cameras and Nike shoes railing against the iniquities of global trade. Beefy truckers from the notorious Teamsters union marched arm-in-arm with environmentalists in turtle outfits. Soon, though, turtles were replaced by teargas as the peaceful protesters in colourful costumes gave way to rioters masked in black handkerchiefs. The debate about globalisation had sprung to life.

Opposition to globalisation is a rallying cry for protesters with all sorts of complaints who demonstrate at every big international meeting: not just Seattle and Genoa, but also Washington DC, Prague, Davos, Quebec City, Gothenburg, May Day in London. Until September 11th, that is. The protests have abated for a while, but the sentiments and arguments that lie behind them have not. Opposition is sure to resurface.

The anti-globalisation movement is led by an unlikely alliance of media-savvy pressure groups and old-fashioned protectionists. Greens make common cause with smokestack industries, consumer activists with trade unions, development lobbyists with rich-country farmers. These 'globaphobes' have all sorts of gripes, many of them contradictory and wrong-headed. Some on the right bemoan the erosion of national sovereignty; many on the left warn against America's negative influence in the Third World. More broadly, globalisation is the focus of popular fears about the might of big business, the pace of economic change and a sense of powerlessness in the face of intangible global forces.

Ralph Nader voiced those fears when he ran for US president in 2000, as did Pat Buchanan when running for the Republican nomination. Naomi Klein captured them in her bestseller, *No Logo*.

The protesters themselves are nothing much to worry about. There has always been – and doubtless always will be – a small minority that is inveterately hostile to capitalism. The discrediting of communism quelled their voices for a while in the early 1990s, but they soon found something else to grumble about: globalisation. So what? Ralph Nader got 3 per cent of the vote. Extreme-left parties in Europe are noxious, but hardly threaten to sweep to power. Equally, some people will always oppose anything that disrupts the settled order. Yet Pat Buchanan and Jean-Marie Le Pen – despite his French election success in 2002 – are isolated bigots. Let them foam at the mouth; just be careful not to pet them.

The real worry is that the overwhelming majority of people who have mixed feelings about capitalism – who enjoy the trappings of material comfort but fret that they or their children might soon lose them – will turn against globalisation. This book is mainly addressed to the millions of people who make up this silent majority. With luck, supporters of globalisation will read it – and hopefully enjoy it – too. But preaching to the converted does little to turn the tide of the argument. It is absolutely essential that the lies and misperceptions about globalisation that are fast becoming conventional wisdom be confronted before it is too late.

Perhaps the most potent – and most pernicious – of the protesters' claims is that companies are now in control. Their brands, it is said, are taking over our public spaces and our minds. Their financial muscle bends our elected representatives to their will. Their freedom to shift factories from one country to another disempowers workers and governments. Their power to frame global rules, notably through the WTO, entrenches their dominance. The upshot is that many workers in America and Europe lose their jobs and the rest have to settle for deadbeat 'McJobs' with lower wages and greater insecurity. Production shifts to the Third World where workers toil in appalling conditions for a pittance to make Nike shoes or Barbie dolls that, thanks to their branding, sell for huge mark-ups in rich countries. Governments connive in this, either because they have bought the corporate line or because their power has leached away. Global competition for jobs and foreign investment causes a 'race to the bottom' that undermines governments' ability to tax and spend, to protect workers' rights and the environment. So globalisation benefits companies at the expense of workers. And it guts our democracy. Our votes are useless, because big global companies call the shots. We can fight back only as consumers, through boycotts and the like, and by co-opting companies into behaving less damagingly.

If companies ruled the world, I would be up in arms too. Making and selling things is important, but less so than freedom, democracy and justice. But the fact is, companies are not in charge. Take brands, for starters. Far from being an emblem of corporate power over consumers, they are signs of companies' weakness. A monopolist has little need for branding: you have no choice but to buy its products. It is only because fickle consumers have a choice between so many competing products that companies rely on brands to try to win their loyalty. The hold that brands have over most of us is pretty tenuous: many people are happy to buy own-label cereal instead of Kellogg's; all of Coca-Cola's branding efforts could not convince people to drink New Coke. Compare it with the grip that patriotism, or love, have on us: many people are willing to die for those. If there is a problem with branding, it is that it convinces some susceptible people, mainly poor kids, to spend – or convince their parents to spend – money they can ill afford. Protecting children is an important issue. But it is far from the worry that brands are taking over the world.

Companies certainly have a strong influence on governments. Sometimes they have politicians in their pockets. That is why money and politics should be kept as separate as possible, and government conducted far more openly. The Enron scandal only confirms that campaign-finance reform is long overdue, especially in America. Even so, companies have a right to lobby governments, just as trade unions, environmentalists and individual citizens do. It is important that their many voices are heard. And it is simply not true that governments merely do companies' bidding. Companies are constrained by competition law: the US government almost broke up Microsoft; the European Commission blocked General Electric, the world's most valuable company, from taking over Honeywell. Companies have to abide by a battery of legislation on everything from workers' rights and health-and-safety procedures to environmental protection and product liability. Bill Clinton raised America's minimum wage. George Bush senior forced companies to slash their sulphur-dioxide emissions. In Britain Tony Blair has introduced a minimum wage, raised fuel tax and imposed a windfall levy on utilities. Corporate taxes make up a bigger share of government revenue than twenty years ago. All of this despite the implicit – or explicit – threat that companies will move abroad if governments don't do what they want.

Perhaps governments are pretty powerful after all. That companies spend so much money lobbying politicians suggests so: why else would companies bother? But how come? Because supposedly footloose companies cannot easily escape governments' authority: they are in fact tied to places in all sorts of ways – by the need to be near their customers, by the need for skilled workers, by all the good roads, schools and hospitals that our taxes pay for. Even if companies were to become more mobile, governments could still collude to nab them, by co-operating over tax raising, for instance. As for the WTO, it is simply governments acting together to regulate world trade: it is their servant, not their master.

It is true that some American and European workers – albeit far fewer than you probably think – have lost their jobs because of competition from the Third World. But trade with developing countries is still only a small fraction of rich-country economies: it is simply too small to have destroyed so many jobs. Most of the decline in manufacturing and worsening of unskilled workers' prospects is due to technological change: computers more readily replace unskilled workers than their more skilled brethren. Governments need to do more to help those who lose out – whether it is because of globalisation or anything else. People need to be equipped with skills to find another job and protected by a decent welfare system in the meantime. But it makes no sense to protect yesterday's jobs at the expense of tomorrow's. Jobs in export sectors pay more than the jobs lost in industries that compete with imports. Protectionism dulls competition and raises prices for everyone. Better, if you think steelworkers or farmers deserve special help, to stuff their pockets with banknotes than to put a spanner in the economy in order to try to preserve their jobs.

Many of the losers from globalisation do not deserve our sympathy at all. They are the cosseted 'national champions' that are incapable of being world-beaters, the fat cats that have gorged themselves at our expense: loss-making national airlines, hopeless nationalised industries, favoured companies run by cronies that have politicians' ears (and pad out their bank accounts). By all means, help the people who work for these companies. But don't protect the companies themselves.

Keeping out imports is not sensible. Nor is it fair. How else than through trade are poor countries going to get richer? Surely international solidarity means buying T-shirts from Bangladesh as well as demonstrating for debt relief? That seamstresses in Bangladesh are paid less than in Britain does not necessarily mean they are exploited. They earn more than they would as farmers. Moreover, conditions in a Nike factory are far better than in a typical local one, as we will see in chapter two. Wages are higher too: studies show that in poor countries workers in foreign firms earn twice the national average. More importantly, 'sweatshops' are generally the first step up on the development ladder – in the 1960s, Westerners used to bemoan the conditions in Japanese sweatshops.

The claims that companies are taking over the world, that global competition prevents governments from taxing, spending and regulating, that globalisation harms the poor, and that our democracy is at risk are not only untrue. They are also dangerous. Convincing people that they are powerless and that governments can no longer intervene for the collective good encourages apathy, frustration and, worse still, anger. It spurs people to take to the streets destructively rather than to engage in a creative debate about what kind of globalisation we want.

The real question

The simplistic row over whether globalisation is good or bad has produced more heat than light. Take, for instance, the bitter wrangle over whether poor countries need freer trade or debt relief. Pro-globalisers point to the overwhelming evidence that freer trade boosts economic growth and thus helps the poor. Whereas income per person in non-globalising poor countries rose by 1.4 per cent a year in the 1990s, it rose by 5 per cent a year in globalising ones – and the poor's income rose in line with average incomes. Anti-globalisers argue that more should be done to help the poor, by abolishing Third World debt, for instance. Yes, indeed. So why not do both? Freer trade and debt relief are complementary, not mutually exclusive. Freer trade helps the poor, but rich-country governments can – and should – do more to help them, notably by cancelling the debts of countries that credibly commit themselves to spend more on providing poor people with schools, hospitals, clean water and so on.

Or consider the notion that if we open our economy, we have to pare back the welfare state. Anti-globalisers, naturally, argue that this means we have to stop globalisation in order to save our hospitals/schools/pensions (delete as appropriate). For right-wingers, this is a convenient canard: governments have to cut social spending, they claim, because globalisation makes it unaffordable. Centre-left governments which fret that voters are unwilling to pay for the better public services they demand connive in this duplicity: we'd love to spend more, they say, but globalisation ties our hands. Nonsense. Denmark and Sweden are among the most open – and most successful – economies and they can afford a lavish welfare state. Indeed, as economies open up, and hence become more vulnerable to the vagaries of the global economic cycle, there is arguably a need for more government insurance, not less. Globalisation and social spending are also complements, not substitutes.

It is time to move the debate about globalisation forward. The important question is what kind of globalisation we want. This presupposes two things: first, that we are still free to determine our future – as individuals, as groups of like-minded people and through the power of our elected governments; and second, that we can to a large extent pick and choose between the bits of globalisation we like and those we don't. The core message of this book is that we can do both. Our challenge is to grasp the opportunities that globalisation offers while taking the sting out of its threats.

If you are a foe of globalisation in all its manifestations, rejoice. Your cause is misguided, but it is not futile. The titans of global commerce can be shackled, trade taxed at every turnpike, the Internet censored.

If you are in two minds about globalisation, you should cheer too. It's not an all-or-nothing, take-it-or-leave-it package; it comes with a wide menu of options. You can have all-American small government or Swedish-style high taxes with cradle-to-grave welfare. You can have free trade in software but not in films. You can allow in long-term foreign investment but keep out hot money. You can choose to welcome more immigrants, or fewer. You can have tighter links within Europe and the Americas or looser ones. Or any combination of the above. John Kay again: 'You can dislike the increasing homogeneity of shopping centres worldwide but still support free trade in manufactured goods. You can favour deregulation of electricity markets but worry about the consequences of worldwide adoption of an Anglo-American model of capital markets. Few components of globalisation are inevitable if there is a genuine popular will to stop them. But mostly there is not.'[7]

If you are a gung-ho supporter of globalisation, this strengthens your argument. If globalisation were simply a technological inevitability, rather than dependent on popular consent, it would be far less desirable. It might deliver economic goodies, but at a hefty price: the loss of democratic choice. Happily, this is not the case. Indeed, if globalisation were the one-size-fits-all straitjacket it is often made out to be, it would probably not last long. If it pinched too many people in too many places, the pressure to cast it off, especially in tighter economic times, would soon become overwhelming. But if people know that they can be cut a bit of slack, globalisation may have a brighter future. Supporters of big government and fans of a slimline state can argue about the appropriate size of government but agree to support globalisation. The French can keep their *exception culturelle* if they want to (although it is baffling that people whose culture is so widely admired abroad are so paranoid about American 'junk'). Developing countries that want to join the world economy but fret about being shipwrecked in a financial gale should by all means free trade but limit capital flows.

I believe that globalisation is generally a good thing. Yes, the world is changing fast. Yes, it can be scary. Yes, some people will lose out at first. But we should opt to live in a more globalised world because it offers greater opportunity for everyone, rich and poor, to make the most of their potential. Globalisation offers a richer life – in the broadest sense – for people in rich countries and the only realistic route out of poverty for the world's poor.

Make no mistake: we can build a better globalisation. It is vitally important that we make the right choices. Our future depends on it.

ONE

Worried Workers

Why globalisation is actually the least of their worries

In North America, the back end of an eighteen-wheeler heading for Mexico, workers weeping at the factory gate, the boarded-up windows of a hollowed-out factory town and people sleeping in doorways and on side-walks have been among the most powerful economic images of our time: metaphors, seared into the collective consciousness, for an economy that consistently and unapologetically puts profits before people.

NAOMI KLEIN, *No Logo*

Having declared free trade and open borders to be America's policy, why are we surprised that corporate executives padlocked their plants in the Rust Belt and moved overseas? Why keep your plant here when you can manufacture at a fraction of the cost abroad, ship your goods back, and pocket the windfall profits that come from firing twenty-dollar-an-hour Americans and hiring fifty-cent-an-hour Asians?

PATRICK BUCHANAN, *The Great Betrayal*

Those days are gone when we deplored the underpayment of
exploited labour in poverty-stricken countries . . . what we
are now deploring is the underemployment it causes in *our*
countries.

VIVIANE FORRESTER, *The Economic Horror*

The overall effect of unregulated global free trade is still to
drive down the wages of workers – most particularly
unskilled manufacturing workers – in advanced countries.

JOHN GRAY, *False Dawn*

The free trade liberals hope that a high-wage, high-skill
America need fear nothing from a low-wage, low-skill Third
World. They have no answer, however to the prospect –
indeed, the probability – of ever-increasing *low-wage, high-skill*
competition from abroad. In these circumstances, neither
better worker training nor investment in US infrastructure
will suffice.

MICHAEL LIND, *The Next American Nation*

Chuck Swearingen is a mountain of a man. His green-and-white
checked shirt is bursting at the seams over his enormous belly. As
he reaches out his huge hand to shake mine, I feel small and vulnerable – and he is just one of the five giant American steelworkers
I have come to have pizza with. But he breaks into a big smile –
'Nice to meet you, Philippe' – and my unease is gone.

Amid all the hoopla about Silicon Valley, Wall Street and the
new Internet economy, it is easy to forget that there is still an
older America too. A less glamorous America that makes ordinary
things that you can drop on your foot. Like steel. America's steelworkers fear that their jobs and their way of life are under threat.
They blame foreign trade. 'We know globalisation is here,' Chuck
explains. 'But we want an equal and level playing field, instead of
whoever has the cheapest labour or can do it cheapest no matter
what rules they play by. We have to monitor the environment,

control pollution. We have safety laws, pensions and healthcare to pay for.' His views are echoed by many other manufacturing workers in the old industrial heartlands of Europe and North America.

Whether you sympathise with them or not, America's steelworkers cannot be ignored. They are in the vanguard of the backlash against globalisation. Unlike the inveterate anti-capitalists, confused college kids or woolly-minded hippies who oppose globalisation in the abstract, they feel they are fighting for their livelihoods. They have so much political clout that even a professed free-trader like George Bush is listening. When I finished writing this book, in early March 2002, the American president had just slapped punitive customs duties on foreign steel – a move that could spark a global trade war.

Where Chuck works is only an hour's drive from Washington DC, but it feels light years away. Sparrows Point is in Maryland, just outside Baltimore, overlooking Chesapeake Bay. Chuck has spent thirty-two of his fifty-two years there, working for Bethlehem Steel, America's second-biggest integrated steel producer. He remembers when Sparrows Point was still a company town. Beth Steel bought the plant in 1916 and around it built a model town that was renowned for its well-kept homes, small-town atmosphere and self-sufficiency. They had their own churches, police and cemetery. The town boomed during the Second World War, when it cranked out steel and ships for the fight against fascism. At its peak, Sparrows Point, which was once America's biggest steel plant, employed 35,000 people. 'We were the highest-paid workers in the area,' says Chuck's colleague, Phil Pack. Now fifty-three, Phil started as an iron-worker apprentice thirty-five years ago – one of the first blacks to break into a then notoriously racist industry. Gordon Jakubowski concurs: 'We were the employment of choice.'

But then decline set in. From 1970 on, wave after wave of layoffs culled the workforce. As early as 1974, the last houses were torn down to make way for a new blast furnace, the largest in the Americas. The raw materials that used to be sourced locally – coal from Bethlehem Steel mines, coke made on site – now come from abroad: iron ore from Canada, coal from Australia, coke from China and Japan, and limestone from Argentina and Venezuela. Sparrows Point now employs only 3,500 people. Even these few remaining jobs may soon be gone: in October 2001, Bethlehem Steel declared bankruptcy, blaming foreign competition. It is now on life-support, awaiting a rescue plan in the legal limbo of Chapter 11 – America's insolvency procedures, which, unlike Europe's, give a company a breathing space to get back on its feet.

Sparrows Point is not a pleasant place. Vast smokestacks puncture the skyline and pollute the air. The scrubland is scarred by the iron ore, coal, coke and limestone that are blasted to make steel and by the slag heaps that are its by-products. Even the chunky steelworkers with blackened faces who toil amid the searing heat and choking dust seem slight set against the outsize building and machinery. It is a desolate wasteland – but working there provides good money.

Very good money, in fact, for work that does not require a college degree. On average, a steelworker at Sparrows Point makes $55,000 a year for a forty-hour week. But many earn as much as $70,000 to $80,000 a year by putting in a further twenty hours or more overtime. For $80,000 a year, you can live like a king in Maryland. 'We are privileged,' concedes Doc Iler, who is fifty and has been with Beth Steel for thirty years. 'When we see our way of life threatened, we're going to resist it.' Steelworkers drive huge SUVs (sport-utility vehicles), like the Ford Expedition, a macho cross between a van and a truck. They live in big houses with lots of land. Some have boats. Their pensions are generous, as are their healthcare benefits: big pluses in a country where so many fear that old age or illness spell destitution. Perhaps most importantly, they can afford to pay to put their kids through university. Chuck has a twenty-one-year-old son in college who wants to go into computers. What if his son wanted to work in steel? 'I would discourage him. There's no future.'

He is probably right. America's steel industry is shrivelling up. A global glut of steel is driving prices down to levels where American producers, with their bloated costs, can no longer compete with their foreign rivals. Phil thinks this competition is unfair: 'We can't go sell steel in Europe, Japan or China 'cause their markets are closed. There's overcapacity so people are selling below cost.' Chuck agrees: 'We can't export 'cause they put up barriers. If we put up barriers they go nuts.'

The truth is a bit more complicated. America's steel industry has long sheltered behind import barriers, yet it has still declined. Trade is clearly only part of Bethlehem Steel's problem. Even Chuck admits: 'We would still be losing jobs if there were no imports. We don't only have foreign competition; we also have domestic competition from [lower-cost] mini-mills. We've got very good contracts from when we were living high on the hog in the sixties.' You can say that again: although steel is a capital-intensive industry (remember all that gigantic machinery), employment costs account for around 40 per cent of Beth Steel's total costs. In a typical manufacturing firm, the figure is around 10 to 15 per cent. The company is hobbled by the huge pension and healthcare costs of its many former employees.

Technological change is also taking its toll. 'Back in the sixties, we used to produce 4 million tons [of steel] with 30,000 people. Now we produce three and a half to four with 3,500 people,' explains Doc. Since Sparrows Point produces almost as much steel as thirty years ago, but with less than an eighth of the workers, most of the job losses are due to cost-saving technology rather than dastardly foreigners. Even so, America's steelworkers are certainly among the losers from globalisation. If America's steel market was thrown open to foreign competition, many more jobs would undoubtedly go.

Whatever the cause is, losing your job can be terrible. 'It is devastating,' says Doc. 'Some of my good friends killed themselves. Families are torn apart. Steelworkers go from making good money to being homeless.' He has worked as a co-ordinator for the United Steelworkers of America (USWA) on its dislocated-worker programme. 'Sometimes we helped find them jobs that only pay $4 to

$5 an hour with no benefits, when they were earning $17 to $18 an hour plus benefits. But they're happy to get them. They need somewhere to hang their hat.' In 1989 the USWA started a career-development programme. 'It didn't make sense to wait until workers are in the street to prepare them for changes.' But finding another job can be very tough. 'Lots of workers have jobs that are unique to the steel industry,' says Chuck. 'They feel totally lost when they lose their job. They have no skills to market themselves for other jobs. They're middle-aged, not skilled to find other work, or too fat and too lazy to find other work. But we've worked hard to get to the positions we've got to. People are protected here. They don't often appreciate that.' Chuck points out that General Electric and Western Electric have recently shut down their local operations. 'Jobs in IT are limited. Jobs in industry were unlimited. Only 20 per cent go to college, 80 per cent don't. Where do they go now? They used to go here. There are lots of working poor.' Jerry Ernest, an even bigger man than Chuck, interjects: 'Unemployment benefit is $280 for twenty-six weeks. I just checked it out. Two hundred and eighty dollars is only a little over a day's wages. We're all worried about layoffs because of Chapter 11. We're teetering.' Thankfully, the USWA has also negotiated a supplementary unemployment benefit for members who are laid off.

Ironically, Bethlehem may yet be saved by a foreign white knight. Robert Stevens, the company's new boss, who took over less than a month before it went into Chapter 11, is adamant that the industry must 'consolidate'. That means mergers, with US or foreign rivals. Even an all-American merger would rankle with some people. 'We are who we are. We'll manage on our own' is a common refrain. Many more would resent a foreign takeover. 'There is still a patriotic pride associated with the company. During the Second World War, Sparrows Point used to produce a ship a day for the war effort,' explains Bette Kovach, Bethlehem's PR woman, who has worked for the company for twenty-five years. But most would swallow their pride if it meant their company survived. 'I love steel. I love Bethlehem. I've worked my whole life here and I'd like to see it continue. If it continues as the US arm of a foreign company, I wouldn't say it's welcome, but it's still worthwhile if it could give our employees security and a livelihood,' she says. 'We're not opposed to foreign ownership,' says Chuck, 'but we'd rather preserve it for ourselves.' What if the choice were between a foreign takeover and taking a pay cut in order to keep the company independent? Chuck laughs. 'We're all capitalist here.' Besides, he adds, 'If they cut wages, no one would work here. Who wants to come work in a filthy place when you could be making the same money for Verizon [a telecoms company]?'

In the old redbrick block that serves as Sparrows Point's headquarters, the facility's boss, Van Reiner, echoes that mixture of pride and realism. 'The process of making things does more than just make things. It provides people with the opportunity to buy a house, raise a family, pay for college education. That is important enough that whose name is on the door doesn't matter. It would be a tragedy if this facility closed. The effect on this area would be catastrophic.' Bethlehem Steel has already shut many facilities, including in 1995 the plant in its home town of Bethlehem, Pennsylvania. Van, a wiry, excitable man, is passionate about steel. 'It's fascinating: making something out of dirt.' Indeed. Like computer chips, which are made out of sand. Would it be a tragedy if the steel plant closed and was replaced by a semiconductor plant? 'Yes. The dislocation would be terrible. And it [the semiconductor plant] just wouldn't open.' The evidence suggests otherwise: despite all the job losses in manufacturing, US unemployment was, until the economy turned down in 2001, at a thirty-year low. Even so, Van exclaims: 'A whole generation would be severely affected. The people who have the new jobs are not the same as the people who lost them. It creates an underclass.' He has a point. Adjusting to change can be painful. But thankfully, the future may be brighter for the next generation. Van's son, who was born in 1975, works as an architectural-graphics-software consultant in Japan, speaks Japanese and set up a dot-com during the Internet boom. He does not share Van's passion for steel: 'He doesn't look at making things like I do.'

Protectionism doesn't work

Some people argue that salvation lies in keeping out imports. Meet
Curtis Barnette, who likes to be known as Hank. Hank looks like an
old-fashioned gentleman. He is deliberately charming. He holds the
door open, pours me a drink, enquires earnestly about my background. His suit is perfectly tailored, his greying hair gelled wet. He
sports a Stars-and-Stripes badge and blue braces to boot. His smooth
voice sounds measured and reasonable, his glasses lend his words
weight and wisdom. He has an impeccable pedigree: chairman
emeritus of Bethlehem Steel (chief executive and chairman proper
from 1992 to 2000), chair of the American Iron and Steel Institute
(and the International one too), member of the US president's advi-
sory committee on trade, and so on. America's steel industry may be
ailing, but Hank himself doesn't seem to be doing too badly. He
personifies the old-school establishment: he lists his friends and
contacts in the US administration starting with President Bush and
Vice-President Cheney and moving exhaustively down. His lavish
law offices at Skadden Arp are literally a stone's throw away from
the White House. He offers to show me the view from the window.

Hank has made good use of his intimate links with successive
administrations. Few industries have been as successful as steel at
obtaining protection from foreign imports. Unfortunately, it has
been rather less successful at making money. This is probably not
a coincidence. Perhaps, as some people claim about communism,
we cannot tell whether protectionism has failed because it was
never really tried. It has not, in recent times, been pushed to its logical extreme: banning all imports altogether. Then, presumably,
we could judge it on its merits. Hank almost concedes as much:
'Remedies [ie, trade barriers] were somewhat effective sometimes,'
he laments. 'But the enforcement of trade law has not been effective for the past five years.'

Indeed. For Hank is not a protectionist, of course. He is far too
savvy for that. No, he believes in 'open markets and market-driven
trade'. But he also believes in 'rules-based trade, with rules that are

properly enforced'. Very reasonable. Who doesn't believe in playing by the rules? But what rules? Rules, which years of his industry's lobbying have helped frame, that conveniently allow the US to slap duties on imports that are deemed 'too' cheap. But too cheap for whom? Not for steel consumers: carmakers, for instance, who can thus sell us cheaper cars. No: too cheap for US steel producers who cannot compete with Europe, Russia, China or South Korea.

Hank puts it slightly differently. 'Many foreign steel markets are closed or cartelised. Foreigners dump their steel in the US market below cost. That is unfair. It causes quantifiable and objectively determined injury. The remedy is to impose tariffs or quotas on foreign steel. Everyone knows that the US market is the target market for excess capacity. Despite protection, ours is still the most significant open market.' Not so, but let it pass. Hank is in full flow. 'We have restructured our industry so far that we can't meet domestic demand any more. America needs around 125 million tons of steel a year and we produce only around 105 million. Imports make up the difference. I'm not against imports, but I'm against imports sold below cost. That is causing injury to our steel industry and to America's national interest. Companies aren't making profits for their shareholders. Workers are losing their jobs and having to accept lower wages. In 1980 we had the capacity to make 155 million tons of steel a year. We've shut down 50 million of that. Then steel employed 500,000 people, now it employs only 165,000. That fall is because of unfair trade and a lack of capital investment.'

Talk of the national interest is a useful cover, especially in these more patriotic times. But why does America need to preserve a steel industry when it can buy cheaper foreign metal? 'We need a strong manufacturing base. Steel is part of that. Our industry has to be profitable, regenerative, modern and technologically advanced. Steel is the engineering material of choice. It goes into cars, tanks, nuclear submarines, aircraft carriers, pipelines, buildings, bridges, tin cans and so on. If our country is substantially dependent on imported products, we lose control over the pricing of the product and the allocation of the product. It's a national public-policy judgement. Dependability of supply is important. September 11th only heightens that.' I ask him whether preserving other industries, agriculture for instance, is also in the national interest. We all have to eat, after all. 'Absolutely. Agriculture is essential too.' That doesn't seem to leave much scope for international trade. Which industries, then, are not essential? 'The market is not free, so we can't judge.' A rather convenient cop-out.

For sure, if a country relies entirely on imports, it could conceivably suffer if a war or blockade cut off foreign supplies. It might therefore make sense to take out insurance against such a calamity by protecting certain critical industries. But this insurance is costly, since we are making things at home that could be imported more cheaply. In the case of steel, it is a pretty hefty cost. One study[1] reckons the cumulative cost to American consumers of higher steel prices since 1969 has been as high as $151 billion (in 1999 dollars). Taxpayers have also had to cough up $23 billion in subsidies. It is only worth taking out that insurance if the perceived benefits it brings are greater than that cost. But just how likely is it that the rest of the world will gang up on America to deny it steel? Incredibly unlikely. And if it were to happen, would America not soon be able to produce steel again? Most probably, yes. And yet the cumulative cost of the insurance is huge. One hundred and seventy-four billion dollars to protect 165,000 jobs: that's over a million dollars a job.

Look at it another way. When people were subsistence farmers, they were self-sufficient. They didn't rely on others for anything. They were also dirt poor. Now we all specialise in a career, and we buy in everything we need from others who have also specialised in this way. Clearly, we are more dependent on others than when we were subsistence farmers. But we are also much richer. And the chances that we will not be able to buy from others whatever we need are pretty slim. Spending billions a year protecting steel for national security reasons doesn't make sense. It's like spending $1,000 a year to insure yourself against the risk that the sun won't ever rise again.

The second weapon in the steel industry's armoury is the claim that dastardly foreigners are selling their steel at unfairly low prices in America. At first blush, it's hard to see how something can be too cheap. If the supermarket is selling apples for a penny a piece, you are hardly likely to protest at this fiendish plot to under-charge you. But when a foreign company sells something in America too cheaply, it is known as 'dumping' – and it's illegal. So if Toyota tried to sell you a foreign-made Corolla for $5,000, what most people would consider a damn good deal would actually be illegal. Now, why is dumping wrong? 'Because it's against the law, and the law should be enforced and obeyed,' Hank explains. Of course, but that is a circular argument. What is the basis for the law? 'Those are the rules we agreed to. The condition for lowering our tariffs was a strong rules-based system. Our tariffs didn't go away because of generosity. They went away because we were assured that we would have rules-based trade.' In short, foreigners are allowed to sell their wares in America on the condition that they don't give Americans too good a deal.

Despite all this protection, or perhaps because of it, American steelmakers are losing the fight. Bethlehem limps on in Chapter 11; LTV has folded. Rather than merge with each other or with for-eign rivals, American steelmakers have stumbled from crisis to crisis on government crutches. Perhaps if they had spent more time and energy trying to go with the flow of economic change, rather than trying to resist it, they would not be in such a sorry state today. There is a glimmer of hope. All the talk is about an overdue consolidation of the industry. Yet despite his denials, Hank still clearly hopes that salvation will come from the govern-ment. 'Here's what needs to be done. We need rigorous enforcement of existing WTO laws. Foreign markets must truly be opened. Foreign countries have to vigorously enforce trade laws in their country, both WTO laws and antitrust. The burden of steel companies' "legacy" health and pension costs need to be taken into account in trade law and assistance. We need international consolidation of companies.' He fails to mention current efforts to reach an international agreement to limit steel production. When prompted, he is sceptical. 'It could be called jawboning.' He prefers the legal certainties of good old anti-dumping.

Trade is not the main culprit

Whatever happens, Hank is not going to end up on the streets. But for workers like Chuck, Phil, Doc, Gordon and Jerry, the stakes are much higher. If they lose their jobs, they may not find another for a long time. There's a fair chance they'll have to settle for lower wages. They may never find work again. Even if they keep their jobs they may see their wages stagnate or even cut. They will probably live in fear of being laid off. The question is: what do we do about it?

Keeping imports out would certainly save some steelworkers' jobs for a while. But it comes at a big price. Not only the direct costs to consumers and taxpayers of tariffs and subsidies. But also the likelihood that other industries will demand protection as well: if steel is special, what about cars, clothing ... you name it? And, most probably, job losses elsewhere. Unless the economy is in a slump, protectionism creates inflationary pressure, which leads to higher interest rates and hence slower growth and job losses. Twelve million people work in steel-consuming industries, compared with only 165,000 in steel. One study sponsored by a group of steel consumers suggests that 20 per cent import duties would save fewer than 9,000 steel jobs but cost over 74,000 jobs elsewhere.[2]

Protecting America's steel industry would also harm more competitive foreign steel producers, like Corus in Britain, ThyssenKrupp in Germany, Posco in South Korea or Arcelor, the new European product of Spain's Aceralia, France's Usinor and Luxembourg's Arbed. Job losses abroad may not trouble Americans, but foreign retaliation should. Europeans might hit back with punitive duties on American cars, for instance. A trade war over steel between America and Europe could spread rapidly to lots of

other industries. Protectionism is bad politics as well as bad economics. As the Great Depression of the 1930s shows, when
protectionist policies get out of hand, they soon impoverish all of
us. But perhaps most importantly, protectionism would actually
save very few jobs in steel – or in manufacturing more generally –
because trade is not the main threat to people's jobs.

The past three decades of globalisation have coincided with two
other trends. The first is the decline of manufacturing in rich-
country economies. The share of manufacturing in Organisation
for Economic Cooperation and Development (OECD) countries has
fallen from nearly three-tenths of the economy in 1970 to just
under a fifth now. Employment in manufacturing has slumped
too. The second trend is a fall in the demand for unskilled workers
in rich countries. People without a college degree are finding it
harder and harder to find jobs. In most OECD countries, they are
two or three times more likely to be unemployed than university
graduates. In Britain and America, but not in continental Europe,
the gap between skilled and unskilled workers' wages has also
widened. Worse, in inflation-adjusted terms, American unskilled
workers' wages have actually fallen over the past thirty years.[3] Even
though more and more people are going to university, and so the
share of the workforce that is unskilled is declining, demand for
unskilled labour is falling faster than supply.

Globalisation is widely blamed for both the decline in manufacturing and the fall in demand for unskilled workers, but both
trends are primarily driven by technology, not trade. Consider manufacturing first. As economies become more productive, they can
produce the same number of widgets with fewer workers. At
Sparrows Point, 3,500 workers produce as much steel as 30,000
once did. Producing more with less is essentially what most economic growth consists of. So unless demand for a product is rising
fast, fewer and fewer people will tend to be employed in sectors
with fast productivity growth. The classic example is farming: we
can now feed ourselves comfortably even though only a tiny fraction of the population works in agriculture. The same is also true

of manufacturing. Global demand for steel has hardly risen over the past thirty years: most of the world's railways have already been built; other metals have taken steel's place. Yet every year manufacturing becomes more productive. So jobs disappear.

The good news is that new jobs replace them. Unemployment in Britain is below one million. As old jobs are destroyed in manufacturing, new ones are created in services. There, productivity growth is often much slower – a nurse cannot readily treat more patients each year, nor can a fitness instructor, a lawyer or a journalist greatly improve their productivity – and demand is rising fast: as we get richer, we tend to consume more services.

These new service-sector jobs are no worse, on average, than the industrial jobs they replace. For every miserable burger flipper, there are many more happy office workers. A survey of European employees[4] found that fewer workers in services than in industry complained about unpleasant working conditions or tasks, boring work, limited working-time flexibility, job insecurity, health problems and so on. Sparrows Point, or a British coal mine, is hardly a pleasant place to work. The only area where services scored (marginally) worse was on anti-social hours. Overall job satisfaction was higher on average in services than in industry. And although the OECD finds that in America average wages in services are 9 per cent lower than in manufacturing, they are 2 per cent higher in France. Over time, moreover, wages in both sectors are rising steadily.

A look at the statistics[5] sheds more light on the shift from manufacturing to services. In 1970, 20.7 million Americans worked in manufacturing. Employment in manufacturing peaked at 22.5 million in 1979. This fell to 19.9 million in 2000: a net loss, allowing for rounding, of 2.5 million jobs out of a total labour force in 2000 of 141 million people. As a share of total employment, the decline in manufacturing has been much more pronounced: down from 26.4 per cent in 1970 to 14.7 per cent in 2000. That is because so many new jobs have been created in services, where employment has risen from 49.0 million to 101.9 million: an extra 52.8 million jobs since 1970.

Britain has lost many more manufacturing jobs than America. In 1970, 8.5 million worked in manufacturing; by 1998 only 5 million did, a net loss of 3.5 million out of a labour force of 28.7 million. Manufacturing used to employ 34.7 per cent of British workers; it now employs only 18.6 per cent. But Britain too has created many new jobs in services: employment has risen by 6.4 million to 19.5 million.

In Germany, 2.5 million jobs were lost in manufacturing between 1970 and 1990: down from 10.3 million to 8.8 million. The figures since then apply to the reunified Germany, and so are not comparable, but between 1991 and 1999, manufacturing employment fell from 11.6 million to 8.7 million: a further loss of 2.9 million jobs out of a labour force of 40.2 million. Germany created an extra 5 million jobs in services between 1970 and 1990, and another 2.3 million between 1991 and 1999, taking the total to 23 million. In 1970, 39.5 per cent of West German workers were in manufacturing; in 1999, 24.1 per cent of unified Germany's were.

Statistical problems mar the French figures too. France lost 1.1 million manufacturing jobs, down from 5.6 million to 4.5 million, between 1970 and 1992. But after that, we have statistics only for jobs in industry, which also includes mining and construction. Between 1993 and 1999, a further 300,000 jobs were lost in industry, bringing the total down to 5.4 million out of a labour force of 25.9 million. Manufacturing's share of total employment fell from 27.5 per cent in 1970 to 20.4 per cent in 1992; industry's slipped from 26.4 per cent in 1993 to 23.7 per cent in 1999. France has also created new jobs in services, where employment has risen by 6.8 million to 16.6 million.

How many of the job losses in manufacturing are due to trade? It is hard to be too precise: pink slips don't come with the words 'trade', 'technology' or 'tastes' on them. But we can still get a pretty good idea. Manufacturing accounted for a quarter of America's GDP in 1970; it now accounts for only 15.9 per cent – a 9.1 percentage-point decline. Over the same period, America's trade deficit in manufacturing has risen from −0.2 per cent of GDP (ie, a surplus of exports over imports) to 3.2 per cent − a rise of 3.4 percentage points, three-eighths of the decline of the share of manufacturing in GDP. But, as Paul Krugman, a top American economist, points out, this overstates the impact of the trade deficit on manufacturing, because we are comparing the fall in value-added in manufacturing with the rise in net imported sales. When imports displace a dollar of manufacturing sales, a big fraction of that dollar would have been spent on inputs from the service sector, which are not part of manufacturing's contribution to GDP. Correcting for this leakage to the service sector, which Mr Krugman estimates to be 40 per cent, each dollar of the trade deficit reduces the manufacturing sector's contribution by only 60 cents. So trade accounts for less than a quarter of the decline in manufacturing's share of GDP: two percentage points out of 9.1.

Rough-and-ready calculations show that trade is to blame for little, if any, of the decline in European manufacturing either. Since 1990, manufacturing's share of GDP has fallen by around six percentage points in Britain, five in France and four in Germany. Over the same period, Britain's manufacturing trade deficit has widened by 0.4 per cent of GDP; France's manufacturing sector has swung from deficit to surplus and Germany's huge surplus has shrunk by 0.5 per cent of GDP. Even without allowing for leakage, trade accounts for only a very small share of manufacturing's decline in Britain and Germany and has actually boosted French manufacturing.

Globalisation is not responsible for much of the decline in manufacturing. Nor is it to blame for much of the worsening lot of unskilled workers. For a start, dismiss the fear that low-wage workers in the Third World will soon be doing all our jobs. The main reason why wages in poor countries are lower is that workers there are less productive. They have less education, less machinery and equipment to work with, inferior management, and so on. They produce less, so they are paid less. As they become more productive, their wages rise. If an employer tried to keep their wages below their productivity levels, a rival one would find it profitable to lure them away with higher pay. True, a monopoly employer like Britain's National Health Service can use its bargaining power to drive wages below competitive market rates. But the NHS is an exception, and as its example shows, pushing wages below productivity levels causes a shortage of staff, which eventually puts upward pressure on wages. Currency fluctuations can also cause productivity and wages measured in foreign-currency terms to diverge – but only temporarily. All the evidence shows that workers' wages are very strongly correlated with their productivity. The fear about ever-increasing competition from low-wage, high-skill workers is nonsense.

But the argument that increased trade with poor countries is causing a fall in demand for unskilled labour is not unreasonable. Skilled labour is relatively abundant in rich countries like America and Britain (as is capital), unskilled labour relatively scarce. The opposite is true in poor countries. So when the two start trading, economic theory predicts that rich countries will specialise in industries that use a lot of capital and skilled labour, poor countries in ones that use unskilled labour intensively. So rich countries' imports from poor ones will mainly be products made with lots of unskilled labour, like shoes. In effect, unskilled workers in rich countries now face competition from those in poor countries. This will tend to drive down their wages.

Fine. But if trade were driving down the wages of unskilled workers who work in import-competing industries, companies in sectors that are sheltered from global competition would take advantage of the fall in wages to hire more unskilled workers. In fact, as we have seen, in rich countries, demand for unskilled workers has fallen across the economy as a whole.

Moreover, trade with poor countries is simply not big enough to account for unskilled workers' misfortune. Despite their meteoric rise, imports from poor countries are still small relative to the size of rich economies. In 1982, imports from non-OPEC (Organisation of Petroleum Exporting Countries) poor countries came to 2.5 per cent of GDP in rich OECD countries. By 2000, they had risen to 3.9 per cent of GDP – an increase of only 1.4 percentage points.[6] In the US, imports from poor countries have risen by 1.8 per cent of GDP, from 1.7 per cent to 3.5 per cent. In the EU, the rise was 1.2 percentage points, from 3.4 per cent of GDP to 4.6 per cent. In the grand scheme of things, this is peanuts. It is hard to see how such a small rise in imports can have widened the earnings gap between American university graduates and high-school leavers by more than 50 per cent. Or how it can be responsible for a near-trebling in the jobless rate of French unskilled workers from 5.4 per cent in 1981 to 15.3 per cent in 1999. Especially since, even as imports from developing countries have risen, so have those countries' wages – and hence their depressing effect on US wages is that much smaller. Whereas in 1960 the average developing-country wage was 10 per cent of the US manufacturing wage, it is now over 30 per cent. Imports from Japan were once seen as low-wage competition. They no longer are.

Strikingly, some of the most open economies – Austria, the Netherlands, Norway and Denmark – experienced neither a large rise in inequality nor an increase in unemployment between 1973 and 1998. Technology, in the shape of computers, is a more likely culprit for unskilled workers' worsening lot. Computers increase inequality not only because they take over the tasks performed by unskilled staff, but also because they enhance the productivity of skilled workers.

That is not to say that some workers in some industries have not been hit by imports from poor countries. Clearly, they have. A comprehensive study by the OECD[7] identified six sectors where imports from low-wage countries are particularly important: clothing and shoes; wood products; rubber and plastics; computer equipment; vehicles other than cars and planes; and some consumer goods such as toys. With the exception of computers, these import-competing sectors have below-average wages, which suggests that they mainly employ unskilled workers. Typically, they paid 15 per cent less than the national average. Imports may harm workers who lose their jobs in these industries if they cannot easily find another one in a sheltered sector of the economy. The study also found that the six export sectors that had benefited most from trade with developing countries – chemical products; drugs and medicines; machinery and equipment; motor vehicles; and (outside the US) iron and steel – paid above-average wages: 10 per cent more, typically.

How big is the hit to workers? Lori Kletzer of the Institute for International Economics in Washington DC has had a look[8] at what happens to workers who lose their jobs in import-competing industries in America. She focuses on five sectors: electrical machinery, clothing, cars, non-electrical machinery and blast furnaces. She finds that nearly two-thirds (63.4 per cent) of workers who lost their jobs in import-competing industries between 1979 and 1999 eventually found another one. On average, those that found another job suffered a pay cut of 13 per cent. Over a third (36 per cent) earned as much as before or more. A quarter took a pay cut of 30 per cent or more. Those who took a hefty pay cut were mainly older, less educated, lower-skilled production workers who had established tenure on their old job. Half of those who found another job did so in manufacturing. Only one in ten went into retail jobs, where they typically had to take a big pay cut.

Dani Rodrik, an economist at Harvard University, thinks[9] that trade does more harm to workers than just costing some of them their jobs: it may also weaken their collective bargaining power. Since companies can more easily shift or outsource production not just to the Third World but also to other rich countries, workers in different countries now compete against each other more than before. This makes workers feel insecure and limits their ability to press for better conditions or wages that are unmatched by productivity gains. There may be some truth to this. But America's total imports were only a seventh of its GDP in 2000, so it is hard to see how trade harms most workers. Imports are two-sevenths of Britain's GDP. If workers' bargaining power has weakened, a more likely culprit is the onslaught on union power led by Ronald

Reagan in the US and Margaret Thatcher in Britain. But has it actually weakened? Wages and salaries accounted for 71.6 per cent of
America's national income in 2000. The fifty-year average is 71.7
per cent. In Britain, where the figures are not comparable with
America's, employee compensation was 55.3 per cent of GDP in
2000, almost unchanged on the average in the 1980s of 55.9 per
cent.[10] Workers in general seem to be faring as well as before.

We cannot say for sure how much trade has harmed unskilled
workers. Economists have tried to crunch the data in all sorts of
ways and have yet to come up with a definitive answer.
Remarkably, though, they nearly all conclude that technology is
responsible for most of the impact. Trade is to blame for less than
a quarter of the increase in inequality. Other factors, such as immigration, falling unionisation and labour-market deregulation, also
played a part.

Welfare to work

In a sense, the whole debate about whether trade or technology is
eliminating jobs is a red herring. Technology is forever destroying
old jobs and creating new ones, yet nobody argues that we should
ban the Internet in order to save the jobs of middlemen. Nor were
the interests of candlemakers allowed to stop the introduction of
electricity. Why? Because technological change makes us richer.
The same is true of trade. Blocking trade is economically equivalent
to smashing up computers. When Americans buy foreign steel,
they are in effect taking advantage of cheaper foreign technology.
The distinction between jobs lost from trade and those eliminated
by technology is political, not economic: it is easier to lash out at
foreigners than at the Internet. Even if trade were responsible for
all the job losses in manufacturing and the entire worsening of
unskilled workers' prospects, it would still be a good thing overall.
The losses to some are more than offset by the gains to many:
cheaper imports, better jobs in export industries, faster economic

growth. So rather than debating whether or not to restrict trade, we should be thinking about what we should do to help men like Chuck.

One option is to wring your hands and do nothing. Job losses are part of the hurly-burly of capitalism. They are an intrinsic part of economic growth. American steelworkers or British coalminers should just fend for themselves. Ironically, Chuck and his colleagues have some sympathy for this view of the world. 'We've always depended on ourselves,' he says. 'You have to pick yourself up and find another job within twenty-six weeks [the length of unemployment insurance]. If you don't, tough.' That is the American way. They are torn between the American dream of individual self-reliance and self-improvement that they were raised to believe in, and their experience, which is that life isn't always that easy. A steelworker cannot overnight become a software programmer, and may find it humiliating to work in a shop. (Although not perhaps as a stripper: see *The Full Monty*.)

Turning a blind eye to job losses and rising inequality is not only inhumane: people who no longer have a job should still have a right to a life. It is also politically dangerous. Losers from globalisation – as well as people who think they are losers, or might be losers – may club together to oppose it and eventually reverse it, as happened in the 1930s, with catastrophic consequences.

Both the heart and the head argue for a different way. We need to do four things to help people cope with economic change. First, invest more in their skills, so that they are better equipped to find good jobs. That means more vocational training, as well as putting more people through university. Second, do more to help those who lose their jobs find other ones: relocation grants, retraining schemes and so on. Third, pay subsidies to people in low-paid jobs, so that everyone has a decent standard of living. Fourth, maintain a generous welfare system, so that the least fortunate do not fall by the wayside. None of this is rocket science. It is the broad thrust of Gordon Brown's policies in Britain. It is also more or less what the Netherlands and Scandinavian countries do.

But it is more problematic in the US, where the welfare net is threadbare. Perhaps America should take a leaf out of Europe's book for once.

It would be foolish to throw away the huge gains from globalisation just because some people lose out. It makes no sense to protect yesterday's jobs at the expense of tomorrow's. Nor is it fair. How else are the poor going to get richer?

TWO

The Poor Profit

*Globalisation is the only route
out of poverty*

Millions of workers are losing out in a global economy that
disrupts traditional economies and weakens the ability of
governments to assist them. They are left to fend for
themselves within failed states against destitution, famine,
and plagues. They are forced to migrate, to offer their labour
at wages below subsistence, sacrifice their children, and
cash in on their natural environments and often their
personal health – all in a desperate struggle to survive.

JAY MAZUR, president of the Union of Needletrades,
Industrial and Textile Workers[1]

The cumulative response to the horror stories of Chinese
prison labour, the scenes of teenage girls being paid pennies
in the Mexican *maquiladoras*, and burning in fires in
Bangkok, has been a slow but noticeable shift in how people
in the West see workers in the developing world. 'They're
getting our jobs' is giving way to a more humane reaction:
'our corporations are stealing their lives'.

NAOMI KLEIN, *No Logo*

Rather than the rising tide of the market lifting all boats, structural adjustment and liberalisation policies with no concomitant obligations on redistribution appear to have sunk some social groups, especially the poor and the vulnerable.

NOREENA HERTZ, *The Silent Takeover*

My concern is not that there are too many sweatshops but that there are too few . . . those are precisely the jobs that were the stepping stones for Singapore and Hong Kong and those are the jobs that have to come to Africa to get them out of backbreaking rural poverty.

JEFFREY SACHS, professor at Harvard University

Tran Van Nam[2] has seen a lot in his forty-one years. He grew up in Vietnam during the war with America. 'The sky used to light up from the bombs. We had anti-aircraft guns on our roof. We used to play with empty cartridges,' he recalls as we chat amid the tanks, missiles and planes at Hanoi's war museum. When he was twelve, in 1972, he would take shelter from the American B52s bombing Hanoi by staying near the Hilton hotel, which served as a prison for captured American airmen. 'We didn't think the Americans would bomb there.' He smiles. Aged nineteen, he was conscripted by Vietnam's communist government to fight in Cambodia. When he returned to Hanoi, he became a government driver, earning a pittance.

Life began to improve when Vietnam started to open up in 1986, under the government's *doi moi* (renewal) policy. Nam got a better job, driving foreign tourists around in a Japanese Nissan rather than a rickety old Russian Lada. The newly legal private shops and markets that opened up everywhere actually sold things that people wanted to buy. 'Things are better now that Vietnam is open. We don't want to live like in Afghanistan or North Korea,' he says. But as he stares wistfully at the statue of Lenin opposite Vietnam's war museum, he still dreams of a better life. 'Hopefully he'll be gone soon. I hate the Communists. They put my father in prison when they liberated Hanoi in 1954. Even now, if I said in public that I hated the Communists, they would arrest me too.' He grimaces. 'I'd also like to have my own car,' he says. 'But it's still too expensive. I make $150 a month. I have a wife and three children, two daughters, fourteen and nine, and a son who's twelve. The import tax on cars is 210 per cent. So a car that in Japan costs $20,000 costs over $60,000 here. It's too much. Maybe it is possible in five or ten years.'

It is not inconceivable. Admittedly, reform in Vietnam still has a long way to go. But Nong Duc Manh, the communist party's general-secretary, has set a target of doubling Vietnam's national income by 2010. Despite the old-fashioned rhetoric ('Our state must be a state of the people, for the people and by the people, based on the alliance of the working class, the peasantry and the intelligentsia and led by the communist party of Vietnam'), that requires more *doi moi*.

If you believe many of the critics of globalisation, people like Tran Van Nam simply do not exist. College kids who have rarely ventured beyond their middle-class suburbs spout on about globalisation only benefiting rich countries, or the elite in poor countries. It is arrant nonsense. Everywhere you look in countries that have opened up to the world there are signs of hope: poor people scrambling to make a better life for themselves. By our standards, many of them are still shockingly poor, but the crucial thing is that they are better off than they were before. It would be criminal to deny them the opportunity of a better life by trying to put a stop to globalisation. It offers them their only feasible route out of poverty.

Globalisation helps

Visit the Third World and you will see poverty so terrible that it is scarcely possible for a pampered Westerner to come to terms with it. One in five of the world's 6 billion people live on less than a dollar a day, almost half on less than two dollars a day. More than 850 million people in poor countries cannot read or write. Nearly a billion do not have access to clean water, 2.4 billion to basic sanitation. Eleven million children under five die each year from preventable diseases.

Alleviating such poverty will not be easy. Yet the evidence that globalisation helps is overwhelming. Start with a study[3] by Jeffrey Sachs and Andrew Warner, two economists at Harvard University. They find that poor countries that were open to international trade grew over six times faster in the 1970s and 1980s than those that shut themselves off from it: 4.5 per cent a year, rather than 0.7 per cent. (Among rich economies, open ones grew by 2.3 per cent a year, closed ones by 0.7 per cent.) That makes a huge difference over time: open economies double in size every sixteen years; closed economies only every 100 years – by which time living standards in open economies would have grown eighty-fold. Another plank in the pro-globalisation case is a study[4] by Jeffrey Frankel, also at Harvard, and David Romer, at the University of California at Berkeley. They find that a one-percentage-point rise in the shares of imports and exports in national income raises GDP by 2 per cent or more.

Then, there are two studies by David Dollar and Aart Kraay, both at the World Bank. The first, 'Growth Is Good for the Poor',[5] crunches data from eighty countries over four decades. It finds that openness to international trade helps the poor by boosting economic growth. This is not a 'trickle-down' effect, whereby the rich get richer and benefits eventually trickle down to the poor: both rich and poor improve their standards of living simultaneously. Improvements in the rule of law also help; reducing inflation is particularly pro-poor. Dollar and Kraay find that the incomes of the poor tend to rise in line with average incomes. When GDP per person rises by 1 per cent, the income of the poorest fifth of the population tends to rise by 1 per cent too. What is true in booms is true in busts. Contrary to what many people

think, the poor's income does not suffer disproportionately in economic crises – although a 10 per cent fall in income when you are
poor is likely to hurt more than a 10 per cent fall in income when
you are rich. Nor is it true, as some people claim, that growth used
to benefit the poor but no longer does: the incomes of the poor
rose in line with average incomes in the 1980s and 1990s as well as
the 1960s and 1970s. In short, Dollar and Kraay show that globalisation boosts economic growth and that a rising tide lifts all boats
equally.

Their second paper, 'Trade, Growth and Poverty',[6] is even more
convincing. Dollar and Kraay find that whereas in developing
countries that are globalising, GDP per person increased by 5 per
cent a year in the 1990s, it rose by only 1.4 per cent a year in non-
globalising ones. This means that living standards double every
fourteen years in globalising countries, but take fifty years to do so
in non-globalising countries – by which time they will have risen
eleven-fold in globalising ones. Better still, the growth in income
per person is speeding up in globalising countries: it is up from 2.9
per cent a year in the 1970s and 3.5 per cent in the 1980s. Yet it has
slowed in non-globalising ones, from 3.3 per cent a year in the
1970s, and has recovered only slightly from the 0.8 per cent-a-year
rise in the 1980s. Moreover, the globalisers are catching up with
rich countries, where GDP per person rose by 2.2 per cent a year in
the 1990s, while the non-globalisers are falling further behind.

The good news is that some 3 billion people live in globalising
developing countries – such as China, India, Brazil, Mexico,
Vietnam and Bangladesh – which have cut their import duties,
witnessed a big rise in trade and attracted lots of foreign investment. The bad news is that 2 billion people live in non-globalising
countries, which include most African and many Muslim countries, where trade is often falling as a share of national income
and which have seen little foreign investment. These countries are
not only failing to open up, they are becoming more isolated from
the rest of the world.

Dollar and Kraay confirm their earlier finding that the poor tend to get richer as fast as the average person does. This does not mean that some poor people don't lose out initially – they do – but it does mean that most of them benefit. Clearly, more needs to be done to make sure that the few losers benefit too; how this can be done I will discuss in chapter thirteen. But the important point is that the poor are generally getting richer in globalising countries.

For sure, foreign trade and investment are not always and every-where a good thing. Sometimes, foreign companies do more harm than good: if they are granted a monopoly, for instance, in exchange for kickbacks to corrupt governments. Sometimes they behave unacceptably, by using slave labour or poisoning the environment. Yet, as we shall see, such abuses can be tackled without blocking the overwhelming majority of beneficial foreign links.

It is also true that foreign trade and investment alone are not enough to make countries richer. Abolishing trade barriers won't do much for war-torn Congo. Internet connections are pretty useless if people can't read or write. Spanking new factories will scarcely improve people's lives if they are dying of Aids. Where governments are crooked, many of the gains from globalisation may end up in Swiss bank accounts rather than in the pockets of ordinary people. Where politicians spend more on weapons than on schools, many of the opportunities of globalisation will be wasted. But none of this is a reason for giving up on globalisation. No country has escaped poverty without trading with the rest of the world.

Without foreign trade and investment, the poor are never going to get richer. Opening the doors to mass migration is politically unacceptable in rich countries. Redistributive taxation from people in rich countries to those in poor ones is also a non-starter. Economic growth through trade is the only answer. It is the only way to raise poor countries' living standards – and it also gives governments the means to do more to combat poverty: money for schools, hospitals and social security.

Even so, we can do more to help the poor. For a start, we should open our markets to their exports. Shamefully, America and Europe still conspire to keep out many of the products that poor countries export, like food and clothing. Yet all too often the debate about globalisation degenerates into a bun fight over whether the poor need free trade *or* debt relief, foreign investment *or* overseas aid, economic growth *or* redistribution from rich to poor. Why not do all of them? They are not alternatives; they complement each other. If only we could get past this dialogue of the deaf, supporters of globalisation and its critics might find plenty to agree on.

Consider Jubilee Plus, the campaign for Third World debt relief. Its cause is a noble one. It is immoral that poor people in poor countries should pay the price for their rulers' wasted borrowing. Yet, for some reason, Jubilee Plus opposes free trade. Perhaps this is because of a blind hatred of markets and capitalism: free trade cannot be good if rich-world companies benefit from it too. How sad! Surely, even if you are anti-capitalist, the ends – helping poor people – justify the means: mutually profitable trade?

The pro-globalisation establishment also gives the impression of caring more about dogma than it does about people. Globalisation is good, they say: economic theory tells us so, and the statistics confirm it. Agreed. But that does not mean we cannot do more for the poor. There are caveats to the merits of cancelling Third World debt – we need to make sure the poor actually benefit from it and that governments do not get their countries into a similar mess again – but let that not blind us to the overwhelming humanitarian case for helping desperately poor countries weighed down by debts they can never conceivably pay back. Nor is it right that the richest country on earth, the US, donates a mere thousandth of its national income in overseas aid – and that mostly to client states like Israel and Egypt. Yes, of course, lots of aid has been wasted in the past. But it is not beyond the wit of man to devise aid schemes that actually help people – witness America's Marshall Plan that helped rebuild war-torn Europe – rather than pay for weapons or five-star hotels for international consultants. Nor is it enough to point out that economic growth lifts all boats and that the poor in poor countries gain from trade as much as the rich. An extra 1 per cent is just one more cent a day on a dollar a day but another thousand dollars a year on a $100,000 a year. Sharing out wealth more equally can go hand in hand with economic growth. Indeed, it is easier to redistribute when countries are growing fast, because it is easier to share out a rapidly expanding pie than a shrinking one.

Making it better

Vietnam provides a good example of how the poor profit from globalisation. Poverty has been cut in half in ten years. In 1988, when *doi moi* was getting started, three-quarters of the population lived on less than a dollar a day. By 1998, 37 per cent did. Of the poorest 5 per cent of households in 1992 – and just think how grindingly poor the poorest 5 per cent were in a country like Vietnam in 1992 – 98 per cent were better off six years later. Ninety-eight per cent. Who said globalisation doesn't help the poor? This wonderful improvement has come about in part because Vietnam's exports of rice, which is mainly grown by poor farmers, have soared. Exports of coffee, seafood and oil have also leapt, as have those of labour-intensive goods, like clothes and shoes.

As you drive out of Ho Chi Minh City (formerly Saigon), you pass seemingly endless paddy fields. Rice farmers are bent double in the muddy water, working with their hands. Buffaloes till the soil. Women in conical hats with striking angular faces carry baskets balanced precariously on a rod on their shoulder. But then the regularity of open fields gives way to bustling new villages with colourful markets and all manner of small businesses. Suddenly, there it is: a gleaming white building that looks like an aircraft hangar. A huge sign on it proclaims 'WE CAN DO IT!' in big blue letters, crowned by a signature red swoosh. Where once there were rice paddies, there now lies a Nike factory.

To be accurate, Samyang is a Nike contract factory. Nike itself does not actually make any shoes or clothes – its expertise lies in design and marketing. It contracts out production to South Korean

and Taiwanese companies. Korean-owned Samyang also has factories in South Korea and the Philippines. Located in Trung An, a
village 32 kilometres north-west of Ho Chi Minh City, the factory
employs 5,200 people, mainly women in their twenties and thirties, nearly all of them local. They make 600,000 pairs of shoes a
month: the Speed Trainer Plus, the Air VS Mazy, the Air Max
Specter and Amplify, the Air Visi Ratic and the Air Zoom Seismic,
according to Ben Hur, the factory's memorably named business
manager. The shoes made at Samyang are shipped around the
world. The boxes piled up in the warehouse are labelled for
Stockport in Britain; Junction City, Kansas; France, Tokyo and
Melbourne, among other destinations.

Nike contract factories are made out to be the dark satanic mills
of the twenty-first century. They stand accused of all manner of
evils: paying their workers – including children – a pittance to toil
for long hours without any rights in appalling conditions. These
exploitative 'sweatshops' are a development dead-end, it is claimed,
not a stepping-stone out of poverty.

I went to Samyang fearing the worst. But I was pleasantly surprised. Its six vast buildings are set among well-kept lawns and a
variety of tropical trees. It looks more like London's Kew Gardens or
a Californian arboretum than a shoe factory. The temperature in
the midday sun is in the low thirties centigrade: I am dripping
with sweat. Inside, fans keep the workers cooler. They are mainly
young women, neatly dressed in turquoise short-sleeved shirts and
dark trousers. Wearing protective goggles, masks or gloves where
necessary, they cut, stitch, mould and glue. Not the most inspiring
work, perhaps, but they are happy to have it.

'This is the only job I've had. I've been here six years. I'm happy
here,' says Miss Thi, a meek young girl of twenty-four. Le Thi Minh,
who is also twenty-four and has been working as a cutter for two
years, agrees: 'I like it here. I used to work in a Vietnamese factory
in Dong Nai province. But it is better here. The pay is better. And
the atmosphere suits my personality.' Pham Thi Mai, twenty-five,
stands out from the crowd with her bright red shirt. She used to

stitch, but is now a supervisor, overseeing thirty-two stitchers. 'It's a good place to work,' she says. 'Working relations are good. I've been here over five years and I'm happy. Before that I worked in a Vietnamese textiles factory. This is better, more convenient. The main problem is communication problems.' Even Nguyen Ngoc Tuan, the union representative, is positive. 'Yes, it's a good place to work. We don't generally have many problems with management, though there can be communication problems. What we really want is consistent orders, so the workers can feel secure in their jobs.' If you boycott Nike, these Vietnamese workers' jobs are at risk.

'Communication problems' is code for difficulties with the Korean managers. Koreans are notoriously abrupt; some would say rude. The Vietnamese are typically self-effacing. This culture clash can cause friction and misunderstanding. Yet in many ways, Samyang is a model factory. Workers earn an average of $54 a month. A pittance by our standards, admittedly. But not as little as it seems. A dollar goes much further in Vietnam than it does in America – five times further, according to the World Bank – because the cost of living is so much lower, so $54 buys as much in Vietnam as $270 does in the US. More importantly, Samyang pays double the local average of $27 a month. It also pays much more than the legal minimum wage in foreign factories of $35 a month in rural areas, $40 in the suburbs and $45 in cities. In state-owned factories, the minimum wage is only $15 a month, while middle-ranking officials may earn $45. Samyang's workers are hardly desperate to leave: two-thirds of them have been with the company for over three years.

Critics often point out that the cost of the labour that goes into making a shoe is only a fraction of its final price. This is a red herring. Labour costs are determined by the amount of labour used, as well as by prevailing local wages – and as we have seen, Samyang pays twice the local average. The price of a shoe is set according to what consumers are willing to pay for it. If this exceeds what it costs to make, then it is profitable to do so. The idea that the gap between the labour cost and the retail price is pure profit for Nike is fanciful. Nike's total profits of $590 million in 2001 were only 6.2 per cent of its sales of $9.5 billion. According to Nike, it pays its contractors an average of $18 a shoe, of which materials account for $11, labour $2, other costs $4 and profit $1. It then marks up the shoes by 100 per cent and sells them to retailers for $36. This covers the product cost, the costs of design, research and development, marketing, advertising, shipping, production management, other sales and business costs, taxes, plus a profit. The retailer marks the shoes up another 100 per cent and sells them to the consumer for $72. Retail costs include the product cost, rent, staff wages, shrinkage, insurance, advertising, supplies and services, depreciation, taxes and profit. Higher-end shoes (over $100) make up only a small portion of overall sales.

That Samyang's workers could not easily afford the shoes they make is also beside the point. Italians who work in a Ferrari factory can scarcely afford one of the sports cars they make. Nor can chambermaids at the Waldorf Astoria afford to spend the night there. People do not work in order to consume what they produce. They do so to earn money to spend on other things.

The benefits of that spending power can be felt for miles around. Since Samyang opened in November 1995, the share of local people earning less than $10 a month has fallen from 20 per cent to 8 per cent. One in five of the locals now earn more than $30, twice as many as in 1995. Over three-quarters now have a television, compared with only a third in 1995. Eight per cent have a phone, four times more than before. Two in three have a motorbike, up from one in three. Samyang's workers and their neighbours are no longer just subsisting; they have a bit extra to spend too. The new bike-repair shops, mini-markets and food outlets testify to that.

Like all Nike contract employees in Vietnam, Samyang staff also get an annual bonus of at least one month's pay; twelve to sixteen days' annual leave plus eight days off for national and international holidays; special leave for personal reasons; and four months' paid maternity leave. Vietnam's labour laws – which are much stricter than in most poor countries: this is meant to be a worker's paradise, after all – are scrupulously enforced. Children under fifteen are not allowed to work; Nike does not employ anyone under sixteen in its clothing factories or under-eighteens in its shoe factories. Workers put in forty-eight-hour weeks: eight hours a day, six days a week, with an hour's break for lunch, which is provided free in the company's sparkling clean canteen. They are only allowed to work 200 hours of overtime a year; they earn at least 50 per cent extra for overtime on working days, double pay on days off and holidays, and an extra 30 per cent at night. Nike factories are closed on Sundays, except for periodic maintenance.

Nearly a third of Samyang's employees are union members. A labour-practices committee was also set up in February 2000 to improve relations between bosses and workers and safeguard workers' welfare. Korean managers are taught about Vietnamese culture; the Vietnamese about Korea's. Workers receive quarterly labour-law training. Posters setting out their rights and benefits are prominently displayed on the walls. Workers who suggest valuable improvements can get a $200 bonus: $18,000 is paid out each year. Locals are increasingly trained to become managers: twenty-two Vietnamese have been promoted to assistant manager since January 2001; the aim is to have 70 per cent local managers by 2002. Samyang provides free evening classes and materials for workers who have not completed high school. It has also donated $37,000 to local charities since 1996. The cost of all this corporate do-goodery is pretty slim: roughly $100,000 a year, on top of labour costs of $4.8 million a year. It is good for the company as well as the staff. Defects have fallen by two-thirds, as has inventory; productivity is up by a third.

The factory is bright, airy, clean and safe. With so much flammable material around, good fire safety is essential. The emergency exits are clearly marked, as are the escape routes, which are clear of clutter. A big fire-evacuation plan is pinned on the wall, and fire drills are held regularly. To prevent injuries, all workers receive safety training. Warning signs are everywhere. Where machines

[handwritten margin note: How indicative is this environment?]

have potentially dangerous exposed moving parts, iron grates pro-tect workers' fingers. Health risks are also minimised. Solvent-based adhesives, which smell awful and can give you a headache or worse, have been replaced by water- or detergent-based glues. The air quality in the factory is tested by US companies, with exposures to harmful chemicals measured against permissible limits set by the US Occupational Safety and Health Administration. Staff get free healthcare and cheap medicines. Pham Chi Tanh, the factory clinic's doctor, says around 150 work-ers a day come to see him, mainly for headaches, coughs and colds. They pay a fifth of the cost of any medicines they need. Samyang aims to be eco-friendly too. Waste is sorted: some is recycled, some reused. Used fabrics and leather, which used to be burned, are now used to stuff sofas and motorbike seats. A waste-water treatment plant is under construction.

Is this all a façade? Is Samyang a Potemkin factory, a sham to show to foreigners? Or perhaps a speakeasy sweatshop, where as soon as outsiders are gone, all sorts of illicit activities take place? I have no reason to think so. Everyone I spoke to seemed genuine. My experience chimes with that of reports from other foreigners – journalists, academics, politicians – who have visited Nike factories in Vietnam. Workplace standards in all Nike factories are also inde-pendently audited by PricewaterhouseCoopers, as well as by CESAIS, the University of Science and Economics in Ho Chi Minh City.

Have conditions at Samyang improved since it became the target of activists' campaigns? Almost certainly. In separate incidents at other Nike contract factories in Vietnam in 1996 and 1997, workers were forced to jog round the factory and lick the floor, and were hit with shoe parts. In 1999, a Korean supervisor at one factory was accused of snapping employees' bra straps. Human-rights activists rightly protested about this. Nike at first tried to deny the charges but eventually responded by cleaning up its act (the supervisor was fired). When I asked Samyang's president, Jack Lee, a wily old man with glasses and a tartan top, whether Nike had forced him to improve conditions at the factory, he replied: 'No. It was our initiative, under Nike's guidance. It's not a condition of our contract with Nike. But it makes sense for us: healthier and happier workers are better workers.' That is not quite true: Nike requires its contractors to abide by local labour laws and to respect its corporate code of conduct.

Nike has had a presence in Vietnam since 1995. It was one of the first US companies to start doing business in the country after Bill Clinton announced the lifting of America's trade embargo on 3 February 1994. Spreading production among many countries reduces the risk that the company will be hammered by political turmoil, economic upheaval or a change in import rules. Nike sources nearly two-fifths of its gear from China, over a quarter from Indonesia and around 15 per cent from both Vietnam and Thailand. Vietnam's political stability was a big plus: the communists have opened up the economy but maintain a tight grip on power. So was its young, highly literate population: nearly three-fifths of Vietnam's 78 million people are under twenty-five; 95 per cent of men and 91 per cent of women over fifteen can read and write. As were its low wages: average income per person was $290 in 1996 (it had risen to $390 by 2000). Samyang also got state aid. 'The government was very encouraging,' says Mr Lee. 'It gave us tax breaks: we didn't have to pay any corporation tax for the first four years, and now we are paying only half the usual rate for the subsequent four. We also didn't pay any duties to import the materials we needed to set up the factory. Our lease for the site is for thirty years, but it can be extended.'

On the downside, Vietnam's roads are poor and narrow and the power supply erratic: Samyang has a back-up generator. Moreover, until a US–Vietnam trade agreement was ratified in late November 2001, America slapped higher customs duties on imports from Vietnam than on those from most other countries. Nike does not make Air Jordan basketball shoes in Vietnam because they would, until recently, have had to pay 30 to 40 per cent higher US import duties than on those made in Indonesia. Cortez running shoes, which sell well in Europe, are made in Vietnam, because the EU does not discriminate against Vietnamese exports.

Samyang is one of five Nike contract factories in Vietnam. Together, they employ over 46,000 people – more than any other private company in Vietnam. (Some of them also make shoes for other Western companies, like Adidas.) Over 22 million pairs of Nike shoes were made in Vietnam in 2000. That adds up to $400 million in exports. Clothing exports were worth a further $50 million. Nike contract factories are the second-biggest exporters in Vietnam, after Japan's Fujitsu. They account for 7 per cent of manufacturing exports and nearly 4 per cent of total exports.

Nine-tenths of the raw materials needed to make Nike shoes are imported. Even the shoeboxes are shipped from the US, because Vietnam does not produce recycled cardboard. Only the rubber is local. So the main benefits Vietnam derives from Nike's presence are good jobs and the transfer of technology and management skills.

To get a better point of comparison, I also visited a locally owned 'no-brand' shoe factory called Husan, in the Tan Binh district of Ho Chi Minh City. My car fought its way through narrow city streets crammed with the ubiquitous *xe om*, literally 'hugging vehicles', the motor scooters that have displaced bicycles. (The bike of choice is a Honda, but a Chinese company has just started selling much cheaper Honda replicas. The first stop for any new owner is to pick up a Honda badge to stick on it: foreign brands are the bees' knees.) Yet the squalor that surrounds Husan – kids picking off rubbish, putrid smells – is a reminder of how poor most Vietnamese still are. The factory building looks decrepit, yet it is only three years old. It burned down in 1998 – nobody died, thank goodness – and has since been rebuilt.

Posing as a student in order to get access to the factory, I quiz Tran Trung Kien, the export sales manager, about Husan. It has been in business since 1992 and now makes 1.8 million pairs of shoes a year, all for export, mainly to Belgium, the Netherlands and Germany. I spot shoes labelled GAT – a rip-off of CAT. It also sells slippers to Germany. Most of its sales go through Hong Kong mid-dlemen, so he can't tell me where the shoes actually end up. But he does say that one of its main customers is Reno, a German clothing retailer. Husan sells the shoes for $3.50 to $5.50 apiece and the slip-pers for $1.50. It imports 60 per cent of its raw materials and sources 40 per cent locally. Unlike Samyang, it pays 45 per cent tax. The fac-tory, which is fully unionised, employs 700 workers. Mr Tran claims that workers are paid $60 a month, but a paysheet on the wall sug-gests they actually make $37 to $52 a month. They work twelve-hour shifts, including overtime. Mr Tran says Husan provides health-and-safety training, but there are no fire exits. The aisles are cluttered with bits and pieces; the machinery is old; and the shattered-look-ing workers are not wearing protective gloves or masks.

Workers at Nike are privileged by comparison. Indeed, people who work for multinational companies are typically winners. Edward Graham of the Institute for International Economics, a think-tank in Washington DC, finds[7] that people in poor countries who work for the foreign affiliates of US firms earn on average double the domestic manufacturing wage. In middle-income coun-tries, like Mexico, employees of US firms earn 80 per cent more than the domestic norm. Even in rich countries, US firms pay 40 per cent more than local ones. (All these calculations exclude the wages of expatriates.) Other studies of Mexico, Venezuela, China and Turkey throw up similar results. Working for an international firm is a boon.

Yet even factories like Husan are a step up from working in the fields or a state-owned enterprise. By and large, people choose to work there rather than elsewhere. It is wrong to judge conditions in a Vietnamese factory by our standards. A Westerner might argue, for instance, that all factories should be air-conditioned. True, it would be more pleasant if they were. But since the cost of air-conditioning is prohibitively expensive and very power-intensive, requiring all Vietnamese factories to fit it would drive many out of business. Many workers would end up unemployed or breaking their backs in the fields in the boiling sun. Would they be better off? Clearly not.

defence of child labour?

Similarly, a ban on all child labour could be counterproductive. If parents cannot afford to keep their kids in school, preventing them from working merely makes their lives more wretched – and may drive them into illicit activities like prostitution. Compare this with Europe and North America, where many university students hold down jobs. Arguably, this detracts from their studies, so a case could be made for banning college students from working: they could then concentrate on their courses. But such a ban would prevent many students from poor families from going to university at all. Aha, you say, but the government could give them bigger grants to compensate. True enough, in rich countries. But that is typically not an option in a very poor country. Governments cannot afford to cover kids' living expenses while they are at school.

It is misguided to stipulate that labour standards should be the same everywhere. They tend to improve over time, as countries get richer. A study by the Brookings Institution in Washington DC found that whereas in countries where income per person is under $500, 30 to 60 per cent of children between the ages of ten and fourteen work, 10 to 30 per cent do so in countries where income per person is between $500 and $1,000. South Korea's example, which I will discuss later in this chapter, confirms this. Even so, there is clearly a basic minimum that should apply everywhere now: slavery is illegal, for instance, and other appalling and abusive conditions should be too.

The sweatshop solution

There is no denying that conditions in some Third World – and even a few rich-world – factories are unacceptably bad. What should be done about them? International pressure can help. Exposing corruption and human-rights abuses, naming and shaming, and so on, can be useful. But it is mostly up to developing-country governments, responding to local pressure, to enforce labour laws that suit their local conditions.

? marshalled via globalisation!

Stopping globalisation is not a solution. Contrary to what critics of globalisation claim, the worst factories are generally local ones producing for the domestic market. That is certainly what two independent studies find.[8] The International Labour Organisation (ILO) found that most child labour takes place in the domestic, not the export, agricultural sector. The truth is that globalisation cannot be blamed for creating most sweatshops – and putting a stop to globalisation would not end worker exploitation. Indeed, the sectors in which sweatshops are concentrated – clothing, shoes, sports goods and toys – account for less than 10 per cent of world goods exports and well under 7 per cent of the stock of US direct investment abroad.[9] So even if some foreign-owned exporters run sweatshops, the overwhelming majority do not. Making multinationals pull out of poor countries would do far more harm than good.

Another possibility is to impose trade sanctions on countries that fail to enforce minimum labour standards. This is what many European and North American trade unions advocate, as do many other critics of globalisation. During the ill-fated World Trade Organisation meeting in Seattle in 1999, Bill Clinton said he shared this aim. But there are all sorts of reasons why this is a bad idea. For a start, it would be a charter for protectionist abuse. We saw how the steel industry has manipulated anti-dumping laws to block imports that it cannot compete with. Uncompetitive industries in rich countries would undoubtedly use alleged labour abuses in a poor country as a pretext for demanding protection from its imports. After all, why else are trade unions in rich countries so keen on the idea? Their responsibility is to their members, not to workers around the world. As a senior American trade-union leader candidly admitted to me in private: 'We don't give a damn about workers in the Third World. We just want to protect our members' interests.' Workers of the world unite? You must be joking. Workers in rich countries see their Third World brothers as rivals. As Phil Pack of Bethlehem Steel admits: 'Yes, we can unite on a common platform of things like freedom of speech. But not on economic issues. Just look at it within the US. We have an interest in steel prices being high; autoworkers want cheap steel.'

Even if the allegations were genuine, sanctions would punish whole countries for the abuses of a few factories. That is clearly unfair. Even if the sanctions were targeted only at, say, the clothing sector, it would still harm the innocent as well as the guilty – and deprive workers in decent factories of their jobs. For sanctions to be fair, they would have to zero in on the few genuinely abusive factories.

Labelling is a better option. Clothing companies that treat their workers decently could advertise this with a logo on their products. One example of this is America's Fair Labor Association's scheme, whereby firms (including Nike) agree to abide by stringent but self-enforced labour standards. It was set up at President Clinton's instigation by a group of clothing companies known as the White House Apparel Industry Partnership. But even this project is far from perfect. It would be better, for instance, if standards were independently monitored rather than self-enforced, with spot checks by well-respected human-rights groups, say. Another problem is that the scheme helps rich-country firms at the expense of equally decent local ones: no poor-country companies bear its 'No Sweat' logo. A third danger is that, under pressure from unions and other critics, it will ratchet up standards too high, and thus needlessly cost jobs in poor countries. Perhaps most importantly, if the aim is genuinely to help workers in sweatshops, rather than just to ease Western shoppers' guilty consciences, it will do nothing to improve conditions in the vast majority of sweatshops, which are locally owned and produce for the domestic market. Surely it is equally terrible if Bangladeshi children are slaving away making clothes for the local market as it is if they are making branded ones for Americans? Or do we only care if they are stitching Nikes?

So here's a thought. Why not lend desperately poor countries a helping hand rather than bashing them with a big stick? Rich countries could pay for schools in poor countries that enforce basic labour standards. The ILO has drawn up four core labour standards:

the right to set up a free trade union, including the right to strike and bargain collectively; the abolition of forced labour; a ban on the worst forms of child labour; and the elimination of discrimination in employment and occupation. All ILO member governments have signed up to these standards, but many do not enforce them. Rich countries could pay into a fund that gave aid to poor countries that the ILO deemed were in compliance with its core labour standards. That would give poor countries a big incentive to clamp down on sweatshops, whoever owns them and wherever they sell to. It would reward good behaviour rather than punishing bad, and it would not be open to protectionist manipulation. If North American and European unions really care about Third World workers, they should back this idea wholeheartedly. So should corporate bashers, if they are interested in more than just hitting out at capitalism. If we genuinely care, we should put our money where our mouth is. Talk is cheap. Dressing up in silly costumes and protesting in the streets is fun. Boycotting Nike is self-righteous. But coughing up more to help the poor is right.

From wigs to riches

In 1960, North Korea was twice as rich as the South. South Korea was poorer than most countries in Africa. Everybody wrote it off, including the World Bank – and even most Koreans. What hope could this war-ravaged, aid-dependent, overcrowded country with few natural resources, little arable land and a tiny domestic market possibly have? 'What do we have to export? Who is going to buy what we make?' the people of the Hermit Kingdom asked themselves. Yet in December 1996, South Korea joined the OECD, the rich-countries' club. Its people are now as rich as the Portuguese. It is the world's biggest shipbuilder and a big producer of steel and semiconductors. We used to buy their wigs (once their third-biggest export); now we drive their cars (Hyundais and Daewoos). It is the world leader in broadband Internet: more than half of South

Korean homes have access to it. Not bad for a bunch of peasants that the Japanese, who ran Korea between 1910 and 1945, once dismissed as 'dogs'.

Of all the many wrong-headed things that Naomi Klein says in *No Logo*, perhaps the most ill-judged is her dismissal of the Asian tiger economies like South Korea. 'Development built on starvation wages, far from kick-starting a steady improvement in conditions, has proved to be a case of one step forward, three steps back,' she claims. 'By early 1998 there were no more shining Asian Tigers to point to, and those corporations and economists that had mounted such a singular defence of sweatshops had had their arguments entirely discredited.' Tell that to the South Koreans. Notwithstanding the huge blow of the Asian financial crisis in 1997, all of them are much, much better off than they were in the 1960s.

Along with Taiwan, South Korea is the most spectacular success story of our era of globalisation. Between 1965 and 1999, income per person in both countries rose by 6.6 per cent a year. That means the average South Korean and Taiwanese is nine times richer than thirty-five years ago. Other star performers cannot quite match up to them: China managed 6.4 per cent; Singapore, 6.3 per cent; Thailand, 5.1 per cent; Indonesia, 4.8 per cent; Malaysia, 4.3 per cent; and Japan, 3.4 per cent. The average Korean born in 1960 could expect to live fifty-four years. Life expectancy at birth is now seventy-five years. South Korea's share of world trade has risen over sixty-fold, from 0.04 per cent in 1962 to 2.5 per cent in 2000. What did the country do right?

Start with what it did not do wrong. In the 1960s, the fashionable plan for going from poverty to prosperity was to industrialise through import substitution. Poor countries should stop importing steel, cars and other industrial products from advanced countries and make them themselves. The way to encourage home-grown industrialisation was to keep out foreign competitors with high import barriers and restrictions on inward investment. These barriers could eventually be lifted, it was argued, once domestic companies had grown strong enough to fend for themselves.

That was the theory. The practice was a disaster. Just look at India. It has a huge population, and hence a potentially large domestic market. So even if Indian companies did not export, they could still get big enough serving the Indian market to reap economies of scale. The market was also large enough to sustain competition between these big firms. If import substitution could work anywhere, surely it was India.

It didn't. India's experiment in industrialisation along national lines bred 'national champions' that actually championed their own interests at the expense of ordinary Indians. Big companies fleeced consumers, selling shoddy goods for inflated prices. Rather than investing their profits in better technology, they chose to lobby for more special favours from government. Bureaucrats who thought they knew best tied the economy up in red tape – quotas, tariffs, permits, licences – that distorted incentives, stifled entrepreneurship and bred corruption. The state poured vast sums into white elephants. The fat cats lived the life of Riley; the poor, often literally, starved. Indian companies did not invest enough. Nor, without the spur of foreign competition or signals from world prices to guide them, did they invest wisely. The economy stagnated. India's already miserable living standards actually fell in the 1960s and 1970s. The epitome of India's failure is the 'Amby', a joke of a car – which is still being made today – based on the outmoded technology of the British Austin of the 1960s. Eventually, India's politicians started to learn from their mistakes. In 1991, they began to open up the economy. Income per person rose by 2.6 per cent a year between 1990 and 1995 and 4.4 per cent a year between 1995 and 2000. But India still has a lot more opening up to do. India's average import duty has fallen sharply from 82 per cent in 1990, but it was still 30 per cent in 1997. The task ahead is huge. Suman Bery of the National Council of Applied Economic Research, a Delhi-based think-tank, compares the reforms India requires to 'restoring a decaying manor house'.

Fortunately, South Korea chose to develop along different lines. Instead of focusing on the domestic market, Korean companies channelled all their energies into selling abroad. Because they had to compete in world markets, they had to relentlessly raise their game. Those that failed to do so, or made investment mistakes, went bust. Those that invested wisely soon flourished.

That is the broad thrust of it. South Korea got rich by exporting. As a share of national income, exports rose from 2.4 per cent in 1962 to 23.7 per cent in 1973. By 1999, they were 42 per cent of GDP. Export earnings paid for imports of better capital equipment that boosted private investment and improved the economy's productivity. But government played a part too. Its philosophy, says Il SaKong, a former finance minister, was 'where the market works, fine; where it doesn't, let's make it work'. For a start, it made a priority of education, which improved workers' skills and boosted productivity. It paid for Korean high-flyers to study in the US, then lured them back home with huge salaries. Second, it made it easy for companies to import the inputs and technology they needed in order to export. Third, it encouraged people to save by raising domestic interest rates. Fourth, it helped companies to invest, by channelling money to them through state-owned banks and by guaranteeing their foreign loans. It ensured that this money was invested productively by cutting off funds from firms that were not successful exporters. Indirectly, the market, not the government, picked winners.

Even South Korea made mistakes. In 1972, it bailed out big companies rather than allowing them to go bust. It then launched a huge drive to develop heavy and chemical industries, such as shipbuilding, cars, steel and petrochemicals, through government-directed import substitution. Some people argue that this industrial policy – rather than the country's export orientation – is responsible for South Korea's stunning success. Yet growth took off before this import-substitution drive and continued after it was abandoned. Studies show that most of the country's growth came from the industries where it had a comparative advantage, like shoes and electrical goods, rather than from government-directed heavy industries. Soon Hoon Bae, a former president of the Daewoo group, concurs. 'Protecting heavy and chemical industries didn't help much,' he told me. Moreover, when the economy ended up in recession with high inflation in 1980, the government changed course. It reverted to its export-oriented strategy, combined with anti-inflationary policies and cuts in import duties. (I will discuss what went wrong during the 1997 Asian financial crisis in chapter eleven.)

South Korea started on the bottom rung of the ladder and climbed steadily up. It takes time to build up people's skills and accumulate capital. At first, it played host to sweatshops where low-paid workers stitched together Nike shoes and the like. The export earnings were ploughed in to improving the country's schools and infrastructure. That in turn made South Koreans more productive and thus able to command higher wages. Nike's factories moved to poorer countries like Indonesia and the Philippines – a shift that Naomi Klein bemoans – and South Koreans moved on to producing higher value-added products. As South Koreans got richer, they demanded improvements in workers' rights and more stringent environmental controls. These higher labour and environmental standards have probably dented their wages a little, but that cost is more than outweighed by the perceived benefits. Along the way, incidentally, South Korea became a democracy. Workers eventually demanded a say as well as higher pay. 'The 1988 Olympics were crucial,' says Soogil Young, an economist who was the country's first ambassador to the OECD. 'They focused the attention of the world on us and put pressure on the government to clean up its act.' Perhaps the Beijing Olympics in 2008 will stimulate change in China too.

Of course, this potted history is a simplification. But the facts of South Korea's development – and North Korea's and Africa's stagnation – are not in doubt. Although there is some disagreement about how that success was achieved, it is obvious that some things were crucial. South Korea got richer through trade. It got richer by saving a lot and investing wisely. It got richer because the government provided schools and infrastructure but also let companies import foreign technology and capital. Globalisation alone did not make South Korea rich. But without it, South Korea could never have succeeded.

Still a ladder up

South Korea's record is truly outstanding. But could it be replicated now? Many critics of globalisation think not. They claim that South Korea and the other Asian tigers, like Taiwan, Singapore and Hong Kong, were able to get rich through trade because they had so few competitors: most developing countries were turned inwards, pursuing import substitution. Now that China and even India are trying to export the same products as other developing countries, the argument goes, export prices are falling relentlessly, trapping poor countries in misery.

It is not an entirely ludicrous argument. Many small countries that export only a handful of commodities have been plagued by falling prices. For instance, Uganda, which gets over half its export earnings from coffee, has seen the average price of its exports fall by a third between 1997 and 2000. Even so, Uganda, one of the few African countries to embrace globalisation, is a success story: its economy grew by 6 per cent a year on average in the three years to 2000.

More importantly, developing countries in general are unlikely to face continually worsening terms of trade. If export prices are falling, the supply of a product must be rising faster than the demand for it. Critics implicitly assume that supply is skyrocketing but that demand is somehow capped. Neither assumption is likely to be true. For a start, developing-country exports are still small relative to the world economy. Total exports from developing countries came to $1.7 trillion in 1999. It sounds big, but it is less than a quarter of world trade and a mere 5.6 per cent of world output. So even if developing-country exports shoot up, the impact on the world economy will be pretty small. Moreover, it is a mistake to assume that all developing countries export the same things. They don't. South Africa's main exports are metals, gold and diamonds. Brazil's are transport equipment, metal products, soybeans and chemicals. China's are machinery and transport equipment, clothes, and computing and telecoms equipment. South Korea's are mainly electronics. And so on. Of course, developing countries sometimes compete with each other, but they are not all making the same things. There is also plenty of scope for developing countries to diversify more. Trade in agriculture and services, which together account for two-thirds of the world economy, is underdeveloped, partly because trade barriers remain high. If they were lowered, the range of products that developing countries could export would be much greater. And, as countries get richer, they move up the production ladder and stop exporting the products they used to sell. South Korea hardly makes any shoes any more; China, Indonesia and Vietnam have stepped in where it left off. Even when countries export the same things, they can still find niches for themselves. Most big rich countries export cars as well as import them: they typically make different cars. Germany sells Volkswagens to the French; France sells Peugeots to the Germans. Also, as developing countries get richer, their imports from other developing countries rise. And, as rich countries get richer, their imports rise too. The clincher is that even though more and more developing countries are pursuing export-led growth, their economic growth is not slowing down. On the contrary, as the Dollar and Kraay study I mentioned at the beginning of this chapter shows, their growth is speeding up. Not for the first time, critics of globalisation are being unduly pessimistic.

Mind the gap

The evidence that globalisation helps alleviate poverty is overwhelming. But isn't the gulf between rich and poor still getting bigger? This is a tricky question. Measuring global inequality is notoriously difficult. It can be measured in many different ways, and the data is often incomplete. One way to measure inequality is the percentage gap between a typical person's income and average income – between the median and mean, to use the statistical jargon.[10] There are around 6 billion people in the world and total world income is around $30,000 billion. So average income is around $5,000 per person. But if everyone if the world stood in a long line, with Bill Gates at the front and the poorest person at the back, the person in the middle would have an income of around $1,000. If everyone had the same income, the person in the middle would earn $5,000. In fact, that person earns 80 per cent less than the average, which is skewed upwards by a relatively small number of rich people. The bigger that gap, the more unequal the world's income distribution is.

François Bourguignon and Christian Morrisson, two French economists at Delta,[11] a research institute in Paris, have charted[12] the change in global inequality since 1820. They find that world inequality increased steadily between 1820 and 1980 – the gap between a typical person's income and the average widened from around 40 per cent to around 80 per cent – but that between 1980 and 1992, inequality fell a little. The historical rise in inequality was overwhelmingly due to differing growth rates among countries, rather than increased inequality within countries. Very broadly speaking, Europe, North America and Japan industrialised, the rest of the world did not.

Ximena Clark, David Dollar and Aart Kraay of the World Bank[13] use a similar method to track changes in inequality since 1960. They find that global inequality rose between 1960 and 1975 but fell between 1975 and 1995, largely because of faster economic growth in China and India, two poor countries that together account for three in eight of the world's population.

Another way to measure inequality is to look at what has happened to people living in extreme poverty. Between 1987 and 1998, the share of the world's population living on less than a dollar a day fell from 28 per cent to 23 per cent. This fall is bigger than the decline one would have seen had everybody's income increased at the same rate over that period. So inequality has fallen somewhat. Again, this is mostly explained by faster growth in China and India, which together accounted for over three-fifths of the world's extreme poor in 1975.

A third way of gauging global inequality is to look at how different groups of countries have fared. The gap between rich countries and the globalising poor ones that Dollar and Kraay identified widened until 1975 but has since narrowed sharply. Globalising developing countries are catching up because their economies are growing faster – although this reduction in inequality was partly offset by rising inequality within China. At the same time, the gap between globalising developing countries and non-globalising ones is growing. In short, poor countries that are globalising are catching up with rich countries; poor countries that aren't are falling further behind. This pattern also holds within countries: the urban, outward-looking coastal regions of China are pulling ahead; the rural inward-looking interior is falling behind. The people who are being left behind are victims not of globalisation, but of a lack of globalisation. So the challenge is to help them join the world economy, not put a stop to globalisation.

Vignettes of hope

Cuba is hardly a poster-child for globalisation: Fidel Castro never ceases to rail against global capitalism. His regime defines itself by its opposition to 'Yanqui imperialism'. Yet his country is utterly dependent on foreign tourism, and its currency of choice is the US dollar. Indeed, the government goes as far as minting its own wannabe dollars, known as convertible pesos, which deliberately mimic the US currency. It all makes the American embargo seem particularly absurd. Castro is not a threat to anyone apart from Cubans.

Some of the Revolution's achievements are real: people are healthy and well educated. Cuba's infant mortality rate is the same as the much richer US's – and less than a quarter of Mexico's. Cubans can expect to live as long as the Danes, and twenty-three years longer than Haitians. Cuba's female illiteracy rate is the same as Greece's. So Cubans are well equipped to lead fulfilling lives. Yet what the government gives with one hand, it takes back with the other. It denies Cubans the chance to make the most of their lives. It clamps down on private enterprise, restricts foreign travel and limits contact with foreigners. Access to the Internet is allowed only through official media, international calls cost several dollars a minute in a country where the average wage is $15 a month, and contact with tourists is controlled by policemen who are on every corner.

What a crying shame! Just think what Cuba could achieve if it embraced the world. Yet even in Cuba, globalisation is making life better. Eddie is a qualified engineer. He works for the government for $15 a month. 'I can't live on that,' he explains. 'I have two sons to bring up.' So he moonlights as a taxi driver for tourists with his taxi-bike. The three dollars I gave him for puffing his way through Havana's grand but dilapidated streets are equivalent to nearly a week's wages. 'Ninety per cent of people want to leave. The Revolution is shit. The government is always controlling us, oppressing us, denying us our freedom.'

Lesotho, a small, mountainous country entirely surrounded by South Africa, is another unlikely beneficiary from globalisation. It is bleak, dusty, isolated and poor. Most people are still subsistence farmers. Even the king of Lesotho, a fat man with a plummy voice who studied at Ampleforth, a Catholic boarding school in Yorkshire, seems a little down at heel: he lives in a seventies palace, with an old-fashioned tape machine. In parliament, the speaker, a woman in a big white wig, cries 'order, order' in Westminster style to noisy MPs who rap their benches and roar their approval or disapproval. Lesotho seems stuck in a timewarp. How, you might ask, could globalisation possibly help?

Actually, how is a tiny, landlocked, backward country going to pull itself up if not by looking to the outside world? That is exactly what it is doing. Lesothans go work in South Africa and send some of their wages home. Increasingly, they also make clothes and shoes for export: Taiwanese companies produce jeans and T-shirts for sale in the US. The country plays an active role at the WTO. Lesotho's income per person has risen by 2.8 per cent a year on average since 1965 – the fastest growth rate in sub-Saharan Africa after Botswana's. Living standards have risen by 160 per cent in thirty-five years. Even in deepest Africa, globalisation can have an impact.

Nor is India, a country that promises much but has so far delivered little, immune. Indians abroad are strikingly successful, yet their country is mired in terrible poverty. The streets of Delhi are crammed with beggars missing arms, legs, eyes. The bureaucrats who meddle in everything are arrogant, incompetent and corrupt. One billion Indians sell less abroad than 5 million Danes or 200 million Indonesians do. Between 1965 and 2000, living standards in India rose even more slowly than in – whisper it softly – Pakistan.

But amid all the squalor and failure, there are pockets of success. In southern India, just outside Bangalore, amid fields where men work with hand-sickles, lies an immaculate complex of buildings with sculpted gardens, water features and a swimming pool. Some tycoon's palace? No: the headquarters of Wipro, a conglomerate spanning everything from vegetable oils to software services that aspires to be India's General Electric.

Amazingly, in a country where the dead hand of government holds everything back, Wipro is a world-beating IT services firm. Among its clients are over fifty of America's top 500 companies, including GE and Compaq, as well as Canada's Nortel Networks and Britain's Transco (formerly British Gas). In 1990, Wipro was valued at 2 billion Indian rupees. Ten years later, it was worth 368 billion rupees (around $6 billion). It is now India's biggest soft-ware-services company, with its shares quoted on Wall Street and pre-tax profits of 7.7 billion rupees in 2000. It is expanding overseas, with sales offices and development centres around the world, including Phoenix, Arizona; Santa Clara in Silicon Valley; and Reading in Britain. Soon it aims to be among the top ten IT services companies in the world.

The striking thing about Wipro is how un-Indian it is. In a country obsessed with hierarchy and formality, where talk takes precedence over action, Wipro is all about merit and delivery. The head of marketing is not a middle-aged man promoted on seniority, but a thirty-two-year-old woman promoted on merit. I asked Sangita Singh about the secret of Wipro's success. On her shelf are books on topics like *Managing the Value Chain*, as well as a teddy bear. Her mobile phone vibrates incessantly. She explains, terribly earnestly, that Wipro stands for 'applying thought'. I see. Or actually, I don't. Perhaps it's the jet lag. Or perhaps it's because, unlike Wipro staff, I have not been trained in 'Vision Break Out', one of the many courses on offer on the company campus.

Sangita certainly 'talks the talk and walks the walk', as she puts it. But I am still perplexed. What else is special about Wipro? 'Azim Premji only hires people with fire in their belly,' she replies. Wipro's boss, Mr Premji, a Stanford dropout who has been called an Indian Bill Gates, is her hero. When asked if she would work for Microsoft for double the money, she says they offered her three times as much and she turned them down. Patriotic pride? Not at all: loyalty to a company committed to quality, empowerment and job satisfaction, she says. And yet fire in your belly is not enough to make you successful. Muslims who burn American flags certainly have it, but it does not make them rich. So why is Wipro a success?

Sudip Banarjee, an old hand who has been with the company since the days when it concentrated on soaps and vegetable oils, explains. Wipro diversified into computing in the 1980s, when India's markets were closed to foreign companies like IBM. It made everything: microchips, computers and software. Its spreadsheet program was called 456, echoing the then-dominant Lotus 123.

When India started to open up in 1991, Wipro suddenly faced foreign competition. The 325 per cent duty on software was eliminated. Duties on computer peripherals were slashed from 146 per cent to between 10 and 20 per cent. Wipro could have become a distributor for foreign companies. Instead, armed with its experience, a skilled workforce (India produces more engineering graduates a year than anywhere bar the US) and low costs (programmers in Bangalore are paid $800 a month, compared with $5,000 a month or more in the US), it decided to globalise and compete. Because East Asia already dominated hardware production, it chose to focus on software services and research and development (R&D): a self-styled 'lab hire'. Pioneers such as GE and Nortel were looking to outsource their software services: Wipro had a market.

Some people might attribute Wipro's success to India's protectionism. Yet hardly any of the companies that prospered behind import barriers are now world-beaters. The truth is that Wipro has succeeded despite, rather than thanks to, the rest of India. It could be floated into the Indian Ocean and still do business. It bypasses India's appalling infrastructure by having its own power supply and leased telecoms links. It is unhindered by the rules and regulations that tie other sectors up in knots: the local government has kept red tape and taxes to a minimum. It is fortunate too that world IT markets are open – and that governments have committed themselves at the WTO to keeping them so.

Wipro's success, as well as that of its arch-rival Infosys, shows that Indian companies can compete in world markets. India's IT exports are growing at 50 per cent a year. They are expected to hit $6.3 billion in fiscal 2000, 15 per cent of India's total exports. More than 180 of the top 500 multinationals outsource their IT needs to Indian companies.

Is Wipro's success replicable? Yes. Already, India hosts call centres for British and American firms. Ex-Wipro staff have started up a host of new IT firms. Indians could also do well in areas such as telecoms, biotechnology and pharmaceuticals. Bollywood, its film industry, could also produce global hits. But to release India's

potential in manufacturing, where its bureaucracy, poor infrastructure and obstreperous unions are harder to dodge, the
country needs root-and-branch reforms. Globalisation could yet
transform India too, if only the government would wholeheartedly
embrace it.

as long as they are 'un-Indian'!

THREE

A Brief History of Globalisation

How our open world emerged

Proceeding three days' journey in a north-easterly direction, you arrive at a city called Shandu [Xanadu], built by the Grand Khan, Kublai, now reigning. In this he caused a palace to be erected, of marble and other handsome stones, admirable as well for the elegance of its design as for the skill displayed in its execution. The halls and chambers are all gilt, and very handsome. It presents one front towards the interior of the city, and the other towards the wall; and from such extremity of the building runs another wall to such an extent as to enclose sixteen miles in circuit of the adjoining plain, to which there is no access but through the palace. Within the bounds of this royal park there are rich and beautiful meadows, watered by many rivulets, where a variety of animals of the deer and goat kind are pastured, to serve as food for the hawks and other birds employed in the chase, whose mews are also in the grounds. The number of these birds is upwards of two hundred; and the Grand Khan goes in person, at least once in the week, to inspect them.

Frequently, when he rides about this enclosed forest, he has
one or more small leopards carried on horseback, behind
their keepers; and when he pleases to give direction for
their being slipped, they instantly seize a stag, or goat, or
fallow dear, which he gives to his hawks, and in this manner
amuses himself.[1]

Marco Polo

Imagine the excitement in Europe at the dawn of the fourteenth
century. Marco Polo has just written the first vivid eyewitness
account of the exotic lands to the east. Europeans knew Asia
existed, but had little idea what it was like. They traded with China,
but only through Muslim middlemen. European merchants could
supply Oriental drugs, silk and spices, but not descriptions of
where they came from. So Europeans conjured up fantasies about
dragons, sorcerers and strange barbaric practices. Suddenly, *The
Travels of Marco Polo* made Asia feel real.

Marco Polo sometimes lets his imagination run wild, and his
reputation has duly taken a battering. Some have even suggested
that he never actually made it to China. But critics are missing the
point. Marco Polo's tales created a fresh consciousness of a world
outside Europe – and a surprisingly advanced one at that. Kublai
Khan, grandson of the much feared Genghis, is no backward bar-
barian. Perhaps the civilised world did not end at Jerusalem after
all.

Kublai Khan's vast Mongol empire provided enough stability for
trade to flourish: a precursor of Britain's role in the nineteenth
century and America's in the twentieth. Europeans – rich ones
that is – benefited: spices not only taste good, they also stop food
from rotting. But with this increase in trade came new ills. The
Black Death, the plague that wiped out a third of Europe's population in the mid-fourteenth century, was imported from Asia by
rats travelling on trading caravans and ships. Europeans had no
immunity to this foreign bug, which is what made it so lethal.
Incas and other native Americans would prove similarly vulnerable

to the germs the Europeans brought with them in the sixteenth century.

Perhaps globalisation began with Marco Polo. Or maybe not. Nobody can say for sure. People have been on the move for time immemorial: scientists reckon all of us originate from Africa. One scholar, Andre Gunder Frank, argues that globalisation is at least 5,000 years old. By 1500 he says: 'there was a single global world economy with a worldwide division of labour and multilateral trade'.[2] That is unlikely: Christopher Columbus had only chanced upon America eight years earlier. But many writers[3] think globalisation began around 1500. In 1498, soon after Columbus discovered America, Vasco da Gama, a Portuguese explorer, sailed around the Cape of Good Hope, Africa's southern tip. This opened up a new trade route to India that bypassed the Arab world. Another Portuguese sailor, Ferdinand Magellan, went one better in 1519–22. He sailed round the globe, proving that the Americas were a new continent (rather than part of Asia) that separated the Atlantic and Pacific oceans, and that the earth was round. A new world had suddenly opened up.

Europeans took to the sea with gusto. They hoped to get rich through trade and plunder. They also wanted to gain glory by winning land for the king and souls for the Church. In Europe: A History, Norman Davies, a British historian, points out that for many Europeans these voyages provided their first meeting with people of different races. If such people actually were human, that is: 'To validate their claim over the inhabitants of the conquered lands, the Spanish monarchs had first to establish that non-Europeans were human . . . Pope Paul III decreed in 1537 that "all Indians are truly men, not only capable of receiving the Catholic faith, but . . . exceedingly desirous to receive it".'[4]

The Portuguese concentrated on commerce, the Spaniards on conquest. The conquistadors were obsessed with dreams of finding untold gold in El Dorado. Later came the Dutch, who muscled in on the Portuguese's lucrative trade with the East Indies, and the English, who colonised North America. Some simply sought a better life; others were fleeing religious persecution too, like the Puritans on the *Mayflower* who landed in Massachusetts Bay in 1620.

By 1600 international sea trade was thriving. The Spanish dominated trade with the New World: 200 ships a year made the crossing to Seville each year. In the 1590s they brought back 19,000 kilograms of gold and nearly 3 million kilograms of silver. The Portuguese and the Dutch handled business with Asia. The Dutch also acted as middlemen: most of Europe's trade flowed through Amsterdam, where the world's first stock exchange was founded in 1602.

The English were the Johnny-come-latelies. In 1600 they set up the East India Company, a precursor of today's allegedly all-mighty multinationals. The Company, soon joined by the Dutch East India Company (1602) and the French Compagnie des Indes (1664), really was powerful. It had a state-chartered monopoly on all commodity trade with the 'East Indies', the lands to the east of the Lebanon. It plundered as well as traded, built forts and block-aded ports, fought battles and captured territory. It was umbilically linked to the spread of English rule in India: Company men ran Bombay, Madras and Calcutta on behalf of the Crown. In 1757 Robert Clive, a Company employee, cemented British rule in India – and won himself a handsome fortune – by defeating the nawab of Bengal at the battle of Plassey. Eat your heart out Exxon: in the eighteenth century, companies really did run parts of the world.

Trade with Asia transformed Europe's tastes. Europeans got hooked on pepper, coffee and sugar. They sipped tea and wore cotton clothes. They swapped their silver, linens and woollens for Oriental silk, porcelain and gold. The discovery of America had an even more profound impact. What could be more French than French beans? More Italian than tomatoes and polenta? More Irish than potatoes? Yet all of them originated in the New World, as did tobacco, cocoa, coca and rubber. It was not all one-way traffic: Marlboro Man's horse came from Europe. So did Kellogg's cereals. Europeans also introduced horned cattle, sheep and sugar to the

Western hemisphere. Later, they imported slaves from Africa: perhaps 12 million (estimates vary from 5 to 20 million) were shipped
to the Americas before 1850.[5] Transatlantic trade in disease was
equally vigorous. Europeans came down with syphilis, the Aids of
its time, incurable until the discovery of penicillin in the 1930s.
Native Americans succumbed to smallpox, pleurisy and typhus.
Last but not least, many Europeans moved to the Americas and
Indies in search of a new life, bringing with them their cultures
and religions.

Between 1600 and 1750 the states on Europe's Atlantic seafront
scrambled for colonial advantage. Their mastery was unchallenged:
they had better ships and guns than the natives. While this created
new links with the Americas and Asia, it drove a wedge between
seafaring states and continental European powers such as Austria
and the German states. Part of Europe was now outward-looking,
part still resolutely turned inward. England benefited most: once a
poor state on the fringes of Europe, it became the hub of the predominant (British) global trading empire.

Contact with new cultures changed the way Europeans saw
themselves. Just as Marco Polo's had, books by European travellers
suggested different – perhaps even better – ways of doing things.
'These works often gave European readers a comparative perspective on the religions, folklore, and culture of the world; and they
handed the philosophers of the Enlightenment one of their most
effective devices for questioning European or Christian assumptions. It hit Europeans hard to learn that the Siamese might be
happier, the Brahmin more sagacious, or the Iroquois less blood-
thirsty than they were themselves.'[6]

Even so, as the Industrial Revolution dawned, Europeans dominated global trade. Yet the Chinese might have given them a good
run for their money. After all, the Chinese developed the compass,
paper, printing, gunpowder and much else long before Europeans
did. Astonishingly, their blast furnaces were apparently producing
as much pig iron in the late eleventh century as Britain was seven
centuries later.[7]

The Chinese made some forays into the Indian Ocean in the early 1400s. Their ships dwarfed the craft that Europeans would arrive on a century later. 'The biggest were about 400 feet long, 160 wide (compare the 85 feet of Columbus's *Santa Maria*), had nine staggered masts and twelve square sails of red silk . . . Between 1404 and 1407 the Chinese built or refitted some 1,681 ships. Medieval Europe could not have conceived of such an armada.'[8]

But the cost of maintaining such a fleet, combined with isolationist urges, put a halt to this seafaring. In 1551 the Chinese emperor made it a crime to go to sea on a ship with several masts, even for trade. Even when Europeans ventured into Chinese waters, China did not emerge from its isolation. The first Chinese vessel to dock in a European harbour was a diplomatic ship that visited London in 1851 for the Great Exhibition. Why not before? In his outstanding *The Wealth and Poverty of Nations: Why Some Are So Rich and Some So Poor*, David Landes, an American historian, argues that the Chinese were smug. Convinced of their own superiority, they lacked curiosity about the rest of the world. And whereas private greed motivated the Europeans, the Chinese state abhorred mercantile success. 'Isolationism became China. Round, complete, apparently serene, ineffably harmonious, the Celestial Empire purred along for hundreds of years more, impervious and imperturbable. But the world was passing it by.'[9] By the time China turned outwards again, it had fallen far behind not only America and Europe, but also most of the neighbours the Chinese looked down on.

Arguably, globalisation was well under way by the time the Industrial Revolution kicked off around 1770. But some economic historians beg to differ. Kevin O'Rourke and Jeffrey Williamson do not dispute that global trade boomed in the sixteenth, seventeenth and eighteenth centuries. They estimate that it rose by just over 1 per cent a year. That may not sound fast, but it was probably faster than the growth of the economy as whole: technological progress (and hence economic growth) was slower in those days. Even so, a rise in trade, they say, does not necessarily imply globalisation. In a genuinely global market, where it cost nothing to ship goods around the world and where there were no import duties, the price of, say, pepper would be the same everywhere. What made importing pepper so lucrative, of course, is that it was very cheap in East Asia and fetched high prices in Europe. But if globalisation was happening, they argue, the gap between pepper prices in Europe and East Asia should have narrowed, bringing us closer to a single global market. It didn't. Why not? Because trade was not free: high import duties nullified the impact of falling shipping costs and trade was dominated by state-sponsored monopolies like the East India Company. Why, then, did trade rise? Sometimes because rich Europeans were getting richer and so could afford more foreign luxuries; at other times because supplies from Asia rose, driving down prices. O'Rourke and Williamson conclude: 'Global trade boomed after 1492 in spite of barriers to trade and anti-global mercantilist sentiment, and it would have been a bigger boom without these anti-global forces.'[10]

It is an interesting academic debate, but it is also quite a narrow one. Although in strict economic terms globalisation might not have been happening in the 300 years after Columbus landed in America, the world was certainly coming together. Until 1520, people weren't even sure the earth was round. By 1800, European settlers peopled the Americas, India was under British rule and the oceans were cluttered with ships ferrying people, goods, ideas and diseases from continent to continent as never before. Even if prices were not converging, the links between far-off places were growing. But O'Rourke and Williamson are right about one thing: what happened next was much more dramatic.

An idea whose time had come

Kings and scholars had long believed in the benefits of trade. But far fewer were keen on _free_ trade. Typically, they were mercantilists: they believed that exports were good and imports bad.

Exports are good because they promote a trade surplus and bring in gold or foreign currency; manufactured exports are particularly good because they supposedly create a lot of added value. Imports are bad because they drain national resources, threaten domestic industry and weaken state power by increasing a country's reliance on foreigners; manufactured imports are particularly bad. So governments need to regulate trade to ensure that merchants' activities serve the national interest. Sound familiar? Unfortunately so. Even today, most mainstream politicians – Bill Clinton and Lionel Jospin to name but two – subscribe to some form of mercantilism, as do many pundits, such as America's Clyde Prestowitz or Lester Thurow. So does Bethlehem Steel's Hank Barnette.

Among the first to question the mercantilist orthodoxy was Henry Martyn, who has been unfairly forgotten by history. In his *Considerations upon the East India Trade* (1701), he argued: 'To employ to make manufactures here, more hands than are necessary to procure the like things from the East Indies, is not only to employ so many to no profit, it is also to lose the labour of so many hands which might be employed [elsewhere] to the profit of the Kingdom.'[11]

But Martyn's eloquent words fell on deaf ears. Adam Smith, a Scottish political philosopher, had more success seventy-five years later with *The Wealth of Nations* (1776). Little of what Smith said was radically new, but he was the first to present a systematic, coherent framework for looking at trade policy. Smith argued that protecting domestic industries reduced competition, allowing them to charge higher prices and leading to sloth and mismanagement. He agreed with mercantilists that protecting a domestic industry would benefit it, but argued that it would harm society as a whole: 'If a foreign country can supply us with a commodity cheaper than we ourselves can make it, better buy it of them with some part of the produce of our own industry, employed in a way in which we have some advantage.'[12] Free trade, he continued, allows the best allocation of society's resources; import regulations distort this pattern and so reduce national income. 'The industry of a country ... is thus turned away from a more, to a less advantageous employment, and the exchangeable value of its annual produce, instead of being increased, according to the intention of the lawgiver, must necessarily be diminished by every such regulation.'[13]

Moreover, free trade, by extending the size of the market, allows a greater division of labour, which increases productivity by allowing greater specialisation. It also encourages the exchange of knowledge about new methods of production and business practices. Smith concludes by dismissing mercantilism as a conspiracy to benefit special business interests at the expense of national welfare: 'Consumption is the sole end and purpose of all production ... But in the mercantile system, the interest of the consumer is almost constantly sacrificed to that of the producer.'[14]

This was powerful stuff, and it began to turn the tide against mercantilism, as Doug Irwin discusses in *Against the Tide: An Intellectual History of Free Trade* (1994). In the early nineteenth century, three Englishmen, James Mill, Robert Torrens and David Ricardo, made a crucial addition to Smith's work. Smith had argued that countries should import goods that foreigners are better at producing. But what if one country was superior to another at producing all goods? Mill showed that trade could still be beneficial: countries should specialise in goods in which they have a *comparative*, rather than an *absolute*, advantage. In other words, they should specialise in what they do best, rather than making everything they do better. Say Tiger Woods is good at gardening as well as being a whiz at golf. He still ought to earn his living on the green and pay someone else to mow his lawn, because his *comparative advantage* – what he is best at – is golf.

Ricardo has received most of the credit for this insight, which he stated in *On the Principles of Political Economy and Taxation* (1817), where he develops the famous example of Portugal and England exchanging wine and cloth. But James Mill expressed it far more clearly in *Elements of Political Economy* (1821):

When a country can either import a commodity or produce it at home, it compares the cost of producing at home with the cost of procuring from abroad; if the latter cost is less than the first, it imports. The cost at which a country can import from abroad depends, not upon the cost at which the foreign country produces the commodity, but upon what the commodity costs which it sends in exchange, compared with the cost which it must be at to produce the commodity in question, if it did not import it.[15]

Mill adds that: 'the benefit which is derived from exchanging one commodity for another, arises, in all cases, from the commodity *received*, not from the commodity given'. In short, exports are not good *per se*; they are the cost of acquiring desirable imports.

This quick look at the intellectual history of free trade is not a digression. The ideas of Smith, Mill and Ricardo helped convince British politicians of the merits of free trade. Britain's unilateral move to free trade kick-started the first big wave of globalisation, which lasted from around 1820 until 1914.[16]

Globalisation takes off

Goods, people and money moved around the globe in the nine-teenth century as never before, as did political ideas and cultural fashions. In 1780 even the best-educated man knew only patches of the inhabited globe ('There was not, even in terms of geographical knowledge, *one* world,' according to Eric Hobsbawm, a British his-torian),[17] and most people's known world was limited to the few square miles around their birthplace. A century later, almost all the world was known, pretty well mapped and starting to be pene-trated by the railway and the telegraph.

Steamships, railways and the telegraph made nineteenth-cen-tury globalisation possible, but it was also a political choice. The British government adopted free trade and convinced others to follow. The Americas were open to the huddled masses of European immigrants: no need for a green card. Britons were free to invest their savings abroad. Contrary to what many pundits claim, globalisation is not an inevitable consequence of improvements in transport and communications. Governments were – and still are – the gatekeepers. China curtailed foreign trade; Britain unleashed it.

Nineteenth-century economic globalisation was in some ways more dramatic than the integration of world markets that has been taking place since 1945. Transport costs and trade barriers fell faster; international capital flows as a share of national output were far larger; and cross-border migration was far greater. The world economy was increasingly bound together in a single network, with a worldwide division of labour and specialisation of production.

A global cycle of boom and bust replaced local economies' traditional cycle of bumper and failed harvests. The discovery of gold in California in 1849 triggered a long global boom (and created, for the first time, a Pacific trade in Chilean cereals, Mexican coffee and cocoa, Australian potatoes, and Chinese sugar and rice); a bank failure in New York in 1857 soon spread misery to Europe; a global slump began in Vienna in 1873. Yet even as the world economy became more integrated, it also became more divided, as countries that prospered drew away from those that languished. The richest country was around three times richer than the poorest one at the start of the nineteenth century, ten times richer at the start of the twentieth and is now sixty times better off.

By 1914 the world was in some ways more globalised than it is now. Britain was at the heart of the world economy, as the US is today. It ruled an empire that swathed the world map in pink, sending out administrators, businessmen, soldiers and clergymen to put their stamp on the colonies. It imported food, cotton and other raw materials from around the world and exported manufactured goods. London was the centre of global finance. Everyone assumed that the world would continue getting smaller. In 1912, Norman Angell, a British journalist, argued in *The Great Illusion* that free trade had made war unthinkable. But conventional wisdom was wrong. The losers from globalisation had already triggered a political backlash against it; the First World War and then the Great Depression sent it into reverse.

Britain's unilateral move towards free trade began at the end of the Napoleonic Wars in 1815. Over the next thirty years, the stranglehold of trading monopolies like the East India Company was broken and protection for domestic industry abolished. This opening up culminated in 1846 in the repeal of the Corn Laws, which split the ruling conservative party. Landowners were aghast at the decision to import cheap food to feed the urban masses.

Where Britain led, others followed. After Louis Napoleon took power in France in 1848, he set about dismantling the trade barriers behind which French industry hid. The move to free trade was sealed by the Cobden–Chevalier treaty with Britain in 1860. Crucially, this contained a 'most-favoured-nation' clause, which stipulated that if, say, Britain lowered its trade barriers to Germany it had to do so to France too. This was a powerful tool for extending free trade to the rest of Europe: by 1866 free-trade pacts covered Belgium, Prussia, Switzerland, Norway, Spain, the Netherlands, the German *Zollverein* (customs union) and Austria. Average import duties on manufactures fell to around 10 per cent from 50 per cent just after the Napoleonic Wars.

Asia was levered open by European colonists and gunboat diplomacy. Britain fought two opium wars (the second together with the French) to force China to buy Indian opium. It picked up Hong Kong at the end of the first in 1842 and established free trade in Chinese ports (and the legalisation of opium) at the end of the second in 1860. The US behaved equally outrageously with Japan: Commodore Matthew Perry's infamous black ships forced Japan to abandon autarky for free trade in 1854. Siam, Korea, India and others were also compelled to open their markets.

Even the United States edged a little towards free trade. Southern landowners, who exported cotton, tobacco and other agricultural commodities to Britain, favoured open markets. But

Northern manufacturers – who moaned about 'unfair' competition from cheap British labour (read Mexican today) – wanted protection for their infant industries. Import duties were lowered a little from the Compromise Act of 1833 until 1860, but by and large the US remained a bastion of protectionism.

The era of freer global trade did not last long. As the boom years of the 1850s and 1860s gave way to the leaner ones of the 1870s and 1880s, country after country began to raise barriers again. When cheap American and Ukrainian grain imports threatened farmers' livelihoods in the late 1870s, continental Europe closed its agricultural markets. Import tariffs were so high that they fully offset the huge falls in transport costs in the four decades before 1914. Responding to pressure from landowners and industrialists, Bismarck moved to protect German agriculture and industry in 1879. France slowly shut itself off over the 1880s, culminating in the penal Méline tariff in 1892. The United States closed its markets too. After the North won the Civil War, it erected further barriers to protect its infant manufacturing industries from European competition, culminating in the highly protectionist 1890 McKinley Act. By the outbreak of the First World War, average tariffs on manufactures were around 20 per cent in many countries (and 44 per cent in the US). Only Britain and Denmark, both net food importers, and Ireland, which was ruled by Britain, kept their markets open.

Even so, better transport was bringing the world together. Shoddy roads and slow sailboats gave way to canals, steamships and railways. (Land transport was so slow in 1789 that the news of the fall of the Bastille in Paris on 14 July reached Péronne, 133 kilometres from the capital, only on the 28th!) Canals sprang up everywhere. They were needed to shift the huge loads of coal, iron, cotton and wool that the Industrial Revolution depended on. By 1820 Britain had four times as many miles of navigable waterway as in 1750; the French soon matched this British feat. In America, the Erie Canal, built between 1817 and 1825, cut the cost of transport between Buffalo and New York City by 85 per cent and the journey time from twenty-one to eight days. Shipping freight from Cincinnati to New York City by wagon and riverboat took fifty-two days in 1817 but only six by canal in 1852. Elsewhere, the opening of the Suez canal in 1869 removed the need to sail around Africa, halving the shipping distance from London to Bombay.

Suez helped sink sailboats: steamships were the future. Whereas sailboats had to be towed along the canal, steamships (which needed too much coal to make travelling around Africa viable) could power ahead. Elsewhere, steamers were racing ahead too: American ones had first travelled up the Hudson River in 1807; British ones had made it up the Seine to Paris in 1816. From 1838 they crossed the Atlantic regularly, at first carrying passengers, post and luxuries, later laden with bulk goods too. Freight charges fell by around 70 per cent in real terms between 1840 and 1910. Similar falls were recorded in Asia.

The invention of fridges allowed Europeans to dine on American beef, shipped chilled by steamer, from the 1870s on. By the 1880s European farmers faced competition – as resented then as it is now – from South American and Australian meat and New Zealand butter. Bananas made their appearance in Europe, and tea and coffee consumption soared.

Railways made an even bigger mark, connecting factories and towns to ports. The railway age started in 1828, when the world's first passenger train ran between Liverpool and Manchester. By 1841 there were 8,500 kilometres of track in the world, by 1851 38,000 kilometres. By 1875, 300,000 kilometres of track on all continents were carrying an estimated 1.4 billion passengers a year and 726 million tonnes of goods, nine times as much as by sea. In 1914 there were over 1 million kilometres of track. Between 1850 and 1910, Britain's railway network nearly quadrupled. Germany's grew ten-fold between 1870 and 1910; France's eighteen-fold. Over the same period, America's rail network multiplied over twenty-seven-fold, from 14,000 kilometres to 400,000. Railways united America's regional markets, spawning national companies in place of local ones. They also brought Europe together: it took twenty days to travel over land from Paris to St Petersburg in 1800, but only a day and a quarter in 1900.

The cost of moving goods around was slashed. In 1868 it cost 177½ pence to ship a quarter of wheat (eight bushels) from Chicago to Liverpool. By 1902 it cost only 46½. Thanks to cheaper transport and lower tariffs, prices across the world converged. Whereas in 1870 wheat cost 58 per cent more in Liverpool than in Chicago, by 1895 it cost only 18 per cent more. The gap between iron and wool prices shrank by a similar amount, as did the difference between cotton prices in London and Bombay. A single global market was emerging.

The world was getting smaller. Jules Verne captured the spirit of the times in his *Around the World in Eighty Days* (1873): Phileas Fogg, a British gentleman, hoped to circle the globe in eighty days, a trip that would have taken nearly a year by sailboat twenty-five years earlier.

The breakthrough in communications was even more remarkable. The telegraph (1835) meant that news could cross the world in minutes rather than weeks. It was as hyped then as the Internet was in the late 1990s. New York was linked to Baltimore in 1844 and to San Francisco in 1864. The first submarine cable between Dover and Calais was laid in 1851, the year in which Julius Reuter set up his eponymous telegraph agency in Aix-la-Chapelle. London and New York were hooked together permanently in 1865: news – about share prices, for instance – that previously took up to three weeks to cross the Atlantic now took less than a day. In 1871 the result of the Derby was flashed from London to Calcutta in less than five minutes. Yet the full resources of the *New York Herald* could not get a letter from David Livingstone in central Africa to New York in less than nine months (1871–2), although *The Times* of London could reprint it on the day following its publication. By 1914 the time for transatlantic cable transmission was down to less than a minute. Before long, Europe was joined to the Far East and Australia too. Unified postal services made rapid correspondence available to all: the great age of letter writing had begun. As the century closed, the telephone (1877) and the radio (1896) brought the world even closer together. In 1900 Europeans and Americans were first able to talk to each other by phone. These new links created a need for agreement on international standards, leading to the birth of the International Telegraph Union (1865) and the General Postal Union (1874).

International trade boomed. It rose 150 per cent between 1780 and 1840, 440 per cent between 1840 and 1870 and a further 420 per cent between 1870 and 1913, by which time it was forty-five times greater than in 1780. Money too flowed across the world as never before. By and large, British savings financed railways, mines and frontier expansion in the New World so that it could produce food for British workers and raw materials for British factories. Britain also lent huge amounts to foreign governments. By 1914 a third of British wealth was invested overseas; more than half of all British savings were invested abroad after 1900. Britain owned 44 per cent of the world's total overseas investments. Two banking families, the Rothschilds and the Barings, dominated global finance. (The Barings were rescued by the British government in 1890 after Argentina defaulted, but their bank bit the dust in 1995 as a result of Nick Leeson's reckless gambling.)

Even more significantly, millions of people were on the move. Around 60 million Europeans set sail for the resource-rich and labour-scarce Americas in the century following 1820, three-fifths of them to the United States – the biggest migration in history. They came from the British Isles and north-western Europe, and later from southern and eastern Europe. Between 1900 and 1910, over a million immigrants entered the US. Most stayed; around a third went home. The US population soared from 10 million in 1821 to 94 million in 1914. Over a million Europeans moved to Brazil, Argentina and Uruguay between 1855 and 1874. Some migrated seasonally: Italian farmhands crossed the seas to pick the harvest in Argentina and Irish labourers went to build American railways before returning home. People were also on the move within Europe. In the 1890s, more Italians emigrated to France and Germany than to America. Around 10 million moved from

Russia to Siberia and central Asia. Around 12 million Chinese and Japanese migrated to East and South Asia. Some 125,000 Chinese workers moved to Cuba between 1853 and 1874 to replace freed slaves; over 100,000 moved to California between 1849 and 1876 after gold was discovered. One and a half million people left India for south-east Asia, south-west Africa, and even the Caribbean. Just as trade caused global commodity prices to converge, so mass migration resulted in a convergence of wage levels. Wages in Sweden, for example, rose from 24 per cent of America's in 1856 to 58 per cent in 1913, a remarkable feat given that American living standards were soaring at the time.

Although California and Australia banned non-white immigration in the 1880s and 1890s, 'all things considered, the greatest international migration of people in history produced surprisingly little by way of anti-foreign labour agitations even in the USA, and sometimes virtually none, as in Argentina and Brazil'.[18]

Political and cultural exchange

The first big wave of globalisation was political and cultural as well as economic. Revolutionary ideas circulated like viruses. As Jonathan Freedland, a journalist for the *Guardian*, has persuasively argued, America's declaration of independence in 1776 was born in Britain: 'The American ideal ... was crafted by people who were either British, of British parentage or who had grown up under British rule – reacting to the British system of government. Their ideas flowed directly from the finest traditions of British radicalism.'[19] This was epitomised by Thomas Paine, the Norfolk Quaker who wrote *Common Sense* (1776), a bold demand for independence for the colonies, and became the chief propagandist for the American Revolution.

America's revolution, in turn, inspired Europe's, in particular France's in 1789. If the Americans could depose the British king, why couldn't the French do away with their far more oppressive

tyrant? Thomas Jefferson's Declaration of Independence had universal relevance: 'We hold these truths to be sacred and
undeniable: that all men are created equal and independent, that
from their equal creation they derive rights inherent and inalien-
able, among which are the preservation of life and liberty, and the
pursuit of happiness.'[20] Tom Paine was at it again in 1791 with *The
Rights of Man*, a radical response to the French Revolution; he also
sat in the French Convention and narrowly escaped the guillotine.

The French Revolution had a far greater impact than America's.
Everywhere in Europe, the oppressed masses now dreamed of lib-
eration from the tyranny of Church, nobility and monarchy, all of
whom quaked at the thought of mob rule and terror. When Europe
was again gripped by (failed) revolution in 1830 and 1848, insur-
rection spread as far as Pernambuco in Brazil and, a few years later,
Colombia.

> France produced the first great example, the concept and
> the vocabulary of nationalism. France provided the codes of
> law, the model of scientific and technical organisation, the
> metric system of measurement for most countries. The
> ideology of the modern world first permeated the ancient
> civilisations which had hitherto resisted European ideas
> through French influence. This was the work of the French
> Revolution . . . Its armies set out to revolutionise the world;
> its ideas actually did so . . . Its repercussions . . . occasioned
> the risings which led to the liberation of Latin America after
> 1808. Its direct influence radiated as far as Bengal, where
> Ram Mohan Roy was inspired by it to found the first Hindu
> reform movement, the ancestor of modern European
> nationalism . . . [It was] the first great movement of ideas in
> western Christendom that had any real effect on the world
> of Islam . . . Its indirect influence is universal, for it provided
> the pattern for all subsequent revolutionary movements, its
> lessons (interpreted according to taste) being incorporated
> into modern socialism and communism.[21]

intellectual globalisation ...

The nineteenth century witnessed a revolution in European political ideas. Liberalism, nationalism and socialism have since taken
hold around the world. Political liberalism – government by consent (including that of a 'loyal opposition'), the rule of law,
individual liberty, religious tolerance, universal human rights – is
perhaps Europe's proudest export. It made steady progress in the
nineteenth century and, despite the challenges of fascism and
communism, continued to do so in the twentieth. It is the basis of
the UN's Universal Declaration of Human Rights, for instance. It is
now well entrenched in many countries. People worldwide demand
their human rights. Nearly all governments at least pay lip-service
to them, although far fewer respect them.

One early victory was Britain's abolition of slavery in 1834. By
the 1850s Britain had forced the African slave trade to close down
(the import of Africans to Brazil fell from 54,000 in 1849 to almost
none in the mid-1850s). It used its economic clout to finally stamp
out slavery in its last bastions, Brazil and Cuba, in the 1880s.
(Slavery in the US was, of course, brought to an end by the North's
victory in the Civil War.)

Economic liberalism – free trade, laissez-faire, respect for private property rights, anti-collectivism – has proved a harder sell.
Although David Ricardo was already teaching political economy in
Cuba in 1818 and liberalism was briefly predominant in the 1850s
and 1860s, its influence waned in the 1870s and 1880s as the
world economy slowed. Even when the economy picked up again
in the 1890s, scepticism about laissez-faire remained. 'Liberalism
was accused of destroying the social order or community which
man had hitherto regarded as essential to life, replacing it by the
intolerable anarchy of the competition of all against all ("every
man for himself and the devil take the hindmost").' *The Communist
Manifesto* (1848) intones: 'it has resolved personal worth into
exchange value, and in place of the numberless indefeasible freedoms, has set up that single, unconscionable freedom – Free
Trade'. The Great Depression of the 1930s dealt liberalism a
hammer blow: the economy could clearly not be trusted to

regulate itself. Liberal ideas have been in the ascendancy again since the 1980s, but are scarcely as dominant as critics maintain. Trade is freer, but most governments remain mercantilist. Privatisation and deregulation have made progress, but rich-country governments still tax and spend a third or (much) more of national income and regulate much of the rest. Genuinely liberal parties are at best political bit-players.

Nationalism, as the 'principle of nationality' is now known, has spread far beyond its roots in western Europe. It was originally a convenient glue for newly created states (such as Italy, which when it was unified in 1870 had not existed as a single entity since the fall of the Roman Empire) or the basis of a claim for self-rule by a minority (such as the Hungarians' demands for autonomy from the Austro-Hungarian Empire). But it has now taken root all over the world. Kurds now demand self-determination, as the Czechs once did. Just as Italy – once dismissed as a mere 'geographic expression' by Metternich, the then Austrian chancellor – has fashioned a national identity around the Italian state since its unification, so Saddam Hussein now endeavours to create an Iraqi nation within the borders of Iraq.

Socialism's success in the twentieth century was just as striking. Despite China's traditional allergy to foreign ideas, this thoroughly European philosophy took root there. In South America, Indian peasants fought guerrilla wars inspired by Marx's ideas. Ethiopia never fell victim to European imperialism but was seduced by the charms of communism. As in the case of nationalism, the conduit has often been a Western-educated elite: Deng Xiaoping studied in Paris, Gandhi in London. The impact of Western ideas on the rest of the world will be discussed further in chapter twelve.

Imperialism too was widely copied, and is equally widely discredited. The concept of empire is ages old, but imperialism – the notion that developed countries should carve up the less-developed world between them – was born in the late nineteenth century (the word itself was coined in the 1870s). Although Spain and Portugal had lost their empires in Latin America in the early

nineteenth century, Britain and France scrambled to divide up
Africa and, to a lesser extent, Asia in the late nineteenth and early
twentieth centuries. The Germans, the Italians and the Belgians
picked up scraps too, while the Dutch consolidated their control
over the East Indies. By 1914 all of Africa except Ethiopia, Liberia
and a small part of Morocco was under European rule. Between
1876 and 1915 a quarter of the world was divvied up as colonies
among half a dozen states. Europeans increasingly ran China's
affairs too. Even the United States assumed the 'white man's
burden' after the Spanish-American War when it occupied the
Philippines, Cuba, Puerto Rico and Guam in 1898 and Hawaii in
1900. Japan eventually joined in the game too, taking Korea and
Chinese Manchuria and occupying much of the rest of China after
1937. Yet the age of imperialism did not last long. Already in retreat
in 1920, when Ireland and Egypt achieved autonomy from Britain,
it was all but dead by 1965.

Imperialism and globalisation went hand in hand in the nineteenth century. Railways and telegraphs made remote parts (and
their raw materials) accessible to the West, which guaranteed its
access to them through colonisation. As a US State Department
official said in 1900: 'territorial expansion . . . is but the by-prod-
uct of the expansion of commerce'.[22] In the age of empire, the
West plundered the Third World. Now, countries choose to open
their borders and trade voluntarily (and so to their mutual advantage). Comparing twenty-first-century globalisation to *Empire*,[23]
as Michael Hardt and Antonio Negri do, is neo-Marxist claptrap.

The birth of a global economy in the nineteenth century had a
burgeoning cultural impact too. Romantic literature and music
(think Keats or Goethe), which seeped across European borders in
the late eighteenth and early nineteenth centuries, did not have
much of an impact in the US until many decades later (Walt
Whitman). Yet by 1875 Charles Dickens' novels had been translated
into ten languages; British culture was spreading throughout the
Empire and the US; and French culture was permeating Latin
America, the Middle East and parts of eastern Europe.

Empire extended European culture far and wide. It enabled missionaries to disseminate Christianity, except where the colonial power discouraged it, as in India, or where Islam prevented it. Educated elites around the world dressed like Europeans and spoke English or French. Hopes for a new universal language, Esperanto, which was devised in the 1880s, soon foundered though.

Emulation was as powerful a force as empire. Japan took aping the West to absurd lengths. In its bid to catch up with the West, nothing was taboo: the simplification, even the abandonment of the Japanese language was considered, as was systematic crossbreeding with Westerners. The Japanese took to eating meat; many converted to Christianity. In the 1870s Japanese 'statesmen and politicians vied in salutes to westernisation. They went about in formal European dress more suitable to a Paris wedding than to everyday business in Tokyo; wore absurd top hats on cropped polls; brandished umbrellas in rain and shine; rode about in carriages; sat in chairs around tables; met in newly built stone structures that rebuked the paper-and-wood buildings of Japanese tradition.'[24]

But it was not all one-way traffic. Improved transport and communications brought 'exotic' cultures to the West too. Japanese influences were felt from the 1860s on, African ones from the early 1900s. Artists moved around as never before and were, unsurprisingly, affected by what they saw: think of the impact of the Pacific on Gauguin. Writers such as Rudyard Kipling, Joseph Conrad and Pierre Loti uncovered India, Africa and East Asia for their readers. Educated Westerners became interested in Eastern spirituality; some even converted to Buddhism. Europeans took up Argentine tango dancing. From 1887 Buffalo Bill's Wild West show, with its equally exotic cowboys and Indians, travelled through Europe.

International tourism took off in the latter half of the nineteenth century. Rich Americans (or sometimes just their wives) flocked to European centres of culture. Rich Europeans developed a taste for spas or summers by the sea. Baedeker produced his first guide to Egypt in 1877. In 1879 Switzerland was already receiving a million tourists a year, 200,000 of them Americans.

Inevitably, people's increased mobility spread disease too. Six cholera pandemics between 1817 and 1923 swept through Asia, Europe and America, killing millions. The influenza pandemic of 1918–19, brought to Europe by US soldiers, killed possibly 40 million people worldwide – more than the First World War did.

Global dislocation

Most people expected the disruption caused by the First World War to be temporary. They had long lived in an open world: they considered it 'normal'. Yet the global economy that had emerged before 1914 fell apart over the next thirty years. The Great Depression that followed the Wall Street Crash of 1929 finally killed it off. In June 1930, the US adopted its infamously protectionist Smoot-Hawley Tariff Act. Imports to America, which had bought nearly two-fifths of the world's exports in 1929, fell by 70 per cent between 1929 and 1932. The US economy shrank by a third. The rest of the world slumped too. The death throes of the global economy highlighted how intimately connected it had been. In 1931, Britain, the champion of free trade for nearly a century, imposed duties on imports from outside the Empire. Other countries followed suit. After Hitler came to power in 1933, Germany explicitly pursued autarky.

The collapse in world trade was remarkable. It had edged up in the 1920s but fell so far in the 1930s that it was scarcely higher in 1948 than in 1913, and still 9 per cent lower than in 1929. The volume of US trade fell by over 20 per cent between 1929 and 1938; Britain's fell by 30 per cent, France's and Germany's by 38 per cent. As a share of national output, trade[25] was still much lower in 1950 than in 1913: down from 22.3 per cent to 18 per cent in Britain, from 17.6 per cent to 10 per cent in Germany, from 17.7 per cent to 10.6 per cent in France and from 5.6 per cent to 3.5 per cent in the US.

International capital flows dried up too. In the seven big rich economies that now make up the G7, they fell from nearly 6 per cent of national income in 1913 to 1.5 per cent in the mid-1930s. Between 1927 and 1933 international lending fell by over 90 per cent. In 1931–2 Britain, Canada, Scandinavia and the United States came off the Gold Standard, the international fixed exchange-rate system that had provided stability for international trade and finance since the nineteenth century. By 1936, the Belgians, the Dutch and the French had abandoned it too.

Mass migration came to a halt. In the first fifteen years of the twentieth century, around 15 million immigrants entered the United States. In the next fifteen, only five and a half million did; in the 1930s, fewer than three-quarters of a million. Migration from Spain and Portugal, mostly to Latin America, dropped from one and three-quarter million in the 1910s to less than a quarter of a million in the 1930s. This despite the huge flood of refugees displaced by war and revolution.[26]

The fragmentation of the global economy contributed to massive political upheaval. To mention only a few things: Hitler took power in Germany; America adopted the New Deal; a socialist Popular Front was elected in France; anti-imperialism gathered strength in Europe's colonies. Only the Soviet Union escaped seemingly unscathed from the Great Depression: revolution in Russia in 1917 had isolated the country from the rest of the world. Between 1929 and 1940 Soviet industrial production tripled. No wonder communism was popular.

Even though economic globalisation was going into reverse, technology was still bringing distant people closer together. Newspapers took off: production doubled in the US between 1920 and 1950. Radio spread news and mass culture even more widely: a medium unknown in America at the end of the First World War was listened to by 10 million households by 1929, over 27 million by 1939 and over 40 million by 1950. The 1920s saw a boom in cinema, with Hollywood films rapidly conquering the world. Hollywood bought up talent from the rest of the world and sold films back to it: movies were initially silent – remember early

Charlie Chaplin – and so an immediately global product. On the eve of the Second World War it produced as many films as the rest of the world combined, radiating the English language and American culture throughout the world. America also exported jazz music, which seduced listeners everywhere. World sport picked up too: the Olympic Games had been revived at the turn of the century; football's World Cup was first played in Uruguay in 1930. Finally, the Second World War itself was the first genuinely global war, with soldiers from every continent fighting and with battles in Europe, Africa and Asia. The dropping of the first nuclear bomb on Hiroshima in 1945 signalled a new era where man could potentially blow up the earth: a new global fear was born.

Globalisation reborn

Our open world was born in the aftermath of the Second World War. The foundations were laid in 1944 at Bretton Woods, in New Hampshire. Its architects were Harry Dexter White, an assistant secretary at the US Treasury, and John Maynard Keynes, the head of the British delegation and perhaps the most brilliant economist of the twentieth century. Their aim was to re-create the international economy that had brought prosperity before the First World War while safeguarding against the dislocation of the 1930s that had led to the Second. So they proposed that international trade be gradually freed, but that speculative capital be tightly controlled. Goods would circulate freely; money would not. Currencies would be made convertible, but their exchange rates would be fixed (albeit adjustable if necessary) against the dollar, which in turn would be pegged to gold. The combination of capital controls with fixed exchange rates gave governments the scope to intervene to manage domestic demand and maintain full employment. If the economy was languishing in recession, the government could cut interest rates to stimulate spending without fearing a run on the currency: thus a repeat of the depression of the 1930s could be avoided.

The immediate aftermath of the Second World War saw integration on other fronts too. The United Nations was designed to provide collective security where the League of Nations had abysmally failed in the interwar years, but it was soon hamstrung as the world settled into two hostile Cold War camps. The North Atlantic Treaty Organisation (NATO) extended America's nuclear umbrella to capitalist western Europe. The Soviet Union responded with its own Warsaw Pact that it foisted on its socialist satellite states in eastern Europe. After the Cold War ended, the UN enjoyed a brief renaissance, but in an era of American hegemony, it has still not lived up to its founders' hopes.

Progress towards European unification has been startling, however. From the modest beginnings of the European Coal and Steel Community (1951), Germany, France, Italy, the Netherlands, Belgium and Luxembourg set up the European Economic Community (EEC) in 1957 with the aim of 'ever closer union' as spelled out in the Treaty of Rome. The six are now fifteen: Britain, Denmark and Ireland joined in 1973, Greece in 1981, Spain and Portugal in 1986, Austria, Sweden and Finland in 1995. From a single currency to a single market, economic integration has been remarkable. So are the stirrings of a common defence policy and an unspoken common foreign policy: the stabilisation of eastern Europe through the prospect of EU membership.

Today's open world

Even though globalisation has been going on for centuries, what is happening now is, in many respects, unprecedented.

Globalisation is more genuinely global than before.[28] In the late nineteenth century, globalisation was driven by Europe and the Americas. The rest of the world was either plundered for raw materials by its imperial masters or ignored and isolated from the world economy. From 1945 until around 1980, globalisation mostly encompassed western Europe and North America, as well as a fistful of Asian exporters: first Japan, then South Korea, Taiwan, Singapore, Hong Kong, Thailand and a few others. So it involved countries that account for roughly a quarter of the world's population. Since then, the opening up of China and the collapse of the Soviet Union and its puppet states have brought another 1.7 billion people into the capitalist world. Many countries in the developing world that had previously tried to develop along national lines, notably Mexico and India, have also opened up. Now, economic globalisation involves countries where roughly two-thirds of the world's population live. The other third are not immune to it, but are still isolated from it.

Transport and communications are faster and cheaper than ever. The cost of sea freight has fallen by two-thirds since 1920; that of air transport by five-sixths since 1930. (A fifth of US imports and a third of its exports now go by plane.) Foreign travel has skyrocketed: tourists made 700 million international trips in 2000, up from a mere 25 million in 1950.[29] A three-minute telephone call between New York and London cost $245 in 1990 dollars in 1930; it is now virtually free on the Internet. People spent 101 billion minutes nattering on international phone calls in 2000, twenty-five times more than in 1975. Emails zip round the world instantly. In late 1995, fewer than 20 million people used the Internet; by 2005 1 billion are expected to. In 2001 more information could be sent over a single cable in a second than was sent over the entire Internet in a month in 1997.[30]

World trade is at record highs. In 2000 goods and services worth $7.8 trillion were traded internationally – $1,300 for every person on earth.[31] Whereas the world economy is over six times bigger than in 1950, the volume of world trade is nearly twenty-two times what it was. Cross-border trade has soared from 8 per cent of world output (GDP) in 1950 to 25 per cent in 2000 – far above the previous peak of 18 per cent in 1914.

A wider range of products is traded than before. In 1914, trade was mainly in commodities, like oil, rubber and grain, as well as manufactures, such as cotton clothes, iron and steel. Now many services are traded too: telecoms, finance, insurance, software, management consultancy and so on. Around a fifth of world trade is now in services. An ever-increasing share of trade is in knowledge and ideas, known in the jargon as intellectual property. Patented Viagra, copyrighted Madonna CDs and trademarked McDonald's restaurants helped America earn $38 billion in royalties and licence fees from abroad in 2000, up from $16.6 billion in 1990 and only $837 million in 1960.

Foreign investment looms larger. In 1985 companies invested a mere $50 billion in factories, equipment and offices abroad. By 2000 their foreign direct investment (FDI) came to $1.3 trillion. In 1982, foreign investment was a fortieth of total world investment; by 2000 it was a fifth. The stock of companies' accumulated FDI totals $6.3 trillion, up from $719 billion in 1982. Assets owned by foreigners came to 56.8 per cent of world income in 1995, compared with the earlier peak of 17.5 per cent in 1914.[32] Although foreign investment was huge a century ago it was limited in its impact. It typically consisted of loans to foreign governments or investments in foreign railways and mines. Now foreigners invest in manufacturing as well as services, buy shares as well as bonds, lend to companies as well as governments.

Multinational companies are more important than before. True, the East India Company and the Hudson Bay Company were once almighty giants, but they were exceptional. A hundred years ago, there were very few multinationals, apart from the United Fruit Company and some mining and railway firms. Companies served foreign markets by exporting, rather than by setting up factories around the world. But in 2000, the 800,000 foreign affiliates of the world's more-than-60,000 multinational companies racked up some $15.7 trillion in global sales – double the value of world trade. Multinationals account for some four-fifths of US trade. Around two-fifths of US trade is between subsidiaries of individual companies.

The growth of multinationals is linked to a big change in manufacturing. Cars, computers, shoes and so on are no longer made in one place. Open up an 'American' PC and you will probably see memory chips from Japan and Korea, a disk drive from a US company in Singapore and a motherboard from Taiwan. Manufacturing production is now dispersed across the world, with each step in the process performed where it is cheapest. Individual components may be made in different countries and assembled in another, while the design and marketing may be done elsewhere. One study[33] found that the production, marketing and selling of one particular 'American' car involved nine different countries. Only 37 per cent of the production value of the car was generated in the US; 30 per cent of the value went to South Korea for assembly; 17.5 per cent to Japan for components and advanced technology; 7.5 per cent to Germany for design; 4 per cent to Taiwan and Singapore for minor parts; 2.5 per cent to Britain for advertising and marketing; and 1.5 per cent to Ireland and Barbados for data processing.

International financial flows have never been bigger. Americans' transactions of shares and bonds with foreigners have soared from 4 per cent of US GDP in 1980 to 230 per cent in 1999. Germans' are up from 7 per cent of GDP in 1980 to 334 per cent in 1998, Italians' from 1 per cent to 640 per cent. The rise in Japan is from 2 per cent in 1975 to 91 per cent in 1998.[34] Banks are lending more and more abroad too. At the end of 1983, banks had $2.1 trillion in foreign loans, bonds and other assets outstanding. This had more than quintupled to $10.9 trillion by the middle of 2001 – and this despite a massive shift in companies' borrowing from banks to capital markets.[35] Currency dealers trade around $1.2 trillion *each day*, up from around $10 billion a day in the early 1970s. Derivatives traders buy and sell $600 billion in over-the-counter currency and interest-rate contracts a day.

Even so, the world economy is still more of a ragged patchwork than a seamless web. Not all parts of the economy are open. Rich countries broadly practise free trade in manufactures – with the notable exceptions of clothing and steel. But they still protect many service sectors, not to mention farming. Foreign airlines cannot fly in America; Japan's tax on foreign rice is 1,000 per cent. Huge swathes of the economy, such as public health and education, are typically provided by governments, and so closed to foreign companies. Even where trade appears free, governments conspire to keep out imports through a variety of means, like fiendishly complicated technical rules and standards, 'safeguard' measures against import surges and 'anti-dumping' duties on foreign products that are deemed unfairly cheap. Poor countries typically have higher trade barriers than rich ones do. But the trade barriers the rich ones do have are particularly harmful because they are mainly in areas like food and clothing, where poor countries typically have a comparative advantage.

Some economics are more international than others. Whereas a huge continental economy like the United States traded[36] only 13 per cent of its GDP in 2000, middling ones like Britain, France and Germany traded 28.5 per cent, 29 per cent and 34 per cent respectively. A small economy like Ireland traded 93 per cent, an even smaller one like Singapore 110 per cent.[37] While some economies are becoming more open, others are not. China traded two and a half times as much in 2000 (25 per cent of GDP) as it did in 1980. The US trades a bit more. Japan trades much less (down from 14.5 per cent of national income in 1980 to 11 per cent in 2000).

Few countries are genuinely global traders. Most trade primarily with a handful of others, typically their regional neighbours. Over two-thirds of western Europe's goods trade is with other countries in the region. Among the fifteen members of the EU, the figure is 63.5 per cent. All EU countries trade more with each other than they do with the rest of the world. The three members of NAFTA also trade mostly with each other. Over half of their exports are within NAFTA, as are two-fifths of their imports. A little under half of Asia's exports are to other Asian countries; nearly three-fifths of Asia's imports come from the region.

So although the world economy is more globalised than it was, it is not as globalised as it seems. Three largely self-contained regional hubs account for three-quarters of it: the EU, which trades a mere 11 per cent of its collective output with the rest of the world; NAFTA, which trades just over 8 per cent; and Japan, 11 per cent. The rest of the world is linked to one, or several, of these hubs through a tangled web of bilateral (or regional) trade agreements.

The pattern of foreign investment is uneven too. Most global FDI flows (85 per cent) come from American and European companies; and 70 per cent of them are invested in the US and the EU. In 2000 Britain was the biggest source (and third-biggest recipient) of FDI in the world, the US the biggest recipient (and third-biggest source). Japanese companies used to invest heavily abroad too, but a decade of economic decline has put paid to that. Developing countries received only 19 per cent of global FDI in 2000, down from a peak of 41 per cent in 1994. The biggest beneficiaries are China, Brazil and Mexico. The poorest countries get very little. → why?

Foreign investment is more important to some countries than others. In 1999 FDI inflows came to 92 per cent of gross fixed investment in Ireland and 32.5 per cent in Britain, but only 17.9 per cent in the US, 17.5 per cent in France, 11.8 per cent in Germany, and a mere 1.1 per cent in Japan. For developing countries, the average figure was 13.8 per cent.

Most countries still have important restrictions on foreign investment in many areas. America's Jones Act requires that vessels used to transport cargo and passengers between US ports be owned by US citizens, built in US shipyards, and manned by US citizens. France jealously protects its privatised utilities from being taken over by foreigners. Foreign supermarkets are not allowed to set up shop in India. Nor does short-term capital flow entirely freely. Many countries, notably China and India, prevent money from moving in and out at will.

Moreover, globalisation has retreated in one important respect. Whereas in the nineteenth century, millions of people were on the move, most countries now keep a tight lid on migration. Ireland lost half its workforce between 1870 and 1910; America's swelled by a quarter. True, in the 1950s and 1960s, 7.5 million people moved to western Europe from its former colonies. But since then, immigration has slowed to a trickle. Now, although American management gurus may jet around the globe without impediment, Indian computer programmers – not to mention Mexican farm hands – struggle to get temporary American work visas. Back in 1900, 15 per cent of the American population was foreign-born; only 10 per cent is now. Less than 2.5 per cent of the world's population works abroad, according to one estimate. Even in the EU, with its much-vaunted free movement of labour, foreign workers accounted for a mere 3 per cent of the labour force in 1998.

The pattern of migration is very uneven. Nearly a quarter of Australians are foreign-born. Other governments count the number of foreigners who live in a country, rather than where residents were born. Foreigners make up just over 5 per cent of the EU's population, but only 1 per cent of Japan's. Foreigners accounted for 3.8 per cent of Britain's population in 1999, 5.6 per cent of France's, 8.9 per cent of Germany's and 19.2 per cent of Switzerland's. Europe admitted nearly half a million asylum seekers in 1999, the US 43,000 and Australia a mere 8,000. Lots of foreigners work in the oil-rich Gulf states; many Filipinos work elsewhere in Asia; lots of people from southern Africa earn their living in South Africa.

Cross-border political co-operation is much greater than it was. A hundred years ago, there was no UN, IMF, World Bank or WTO, let alone the EU. As Martin Wolf, the chief economics commentator at the *Financial Times*, has remarked: 'The nineteenth century was a world of unilateral and discretionary policy. The late twentieth century, by comparison, was a world of multilateral and institutionalised policy.'[38] There were far fewer international pressure groups, bar the Anti-Slavery League and the Second (Socialist) International. Instead, there was empire: Britain owned a quarter of the world; France big chunks of Africa; the US Cuba, Puerto Rico and the Philippines.

Globalisation is also more of a challenge to national governments than before, because they have become so much bigger and taken on so many new tasks. A century ago, governments taxed and spent so little that few worried about an eroding tax base or the burden of paying for the welfare state. In 1913, public spending was a mere 7.5 per cent of GDP in the US, 12.7 per cent in Britain, 14.8 per cent in Germany and 17 per cent in France; the respective figures in 2000 were 29.4 per cent, 39.2 per cent, 42.9 per cent and 51.4 per cent. Governments had yet to write the reams of rules on labour rights, environmental protection, product standards, health-and-safety requirements and so on that set countries apart today.

Perhaps most importantly, globalisation is now more pervasive than ever. True, in 1914,

> the inhabitant of London could order by telephone, sipping his morning tea in bed, the various products of the whole earth, in such quantity as he might see fit, and reasonably expect their early delivery upon his doorstep; he could at the same moment and by the same means adventure his wealth in the natural resources and the new enterprises of any quarter of the world, and share, without exertion or trouble, in their prospective fruits and advantages; or he could decide to couple the security of his fortunes with the good faith of the townspeople of any substantial municipality in any continent that fancy or information might recommend . . . Most important of all, he regarded this state of affairs as normal, certain, and permanent, except in the direction of further improvement, and any deviation from it as aberrant, scandalous and avoidable.[39]

Yet the inhabitant that Keynes was describing was a rich gentleman, not the proverbial man on the Clapham omnibus. Internet shopping, foreign holidays and international share trading are now open to the majority of people in rich countries, as well as to a growing minority in poor ones. Even remote African villages have radio and television – though perhaps not the laptops in the IBM advertisements. Globalisation is also more intense and immediate. In a mass-media world, people and events across the globe *feel* closer. However shallow and sentimental our emotions may be, many people do feel affected by famine in Africa, sweatshops in Asia and logging in the Amazon. (But although many people were moved by the wars in Rwanda and Bosnia, far fewer felt affected by the war in Angola or that between Armenia and Azerbaijan.) September 11th had such a global impact in part because people watched it live on TV. Within minutes of the tragic events, millions of people everywhere were emailing each other and texting each other on their mobile phones.

Why the world hasn't changed (that much)

New York. September 11th 2001. The world seems to stop. Transfixed by the terrible images on our TV screens, we all freeze in horror and disbelief. The scenes scarcely bear recounting: the second plane, that flying firebomb, piling into the smoking skyscraper; miniature people leaping desperately, arms flailing, into the void; the awesome Twin Towers of steel and glass collapsing into rubble; the ghoulish figures of New Yorkers caked in dust fleeing for their lives. Instantly iconic, these vignettes of America under attack from unseen assailants will haunt us for years.

The attack on the World Trade Center was aimed at a symbol of American – and global – capitalism, the very heart of Wall Street and the world economy. It highlighted how the oceans and border posts that once allowed America to live apart from the rest of the world now offer little protection from terrorism. Osama Bin Laden's attack on America was conceived in Afghanistan, nurtured in Germany, developed in Britain and financed through international banks. Any illusions that Americans harboured of living apart from the rest of the world are shattered. Until September 11th America still *felt* inviolate. Now it feels violated. Americans no longer feel safe from attack on American soil. Isolationism is no longer an option.

Scarcely pausing for grief, pundits were quick to declare globalisation dead and buried amid the wreckage in Manhattan. John
Gray, a professor of political philosophy at the London School of
Economics and the author of *False Dawn: The Delusions of Global
Capitalism*, proclaimed: 'The atrocities in Washington and New York
did more than reveal the laxity of America's airport security and the
limitations of its intelligence agencies. It inflicted a grievous blow to
the beliefs that underpin the global market ... The lesson of 11
September is that the go-go years of globalisation were an interreg-
num, a time of transition between two epochs of conflict.'[40]

This couldn't be further from the truth. The case for globalisation is as strong as it was before September 11th. In fact, it is even
stronger: spreading the benefits of globalisation to the many poor
Muslims who are so hostile to the West would doubtless take some
of the sting out of their hatred. The terrorist threat also underscores the urgency of shaping the kind of globalisation we want.
Governments are impotent? Tell that to the Taliban.

Even so, might a renewed emphasis on securing national borders put a stop to globalisation? Stephen Roach, the normally
perceptive chief economist at Morgan Stanley, an American investment bank, has argued as much: 'Terrorism puts sand in the gears
of cross-border connectivity and the result threatens the increasingly frictionless world of globalisation. The tragic events of
September 11th have, in effect, levied a new tax on such flows. The
security of national borders will now have to be tightened – hardly
a costless endeavour. That will affect more than airports and shipping ports. The porous borders of Canada and Mexico, the conduits
of increasingly seamless NAFTA linkages, will be tightened too.'[41]

Mr Roach can be forgiven for overreacting: Morgan Stanley had
offices in the World Trade Center. But even the carnage of
September 11th is not enough to spell globalisation's demise.
Admittedly, commercial insurance premiums for American firms
rose in the six months after September 11th, as did air-freight costs –
by 15 per cent, the World Bank estimates, but that is not big
enough to have much of an impact on international trade,

especially since most goods travel by sea. A study[42] by Craig VanGrasstek, an American trade expert, found that shipping costs for American imports had not risen since September 11th. Nor are multinationals abandoning their foreign investment plans, according to surveys[43] by the United Nations, AT Kearney, PricewaterhouseCoopers and others.

Global recession poses a bigger threat to globalisation than terrorism does. It sharpens economic choices and increases the temptation to blame foreigners for domestic woes. The growth in world trade stalled in 2001, while the UN reckons[44] FDI flows fell by 40 per cent, although it attributes this mainly to the end of the global merger boom. If the economic climate turned very sour and countries reacted by becoming protectionist, globalisation could be at risk. But thankfully, partly as an unintended consequence of September 11th, WTO member governments finally agreed to launch a new push to free up world trade in Doha, the capital of Qatar, in November 2001. There is life in globalisation yet.

FOUR

Brand New World?

Why brands are not all-conquering beasts

Quite simply, every company with a powerful brand is attempting to develop a relationship with consumers that resonates so completely with their sense of self that they will aspire, or at least consent, to be serfs under these feudal brandlords.

NAOMI KLEIN, *No Logo*

Expressing its aspirations, its soul, its sense of family, the brands humanised the corporation, lifted it from the land of goods and services up to an exalted moral plane.
Branding dressed the mercenary workings of the market in the fine clothes of civilisation. They gave business a 'holy mission', in the words of the irrepressible Tom Peters. Branding thus has a hidden but most definite political purpose . . . The shoes, the computers, the staplers and the radios may be manufactured in sweatshops in Indonesia, but don't think about that – that's just economic nature. The corporation proper is the set of core values: a bright,

shining thing that follows its dreams and lives forever in
single-minded dedication to a noble purpose. When we walk
past a billboard or ride on a corporate-sponsored bus, it is
the little lies of branding that irritate us – 'Life tastes good',
'Is This a Great Time or What?' – but the big lie of branding,
the virtuous pretence of the corporation, is the one that
degrades the lives of us all.

THOMAS FRANK, author of *One Market Under God*[1]

David Beckham seems to have sported every trendy haircut under
the sun. With one notable exception: he did not succumb to the
craze for shaving Nike's trademark 'swoosh' into one's hair. A fashion slip-up by his advisers? Unlikely. Although Beckham could walk
out on Manchester United football club, or even Posh Spice, he'd
find it harder to breach his sponsorship deal, worth up to £10 million over seven years, with Nike's bitter rival, Adidas.

Brands have never held so much sway. Their logos transform
ordinary things into objects of desire. Their cachet persuades us to
part with inflated sums for commonplace items. Their images
permeate our culture, pervade our consciousness and pervert our
sensibilities. Their grip on us is so strong that the companies that
own them in effect now run the world. No wonder they are so valuable: Coca-Cola's brand is worth $68.9 billion, Microsoft's $65.1
billion and IBM's $52.8 billion, according to Interbrand, a brand
consultancy.[2]

Or so, at least, it is claimed. Brands arose from much humbler
origins: as badges of quality and consistency. They were born in the
nineteenth century, when people started to buy products made in
far-off factories from salespeople who were strangers, rather than
local produce sold by familiar faces. A brand's reputation was a substitute for people's trust in a local shopkeeper. Just as a village
trader had an incentive not to rip you off if he wanted your repeat
custom, so Lipton's desire to see city-dwellers flocking back to its
tea houses day after day guaranteed a good cup of char. Same story
for Kellogg's cornflakes, Quaker Oats or Aunt Jemima's pancakes in

early twentieth-century America. 'Brands were the first piece of consumer protection,' says Jeremy Bullmore, a former director of J. Walter Thompson, an advertising agency. 'You knew where to go if you had a complaint.'[3] Unsurprisingly, people were willing to pay a little more for the peace of mind of knowing what they were going to get.

Brands still fulfil this essential role. Would you order online from a retailer you don't know and trust? I've made that mistake, and got stung. So there's a lot to be said for Amazon.com's honesty and reliability, even when it doesn't have the keenest prices. Amazon has a huge incentive to maintain its reputation precisely because this allows it to charge a little extra. (One American study found that 51 per cent of price-minded shoppers didn't choose the cheapest offering on a price-comparison website. Shoppers were willing to pay a 3.1 per cent premium for a brand name and a 6.8 per cent premium at places where they'd shopped before.)[4] That is true in spades in the Third World. Better to park your savings at Citibank than at a local bank run by the corrupt president's son. For all their blandness, the reliable uniformity of Hilton, Sheraton and Hyatt hotels has helped ensure their success from Kinshasa to Karachi, and doubtless soon in Kabul too.

As choice proliferated, brands helped simplify buying decisions. Don't waste time assessing all the different kinds of toothpaste on the supermarket shelves, just reach for Colgate. When competition was less fierce and consumers less savvy, companies could keep their customers loyal – and the profits rolling in – year in year out without having to shell out much to maintain their brands.

It was good while it lasted. But times changed. Improvements in manufacturing enabled new competitors to match established brands' quality, but at a lower price. Consumers eventually realised that the difference in quality, if any, between a branded good and its unbranded brethren did not justify the hefty mark-up. The watershed was Marlboro Friday, on 2 April 1993, when Philip Morris slashed the US price of Marlboro cigarettes by 20 per cent to try to claw back some of the market share it had lost to its cheaper rivals. Pundits were quick to bury brands: if even Marlboro Man, around since 1954 and the longest-running campaign in ad history, could not protect Philip Morris, surely all other brands were doomed too. Brands were also under attack from supermarkets' own labels: why buy Colman's mustard if Tesco's is cheaper, just as good, and may even secretly be made by Colman's?

In response to this new challenge, brands rebranded themselves. They now aspire to be much more than just corporate kite marks. They aim to associate a product or company with an image, a set of emotions, a way of life. Those brands are then expressed through a logo, advertising and so on. Essentially, then, a brand is now an idea. Nike is no longer a mere purveyor of over-engineered trainers: it is trying to sell individual achievement through sports. 'Our identity is more than a swoosh splashed on a product. Our identity is the relationship we have with the world we touch. It's a relentless search for the innovative, the unconventional, the ingenious – born of the desire to express our passion for the athlete by continuously finding new ways to help reach athletic potential,'[5] declares its corporate website. If you wear Air Jordans, some of Michael Jordan's magic might just rub off on you. (Peter York, a British management consultant, has gone as far as to argue that Nike's swoosh 'means precisely what the crucifix meant to an earlier generation in ghettos – it promises redemption, vindication and a way out'.) Coca-Cola does not just sell fizzy drinks; it provides 'refreshment, value, joy and fun'.[6] Philip Morris tries to associate smoking Marlboros not with cancer, but with the rugged individualism of a mythical Western cowboy. Starbucks offers more than overpriced insipid coffee: 'It's the romance of the coffee experience, the feeling of warmth and community people get in Starbucks stores,'[7] waxes its chairman, Howard Shultz.

If companies are in the business of building brands, not products, they may reshape themselves along those lines. As Chris Foges, a London-based writer on design and branding, points out: 'BMW now proceeds from the point that it is not a car manufacturer but a brand that is all about precision engineering and quality. From that viewpoint, it could just as easily make designer furniture or niche gadgets as cars. This would be accepted by its customers, as this is how they now perceive BMW.' Virgin has stretched branding to its logical (and ludicrous) extreme. It has plonked its logo on almost anything (planes, trains, music, mobile phones, make-up, mortgages, radio, cola, wine) and then relied on its perceived hipness – and free publicity from yet another failed attempt by Richard Branson to fly round the world in a hot-air balloon – to lift sales.

Companies try to add magic to their brands in a variety of ways: by a relentless barrage of advertising (Procter & Gamble spent $3.2 billion advertising brands such as Pampers and Pringles in 2001), as well as by more creative marketing, such as sponsorship (Nike sponsors Tiger Woods, Arsenal football club and Brazil's national soccer team, among many others), cross-promotion (McDonald's meals linked to Disney films) and PR stunts (in 1985 Coke became the first soft drink in space). Branded clutter is now ubiquitous: salmon-pink London cabs advertise the *Financial Times*; Mondrian-like sweatshirts are emblazoned with the words Tommy Hilfiger; Flat Eric, the glove puppet from ads for Levi jeans, has become a global star, while the anodyne soundtrack to the ad by Mr Oizo shot to the top of the music charts. With luck, all of this puff gives companies an edge over the competition and enables them to charge a premium.

It's no longer just companies that are in on the act. David Beckham is a brand. So were the Spice Girls. Britain almost became a brand in 1997, when the concept of 'Cool Britannia' – dreamt up by Geoff Mulgan and Mark Leonard of branded think-tank Demos – was briefly acclaimed in Downing Street and *Newsweek* declared London the coolest capital city on earth. With typical hubris, Wally Olins, a corporate-identity consultant, wants to try rebranding the European Union. Even – perish the thought – *No Logo* has become a brand.

So far, so innocuous. Marketing men have always been full of hot air. But Naomi Klein and others argue that brands have become altogether more sinister. It is worth quoting her argument at some length, so as not to be accused of distorting it.

Power, for a brand-driven company, is attained not by collecting assets *per se*, but by projecting one's brand idea on to as many surfaces of the culture as possible: the wall of a college, a billboard the size of a skyscraper, an ad campaign that waxes philosophic about the humane future of our global village . . .

In this way, these corporate phantoms become real. If we think of a brand-driven company as an ever-expanding balloon, then public space, new political ideas and avant-garde imagery are the gases that inflate it: it needs to consume cultural space in order to stave off its own deflation . . .

The goal now is for the brands to animate their marketing identities, to become real-world, living manifestations of their myths. Brands are about 'meaning', not product attributes. So companies provide their consumers with opportunities not merely to shop but to experience fully the meaning of their brand. The brand-name superstore, for instance, stands as a full expression of the brand's lifestyle in miniature . . .

But this is only the beginning. Nike, which used just to sponsor athletes, has taken to buying sporting events outright. Disney, which through its movies and theme parks has sold a bygone version of small-town America, now owns and operates its very own small town, Celebration Florida.

In these branded creations, we see the building blocks of a fully privatised social and cultural infrastructure. These companies are stretching the fabric of their brands in so many directions that they are transformed into tent-like enclosures large enough to house any number of core activities, from shopping to entertainment to holidays. This is the true meaning of a lifestyle brand: living your life inside a brand. Brand-based companies are no longer satisfied with having a fling with their consumers, they want to move in together.

These companies are forever on the prowl for new and creative ways to build and strengthen their brand images. This thirsty quest for meaning and virgin space takes its toll on public institutions such as schools, where, in North America, corporate interests are transforming education, seeking not only to advertise in cafeterias and washrooms but to make brands the uncritical subjects of study. Maths textbooks urge students to calculate the circumference of an Oreo cookie, Channel One broadcasts Burger King ads into 12,000 US schools and a student from Georgia was suspended last year for wearing a Pepsi T-shirt on his school's official 'Coke Day'.[8]

And that's not all. Not content with gutting our culture of substance and substituting their vacuousness, brands are also usurping youth identity. For young people today – although presumably not for Klein herself – 'generational identity [has] largely been a prepackaged good and ... the search for self [has] always been shaped by marketing hype, whether or not they believed it or defined themselves against it. This is a side effect of brand expansion that is far more difficult to track and quantify than the branding of culture and city spaces. This loss of space happens inside the individual; it is a colonisation not of physical space but of mental space.'[9] Goebbels, it seems, was not a patch on Nike. Nowhere is safe: brands are taking over the world.

Don't believe the hype

Rewind to 23 April 1985. Amid the greatest fizz in corporate history, the biggest brand in the world, so powerful that its slogan was simply 'Coke is It', replaced its ninety-nine-year-old flagship soft drink with New Coke, a sweeter, more Pepsi-like brew. 'The best has been made even better,' exclaimed Robert Goizueta, Coke's late boss, at the press launch. 'The world's largest soft-drink company has developed an improved taste for the world's number one soft drink. Some may call this the boldest single marketing move in packaged goods history. We simply call it the surest move ever made because the new taste of Coke was shaped by the taste of the consumer.'[10] Yet a mere seventy-seven days later, after New Coke had been compared to 'sewer water', 'furniture polish', 'Coke for wimps' and, worst of all, 'two-day-old Pepsi',[11] the mightiest global brand beat a humiliating retreat. Old Coke was reintroduced as Coca-Cola Classic; New Coke was left to go flat.

Brands are not as omnipotent as Naomi Klein, Thomas Frank and others make out. Critics take the hype that surrounds brands too seriously. Brands might aspire to take over the world, but that doesn't mean they have succeeded.

Undeniably, we live in an increasingly consumerist culture. Which is great, in many ways. Few people would swap our world of material plenty for a more ascetic life. Just ask east Europeans how much they enjoyed their unbranded world. (When I was in Moscow in 1991, GUM, the famous department store, was holding an exhibition of Western consumer goods: Ariel washing powder you could ogle but not buy. Russians filed by in silence. Procter & Gamble would not even dare to dream of such brand worship in the West. Such was the depravity that the failure of the Soviet model to deliver the goods led to.) Companies tend to produce things because we want them, or because we find we want them after they have tempted us. Sony televisions are not foisted into people's living rooms and people forced to watch them. Pepsi is not poured down our throats. Safeway does not drag us away from local stores and herd us through its aisles. Deep in human nature, there is clearly a desire to have more.

It is also true that we in the West increasingly define ourselves by what we consume. As the old divisions of class and religion blur and fade away, we are freer to define our own identity. For most people, where they grew up and live is still crucial. For many, so is their job. For some, their race or their sexuality is also important. People increasingly define themselves by their values too: green, liberal, New Age, pro-choice, anti-abortion, whatever. And yes, of course, we also make a statement about ourselves through the clothes we wear, the car we drive and so on.

Nothing radically new there: a rich lady who might once have showed off by wearing a generic luxury product, like a fur coat, might now display her affluence by carrying a branded one, like a Louis Vuitton handbag. Poorer people might try to capture some of that mystique by dabbing on Gucci perfume. Superficial? Sure. But are the brands corrupting us? Arguably not. If we are merely choosing the product that best matches our tastes or that best conveys the message we want to send out about ourselves, then we are using the brand, rather than it using us. Owning a Louis Vuitton handbag is not what makes the rich lady a snob, it is merely the way that she chooses to express her perceived social superiority. Some may tut that poor people should not be 'wasting' their money on Gucci perfume, but who are they to dictate how people spend their money? In this 'brand new world', consumers, not brands, hold the whip hand: they choose the brands, which have to cater to their every whim.

Think, for a minute, about what brands mean to you. Do you really feel like Michael Jordan when you put on a pair of Nikes? Did you genuinely think, when you bought the shoes, that they would somehow transform your life? Of course not. The swoosh, and all the hoopla that surrounds it, distinguishes a Nike shoe from any old shoe. Nike may be fashionable, but that is a far cry from the extravagant claims made about its brand. You were willing to pay a premium for Nike, but you can afford to: even pricey shoes make up only a small part of all but the poorest Westerners' budget.

I have to confess: I wear Nike shoes and clothes (although I steer clear of Starbucks – I look for romance from lovers, warmth from my family and community from friends, not from a coffee shop). Am I being conned? Perhaps. Was I, at some level, persuaded by its marketing that its stuff was cool and that by extension wearing it made me cool? Quite possibly. But so what? I happen to like my

Nike gear, just as there are many Nike products that I don't like. I don't mind paying a little extra for them, although I baulk at spending over £100 on sports shoes. Do I think wearing Nike makes me an athlete? No. Has Nike 'colonised' my mind? Of course not.

The fear about brands – that we are being brainwashed into shelling out for things that we don't really want and manipulated into defining ourselves through the products we buy – is overdone. There is something terribly patronising about *No Logo*: I am intelligent enough to see through brands, Klein implies, but most poor saps are not. Yet most people are not as stupid and gullible as she makes out. As she acknowledges in her book, Nike's spell is not so powerful that inner-city blacks cannot rebel against it. Most people eventually realise that buying things is not enough to make them happy.

It is an old communitarian trick to claim that enlightened individuals – Lenin or Hitler, for example – know what the people really want, that the views and preferences people express are not what they would think if only they could break free from their social conditioning. The assault on brands is a new, intellectually feeble twist on this old theme. But the sentiments that lie behind it are equally obnoxious. They hint at fascism, all in the name of the people.

Brands are not all-powerful drugs that force us to part with our money unthinkingly. They are marketing devices that help companies attract and hold on to customers. Such emotional manipulation is not easy. Despite its huge marketing budget, Procter & Gamble has largely failed to create successful brands around its products: anyone know what Tide stands for beyond washing powder or Crest apart from toothpaste? Nor is conveying a brand through advertising straightforward. Absolut's witty vodka ads have gone down better than Smirnoff's drunken delusions. The future of mobile phones belongs to Orange, not BT Cellnet (now O_2). Even with all the big-money backing in the world, brands sometimes flop: witness New Coke.

When branding does succeed, its hold on us is at best tenuous and transitory. Brands' individual values wax and wane (Starbucks up, Nescafé down). Nor is a brand's success unrelated to the actual quality of the product being provided: whereas countless much-hyped dot-coms were shooting stars, Amazon survives. Even according to Interbrand, which has every incentive to exaggerate the importance of brands in order to justify its inflated consultancy fees, Nike lost 5 per cent of its brand value between 2000 and 2001. Coca-Cola was down 5 per cent too. McDonald's, another of Klein's pet hates, is down 9 per cent. Kellogg's, second less than a decade ago, has slipped to thirty-ninth in the latest league table. The Body Shop has lost much of its ethical halo, as has Ben & Jerry's ice cream since its owners sold out to Unilever in 2000.

Brands' collective growth is partly a boom-time phenomenon. The US has recently enjoyed its longest economic expansion in history: ten years without a recession. Britain's economy has had a good run too. In the good times, people feel flush – and flash. They are more willing to splurge on expensive shoes and overpriced coffee than when times are tight. Already, as times get tougher, brands are suffering. For what it's worth, of the seventy-four brands that appear in Interbrand's top 100 ranking in both 2000 and 2001, forty-one declined in value between 2000 and 2001, while the combined value of those seventy-four fell by $49 billion – to an estimated $852 billion, a drop of more than 5 per cent. Cheap own-label products are making a comeback.

Far from being unassailable, many brands are on the rocks. If they are making ever more desperate attempts to win us over, it is typically a sign of weakness, not strength. Often, little else distinguishes companies' products: there is a limit to how many clever new shoe technologies can be invented in a year – and any that are can quickly be copied. According to Marketing Intelligence Service, a consultancy based in Naples, New York, 31,432 new products were introduced in North America in 2000, almost all of them competing with products in existing categories. The branding sound and fury reflects the ferocity of competition – and hence the precariousness of corporate power – in what would otherwise be commodity markets. BT didn't need branding when it was a monopoly. Nor do government agencies like the US Department of Health.

Consumers are more fickle than before. DDB, an advertising agency, found that whereas in 1975, 66 per cent of American consumers in their twenties said they stuck to well-known brands, only 59 per cent did in 2000. Among those in their sixties, brand loyalty slumped from 86 per cent to 59 per cent.[12] As David Lubars, a senior advertising executive in the Omnicom Group notes: 'consumers are like roaches – you spray them and spray them and they get immune after a while'. Young people are particularly cynical. Even Nike is struggling to reach them: its US revenues in the second half of 2001 were only 3 per cent up on a year earlier; athletic shoe revenues were down 2 per cent.

'Mass marketing has become a very hard thing to do because people don't like to be seen as "normal" any more – they all want to be seen as individuals,' says Martin Hayward, chairman of the Henley Centre, a London-based forecasting group. 'The bigger you become, the less appealing you become. It's a dilemma: somehow you have to find a way of exploiting the behind-the-scenes benefits of being big, yet at the point at which you touch the consumer, you have to be seen to be small.'[13]

Brands, it seems, are passing their sell-by date. Perhaps they need another rebranding. The truth is that although brands may aspire to control us, we in fact usually control them. They stand or fall on the basis of our whims and fads. So what, if anything, is the problem with them? There is the risk that the branding of culture 'ends up causing the event to be usurped, creating the quintessential lose-lose situation. Not only do fans begin to feel a sense of alienation from (if not outright resentment toward) once cherished events, but the sponsors lose what they need most: a feeling of authenticity with which to associate their brands.'[14] But this is largely self-correcting. If consumers turn against cultural events, like those at Britain's ill-fated Millennium Dome, where branding usurps the content, companies will change tack, just as the reaction against the fad for oversized logos on clothes sparked a return to more discreet branding.

In its critique of *No Logo*, entitled 'Pro Logo', *The Economist* goes further. It argues that people actually like lifestyle brands because 'they add fun and interest' and 'have a cultish quality that creates a sense of belonging'. It quotes – apparently approvingly – the irrepressible Mr Olins: 'In an irreligious world, brands provide us with beliefs. They define who we are and signal our affiliations.' I wouldn't go that far. Billboards along American freeways may literally add colour, but they also obscure an often beautiful landscape. As for the 'beliefs' that brands try to embody, they are shallow indeed. Religion may be in retreat, but people still have strongly held beliefs, in justice or freedom, for instance. The cult of sporting excellence was not created by Nike; it is as at least as old as ancient Greece and more recently stems in part from the liberal philosophy of individual achievement.

A genuine fear is that the swoosh may convince some impressionable poor people to buy shoes they can ill afford. In practice, this boils down to poor kids and teenagers. 'Sometimes a mother will come in here with a kid, and the kid is dirty and poorly dressed. But the kid wants a hundred-twenty-buck pair of shoes and that stupid mother buys them for him. I can feel that kid's inner need – this desire to own these things and have the feelings that go with them – but it hurts me that this is the way things are,' says a shopkeeper whom Klein quotes.

Bombarding kids with ads, at home or at school, can cause problems. Channel One should certainly not be allowed to force kids at school to watch ads. Convincing poor teenagers in inner cities that they must have a £100 pair of Nikes is pretty despicable. (Having said that, teenagers have long placed an exaggerated importance on looking cool. If Nike shoes weren't cool, something else would be.) Where there are abuses, governments should intervene: through tighter controls on advertising aimed at children, for instance. Even so, the real issue is not Nike shoes, but child poverty. Nobody frets if a rich kid wears £100 trainers.

So the biggest problem may actually be that critics' obsession with brands diverts attention from genuinely important political problems. Ms Klein takes aim at the left's single-minded pursuit of equality for women, blacks and others for blinding it to bigger political issues. 'In this new globalised context, the victories of identity politics have amounted to a rearranging of the furniture while the house burned down,' she intones. 'Though girls may indeed rule in North America, they are still sweating in Asia and Latin America, making T-shirts with the "Girls Rule" slogan on them and Nike running shoes that will finally get girls into the game.' Yet she is guilty of a similar sin. 'One can't help thinking that one of the main reasons black urban youth can get out of the ghetto only by rapping or shooting hoops is that Nike and the other multinationals are reinforcing stereotypes of black youth and simultaneously taking all the jobs away.' Really? Surely poor schools or broken families are more to blame? Rather than campaigning against Michael Jordan ads, people should be fighting for more government spending to alleviate child poverty and revive inner cities.

There is, to be fair, another worry. Klein links it to the growth of brands, but its validity does not stand or fall on her analysis. It is that companies' sheer size and global reach makes them the real masters now. Amid an apparent cornucopia, it is claimed, they are in fact restricting consumer choice. Workers are now at their mercy, politicians in their pockets. Where governments once regulated companies, companies now dictate to governments. Brands do not run the world. But perhaps companies do.

FIVE

Giants with Clay Feet

Why companies don't run the world

Corporations are much more than purveyors of the products we all want; they are also the most powerful political forces of our time . . . Shell and Wal-Mart bask in budgets bigger than the gross domestic product of most nations . . . of the top hundred economies, fifty-one are multinationals and only forty-nine are countries.

NAOMI KLEIN, *No Logo*

All the goods we buy or use . . . are increasingly controlled by corporations which may at their whim choose to nurture, support or strangle us . . . Business is in the driving seat, corporations determine the rules of the game, and governments have become referees, enforcing laws laid down by others.

NOREENA HERTZ, *The Silent Takeover*

A long, a very long and very patient, secret and surreptitious process conducted in the shadows must have led to that abandonment which has facilitated the hegemony of a now anonymous private economy, grouped by means of massive mergers on a world-wide scale into intricate networks, so inextricable, mobile and ubiquitous that it is difficult to locate them. They thus evade everything that could restrain, oversee or even observe them . . . They need not bother much about states, which compared to themselves are often so powerless and helpless.

Viviane Forrester, The Economic Horror

If people think corporations are powerful, they haven't been in a corporation. We are by no means powerful – we are confined and restricted in what we do. Consumer choice doesn't allow us to have unfettered power.

A company boss, quoted in The Silent Takeover

On New Year's Eve 1600, Queen Elizabeth I granted a monopoly on trade with the East Indies to 218 knights and merchants of the City of London. The East India Company aimed to break the Dutch grip on the lucrative spice trade with the East Indies, but it soon ditched its original goal and focused its energy on India instead. There it made huge profits, mainly by exporting cloth to England. By 1717, when the Mughal emperor exempted it from paying customs duties in Bengal, the Company had set up trading posts along the east and west coasts of India, and big English communities had developed around its settlements in Calcutta, Bombay and Madras. But it was in 1757 that the Company really became powerful. Robert Clive, a Company official who had previously put paid to French ambitions in India, defeated the army of the nawab of Bengal at the battle of Plassey. The Company became, in effect, the ruler of large parts of India. It had an army, a trading monopoly and – after 1765, when it won the right to collect customs in Bengal on behalf of the Mughal emperor, a privilege that company officials used as a licence for plunder – tax-raising powers. It had genuinely usurped the powers of a state.

But then the British government intervened. Through Lord North's India Bill, also known as the Regulating Act of 1773, Parliament reasserted control over the Company's affairs and placed a governor-general in charge of all its possessions in India. By the East India Act of 1784 the government assumed more direct responsibility for British activities in India, although the Company continued to control commercial policy and lesser administration. Parliamentary acts of 1813 and 1833 ended the Company's trading monopoly. Finally, after the Indian Mutiny in 1857, the Crown took over sole responsibility for running India. When the East India Company was finally dissolved in 1874, *The Times* reported: 'It is just as well to record that it accomplished a work such as in the whole history of the human race no other company ever attempted and as such is ever likely to attempt in the years to come.'

Until now? Captains of industry – the name itself suggests almost military might – now rule over vast empires with outposts dotted around the globe. Their valiant exploits are lionised, their titanic struggles for world domination chronicled with awe. Their faces adorn business magazines and, increasingly, mainstream ones too. Their biographies sell millions. Governments everywhere court them. Welcome to the new age of big business.

Companies have expanded almost as much as their bosses' egos. Some have grown mainly because they are successful: Tesco, Wal-Mart or Starbucks, for instance. Many others have tried to buy success by gobbling up their rivals. The late 1990s witnessed an unprecedented merger boom. At its peak, in 2000, the value of mergers and acquisitions completed worldwide topped $3.7 trillion, of which cross-border deals came to $1.1 trillion.[1] The ten biggest mergers of all time have all happened since 1998.

Everywhere you look, companies have been mating with gay abandon. In computing, Compaq bought Digital Equipment and is hooking up with Hewlett-Packard. In mobile phones, Britain's Vodafone snapped up America's Airtouch in 1999 and then swallowed Germany's Mannesmann for $173 billion[2] in 2000 – the biggest takeover ever. Deutsche Telekom acquired Voicestream and

One-2-One (now T-Mobile), while France Telecom bought Orange. In America's telecoms market, SBC Communications has taken over two of the other six Baby Bells spun off from AT&T: Pacific Telesis and Ameritech. Bell Atlantic and GTE combined to form Verizon; WorldCom took over MCI. In aerospace, Boeing bought McDonnell Douglas. In retailing, America's Wal-Mart's purchase of Britain's Asda was followed by the French marriage of Carrefour and Promodès. In drinks, GrandMet and Guinness combined to form Diageo, which makes Smirnoff vodka, Johnnie Walker and J&B whisky, Gordon's gin, Malibu, Baileys and Guinness. In the car industry, Germany's Daimler Benz, which makes Mercedes, got hitched to America's Chrysler; France's Renault got its hands on Japan's Nissan; and Ford took over Volvo. In pharmaceuticals, Pfizer, which makes Viagra, bought Warner-Lambert; GlaxoWellcome (itself the product of Glaxo and Wellcome) and SmithKline Beecham became GlaxoSmithKline; Switzerland's Ciba and Sandoz formed Novartis; and Sweden's Pharmacia combined with America's Upjohn. In the oil industry, Exxon (which trades as Esso outside the US) bought Mobil; Britain's BP guzzled up America's Amoco and Arco in quick succession; Total, Fina and Elf all combined; and Chevron bought Texaco. In banking, Citicorp merged with Traveler's Group to form Citibank, Chase Manhattan bought JP Morgan, Morgan Stanley snapped up Dean Witter and Discover, Swiss giants UBS and SBC merged, HSBC bought Midland, Lloyds acquired TSB, Royal Bank of Scotland swallowed NatWest, France's BNP snaffled up Paribas. In accounting, PriceWaterhouse and Coopers & Lybrand became PricewaterhouseCoopers. In media, Disney grabbed ABC, Viacom nabbed CBS, Germany's Bertelsmann bought America's Random House and France's Vivendi bought Canada's Seagram, which owns Universal's film studio and Universal Music, the world's biggest record company. Last but not least, as this frenzy of deal-making reached fever pitch in early 2000, America Online, the king of new media, took over Time Warner, the biggest old-media baron, for $94 billion, to form AOL Time Warner (which owns Time Warner Books, of which Abacus, the publisher of this book, is an imprint). Even the usually sober *Economist* got carried away. 'For once the superlatives and the hype seem justified,' it declared. 'It is, to use an expression much beloved of Intel's Andy Grove, an "inflection point".'[3] Indeed it was, for it marked the peak of the merger boom. As the stockmarket bubble burst and the world economy slowed, merger activity slumped to $1.9 trillion in 2001 and is at its feeblest for nearly ten years so far in 2002.

Companies are not only bigger than ever. They are more international too. The United Nations reckons there are over 60,000 multinational companies, with over 800,000 affiliates abroad.[4] Their foreign affiliates made estimated sales of $15.7 trillion in 2000, twice world trade of $7.8 trillion. Together, they invested $1.3 trillion abroad in 2000, bringing their total foreign assets to $21.1 trillion. Big firms own the bulk of this foreign investment. In 1999 the top fifty American multinationals owned 52.1 per cent of America's foreign-investment stock. The equivalent figure for Germany was 55.5 per cent, for France 59.0 per cent (in 1995), for Britain 79.0 per cent.[5]

Together, the top one hundred non-financial[6] multinationals owned $2.1 trillion in foreign assets in 1999, and $5.1 trillion in total assets. They had sales of $4.3 trillion and employed 13.3 million people. The biggest, ranked by foreign assets, is America's General Electric, which had $141.1 billion of them in 1999. Second was Exxon Mobil with $99.4 billion; third Shell, with $68.7 billion.

Let us not kid ourselves: these companies are not fluffy do-gooders. They are in it for the money, pure and simple. That is one reason why the current fad for 'corporate social responsibility' is not the blessing it is made out to be, as will be discussed in chapter seven. But even though companies are pursuing profits, it does not necessarily mean they profit at our expense. The beauty of competition is that it enables consumers, and society as a whole, to benefit from companies' self-interested actions. Adam Smith was right when he remarked that: 'It is not from the benevolence of the butcher, the brewer, or the baker that we expect our dinner, but from their regard to their own interest.'[7] If you find it hard to believe that good can come from seeking profits, consider what would happen if companies didn't try to make a profit. They would soon go bust, and the jobs and products they create would disappear.

Nor are multinationals the demons they are made out to be, as an OECD study makes clear.[8] For a start, foreign firms pay their workers more than the national average – and the gap is widening. In America, for example, foreign companies paid 4 per cent more than domestic ones in 1989; in 1996 they paid 6 per cent more. They are creating jobs faster than their domestic counterparts are. The workforce of foreign firms in the US rose by 1.4 per cent a year between 1989 and 1996, compared with an annual rise of 0.8 per cent for domestic ones. In both Britain and France employment at foreign outfits increased by 1.7 per cent a year; at domestic ones it fell by 2.7 per cent. Moreover, foreign companies spend heavily on research and development (R&D) in the countries where they invest. In 1996 they accounted for 12 per cent of America's R&D spending, 19 per cent of France's and a remarkable 40 per cent of Britain's. Indeed, in some countries foreign companies spend more of their turnover on R&D than domestic ones. In Britain, for example, foreign firms spent 2 per cent of their turnover on R&D, domestic ones only 1.5 per cent. Lastly, foreign firms tend to export more than domestic ones. In 1996 foreign companies in Ireland exported 89 per cent of their output, domestic ones only 34 per cent. The big exception is America, where domestic firms exported 15.3 per cent of their output, foreign ones only 10.7 per cent.

Companies bring us many bounties. But even so, have they got too big for their boots? Are these globo-mega-corps the new Big Brothers? Naomi Klein and Noreena Hertz certainly think so. David Korten has even written a book entitled *When Corporations Rule the World*. Their arguments are rarely expressed cogently, but they go something like this. Companies wield power through their brands, which have been known to hypnotise even the most hardened Taliban fighters into submission. Their sheer size also gives them clout – fifty-one of the world's hundred largest economies, they claim, are now corporations and only forty-nine are nation states. Moreover, the control that a few big players apparently have over many global industries gives them a stranglehold over our lives. Finally, there is companies' ability, through a mixture of bribes and threats, to get governments to do their bidding – or to avoid their writ entirely. Move over George Bush, Bill Gates rules OK.

Size isn't everything

Who would have thought that the fate of a disused oil rig could cause such commotion? In 1995, Shell, an Anglo-Dutch oil company, planned to dispose of its Brent Spar oil platform by sinking it in the Atlantic Ocean, 150 miles off the coast of Scotland. But Greenpeace, the environmental campaign group, objected – wrongly, it later turned out – that disposing of it on land was more eco-friendly. When Shell started to tow the rig away for disposal on 30 April, Greenpeace activists in a helicopter tried to intervene by landing on the Brent Spar. They were beaten off with water cannon, but the video pictures were soon on TV screens across the world. Protesters swamped Shell petrol stations throughout Europe and drivers filled up elsewhere. The company dug in its heels. But then, on 20 June, the unthinkable happened: Shell backed down. The world's second-biggest company by sales had been humbled by a handful of media-savvy eco-warriors.

Far from giving companies power over consumers, brands actually give people more influence over companies' behaviour. If what you are selling is image and reputation, you are incredibly vulnerable to anything that is perceived to damage them. Compare the ineffectiveness of the consumer boycotts of old – like the longstanding campaign against Nestlé for selling powdered baby milk to poor countries – with how Nike has bent over backwards to dispel allegations that its products are made in sweatshops. As companies increasingly make a virtue of being 'socially responsible' – of being good employers, kind to the environment and generous contributors to the community, rather than mere money-making machines – their vulnerability can only increase. Klein herself actually admits this: 'Brand image, the source of so much corporate wealth, is also, it turns out, the corporate Achilles' heel.' Exactly: if brands are such fragile constructs, they are scarcely the basis for world domination.

Nor is companies' size all it's cracked up to be. The world's most valuable company, America's General Electric, was worth a whopping $370 billion at the end of January 2002. The company with the biggest sales in 2000, America's Exxon Mobil, had a turnover of $206 billion; it also made the biggest pre-tax profits, of $27.5 billion. These are staggeringly large figures. Yet relative to the market and economy as a whole, they are still pretty small. Exxon Mobil's profits are a mere 0.3 per cent of US national income and 0.09 per cent of world income. GE's market capitalisation was only 2.7 per cent of the total value – $13.6 trillion – of companies quoted on American stockmarkets and 1.4 per cent of the world total of $26.3 trillion. In fact, the top hundred quoted US companies account for a much smaller share (46 per cent) of America's total stockmarket capitalisation in 2000 than they did in 1980 (62 per cent).[9] Even the hugest companies are not as big as they seem.

But what about the much-repeated 'fact', highlighted by both Naomi Klein and Noreena Hertz and repeated by countless others, that fifty-one of the world's hundred largest economies are now corporations and only forty-nine are nation states? It is simply not true. The statement is arrived at by comparing companies' sales and countries' gross domestic product (GDP). But this is like comparing apples and pears. Imagine a market trader who sells £1,000 of fruit and vegetables a week. Is he richer than a lawyer who earns £900 a week? If you use Klein's and Hertz's flawed methodology, yes he is: £1,000 is, after all, bigger than £900. But taking into account that the fruit and veg that the trader sold cost £500, he makes only £500 a week. Who makes more? The lawyer, clearly. Similarly, a company with sales of $20 billion is not 'bigger' than a country with a GDP of $15 billion if its value-added (the difference between the value of its sales and the cost of the inputs it buys from suppliers) is only $5 billion. It is truly shocking – or perhaps conveniently dishonest? – that Naomi Klein, who has lectured at Harvard and Yale universities, and Noreena Hertz, an academic at Cambridge University no less, can make such a schoolgirl error.

A less misleading comparison – between companies' value-added and countries' value-added, their GDP – reveals that only two companies make it into the top fifty creators of value-added, and thirty-seven into the top hundred.[10] The biggest company by this measure in 2000, Wal-Mart, created value-added of $68 billion, around the same as Chile's GDP. The second-biggest, Exxon, created $53 billion in value-added, around the same as Algeria's GDP. Yet the US economy is 200 times bigger than Wal-Mart; Japan one hundred times greater; China twenty times bigger. Even small countries like Belgium, Sweden and Austria are three to five times larger than the largest multinational. The value-added created by the largest fifty corporations represents only 4.5 per cent of the value-added created by the largest fifty countries.

More importantly, inferring from companies' size that they are as powerful as countries is fatuous. Companies and countries are very different. Companies have to attract capital and workers that are free to move elsewhere; they also have to persuade customers to buy enough of what they produce to earn sufficient profits to pay shareholders and workers an acceptable return. Companies that fail go bust or get taken over. States, on the other hand, can impose taxes and regulations. Mighty Exxon pays taxes even in tiny Luxembourg: Esso's largest service station in the world is at Wasserbilig, in the Grand Duchy. If Exxon developed an oil field in Algeria, the Algerian government could tax it, or even nationalise it. Even tinpot states can arrest or conscript their citizens and fight wars. All of Wall Street's combined financial clout could do nothing to avenge the destruction of the World Trade Center – but the American government could. A handful of states can blow up the earth. And unfortunately, even states that fail to deliver the basics for their citizens – like food and security, let alone prosperity and freedom – rarely disappear. The only 'companies' that have powers remotely comparable to those of states are the drug cartels. Colombia's earn billions of dollars a year, control parts of the country, have private armies and operate outside the law.

Wal-Mart seems puny in comparison. Indeed in some ways, Wal-Mart is weaker than some small stores. Because it faces fierce competition from other retailers, it has less scope to mark up its prices than the only shop in an isolated skiing village does. Even the biggest companies can be constrained by competition.

Take a behemoth like British Telecom. When it was a nationalised monopoly, and so theoretically owned by the people, it treated its customers with disdain. They had to wait months to have a phone line connected. Their complaints were ignored. BT could afford to treat its customers badly because they had no alternative supplier. For BT, read France Telecom, Deutsche Telekom, or AT&T before it was split up.

Competition makes all the difference. BT is bigger than it was twenty years ago (as are all the other telecoms companies I mentioned). Yet in the now fiercely competitive market for international phone calls, it is just one provider among many. Its prices have fallen and its service has improved. It has to offer its customers what they want or it will lose their business. Compare that with the market for local calls, where BT is still dominant. Because it faces little competition, it can still hold customers and the government to ransom – by delaying the roll-out of broadband Internet, for instance.

Or consider General Motors. Its turnover totalled a massive $179 billion last year. By comparison, its customers may earn as little as $30,000 a year. Surely, then, GM holds the whip hand? Not at all. Because it faces competition, it is at the mercy of its customers. It has to offer people what they want – better cars for lower prices – or it will lose their business.

Rewind to the 1960s. GM's sales were a fraction of what they are now. Yet it had much more power. It could produce overpriced,

shoddy cars, and still people bought them. Why? Because competition from Ford and Chrysler was pretty slack. Enter the Japanese. In
the 1970s and 1980s they challenged GM's dominance. They produced better cars that cost less. GM lobbied the government for
protection against this 'unfair competition'. The government rode
to the rescue. What's good for GM, it was still thought, was good
for America. Eventually, though, Americans got the cars they
wanted. Not only from Toyota, but also from GM, which finally
responded to the foreign competition by listening to consumers'
demands.

If you are worried about corporate power, you should support
globalisation. Freeing trade curbs domestic giants by exposing
them to foreign competition. BT, France Telecom and Deutsche
TeleKom now trample on each other's turf, as do new companies,
big and small, like Vodafone and Virgin. Closed domestic markets,
where national champions can cosy up to government, are much
more likely to be monopolised than global ones. Even though many
global companies are bigger than before, they are not necessarily
more powerful. It is the absence of competition, not size, that gives
companies clout.

If companies were taking over the world, you'd expect them to
be grabbing a bigger slice of the economic pie. The reason they
exist, after all, is to make profits. Yet that's not happening.
Companies' profits go up and down with the economic cycle: fatter
in booms, leaner in busts. From a recent peak of 12.6 per cent of
national income in 1997, US corporate profits fell to 11 per cent in
2000 and 9.3 per cent in 2001.[11] That is in line with the average over
the last fifty years of 10.5 per cent. Profits reached a post-war peak
of 14.7 per cent of national income in 1950 and dipped to a trough
of 7.7 per cent in the deep recession of 1982. The figures for Britain,
which cannot easily be compared with those in the US, show a
similar stability. The gross operating surplus of financial and non-
financial corporations was 17.7 per cent of GDP in 2000, down
from 19.8 per cent in 1997 and in line with the average in the
1980s of 17.2 per cent.

Nor is size any guarantee of business success. In 1912, US Steel was the world's biggest industrial company. Its market value was equivalent to two-thirds of all the money then in circulation in America. Now it's a midget, valued at just $1.6 billion in January 2002. Granted, steel is less important now that it was then, but even within its industry US Steel has slumped: it is not even among the world's top ten steel producers.[12] Only General Electric, Exxon and Shell have remained among the top dozen companies since 1912. Other former giants – Britain's Austin Morris in Britain, America's Ling-Temco-Vought, Japan's Aikawa, Germany's Reemtsma – are long forgotten. One-third of the top companies of 1912 have grown over the course of the century (or are part of a successor company that has); the remaining two-thirds are relatively smaller now than they were then.[13] In the long run, most large companies fail. Some go bust: spectacularly so in the case of Enron, once America's seventh most valuable company. Most decline and are then bought up by nimbler rivals: like Midland Bank, once the world's biggest bank, which has been gobbled up by HSBC.

Even over a shorter period, companies wax and wane with startling frequency. Only thirty of the top fifty industrial companies in 1980 were still in the top fifty in *Fortune* magazine's 2000 list. Only nine of the top twenty were still in place, and five of the top ten. The same applies over an even shorter time-frame, the six years to 2000. Among industrial companies, fifteen of the top fifty, four of the top twenty and two of the top ten fell out of favour between 1994 and 2000. Among service companies, the turnover was even more rapid. Twenty-nine of the top fifty, nine of the top twenty and three of the top ten fell from grace in a mere six years.[14]

Many of the world's largest companies were pygmies twenty years ago. Microsoft, founded in 1975, was hardly a household name. Nor was Oracle, which was set up in 1979, Sun Microsystems (1982) or any of the other new firms in the computer industry that IBM once dominated. Cisco Systems was only born in 1984, AOL in 1985. Same story in mobile phones: the old telecoms providers and manufacturers have been eclipsed by upstarts like Vodafone, established in 1982, and Nokia, which in the early 1980s was a small Finnish company that sold rubber boots and toilet paper. Wal-Mart was a fraction of the size it is today. So much for big companies' impregnability. As John Kay rightly says: 'Size is not a sustainable competitive advantage. It can be replicated, and will be, by a company that has a true competitive advantage.'

Academic studies show that most mergers flop. They are typically products of management fads and corporate hubris rather than sound business logic. The fashionable conglomerates of the 1970s and the asset plays of the 1980s were subsequently unwound. The products of the latest, and biggest, merger wave are unlikely to be exceptions. Companies that have recently been combining will doubtless soon be splitting and shrinking. A survey by KPMG Consulting[15] released in February 2002 suggests that more than a third of the biggest international takeovers agreed at the height of the bull market are already being unwound.

'Pushing these huge – and costly – deals [was] the almost universal belief that industries will become more concentrated as the world's markets become more globalised,' says Pankaj Ghemawat, a professor of business administration at Harvard Business School. 'The spoils of the market are supposed to go to a select few in each industry. And companies believe that if they are going to be among the winners, they will have to shore up economies of scale in manufacturing, branding, and research and development. That's how they hope to scare off potential competitors and sew up new markets. From this perspective, cross-border mergers are a do-or-die proposition. If you want to survive, let alone thrive, you must be one of the world's biggest players.'[16]

Yet, as Mr Ghemawat points out, there is no evidence to support the belief that the winner takes all in a global economy. Empirical research shows that global, or globalising, industries have actually witnessed steady decreases in concentration since the Second World War. In 1970, the hundred biggest manufacturing firms in America produced 33 per cent of industrial output. In

1990, they still produced 33 per cent. In Japan their share slipped from 22 per cent to 21 per cent. In Britain it fell from 40 per cent to 36 per cent, in Germany from 30 per cent to 23 per cent.[17] All sorts of industries – oil, cars, aluminium – are less dominated by a few big players than before. The peak of concentration in the car industry was probably in the early 1950s, when America's Big Three made three in four of the world's cars. In 1969 the three largest car producers, General Motors, Ford and Chrysler, made half the world's cars. In 2001, the top three (GM, Ford and DaimlerChrysler) made just under half the world's cars. All the mergers, alliances and consolidation have only offset the larger players' loss of market share.

That is even more so in high-tech industries. Between 1988 and 1998, the top five companies' share of worldwide sales in computer hardware, computer software and long-distance telephone calls fell by 15 to 30 percentage points. That should not be too surprising, since it is what economic theory predicts. Say five countries have four domestic producers each. They then open their markets and ten companies go to the wall: there are still more companies (ten) in the new single market than the five there were in each domestic one previously. Only in industries where being big dramatically lowers a company's costs are we likely to see very few firms survive.

Even then, the number of companies in an industry is a poor guide to how much competition there is. There are many vitamin makers, yet the US Department of Justice found eight of them guilty of running a cartel. Only two companies make big passenger planes, yet Boeing and Airbus compete fiercely. Conceivably, a single-firm industry could still be competitive if the threat of entry by a rival kept prices low. Often, industries where lots of companies survive are less competitive than those with only a handful of strong players. That is certainly so in the airline industry, where restrictions on who can fly where have kept moribund national airlines alive. This is starting to change: that Sabena, Belgium's national airline, went bust in 2001 signals a rise in competition, not a reduction in it. Similarly, signs that America's fragmented steel industry may finally be starting to consolidate are a response to more competition not a harbinger of less. There is no easy way to tell how much competition, there is in a market. That is why antitrust watchdogs have to be eternally vigilant.

Competition is not a cure-all. Markets sometimes fail. Some companies gain an unhealthy monopoly: Microsoft, for instance. Others are able to fix prices, like De Beers in the diamond market. Adam Smith's warning that 'people of the same trade seldom meet together, even for merriment and diversion, but the conversation ends in a conspiracy against the public, or in some contrivance to raise prices'[18] is as relevant as ever. Companies may also be able to exploit their workers, if there is high unemployment, for instance. They may fail to consider the damage they cause by polluting. They may be able to con consumers who lack adequate information, and so, for instance, sell them inappropriate pensions. And so on.

For all those reasons, governments often need to intervene. Granted, they don't always do what's right. Sometimes, they fail to intervene when they should. Often, they make mistakes when they do. Sometimes, corporate lobbying efforts have an undue influence on what they do. For instance: in 1997 Britain's incoming Labour government excluded Formula One motor racing from a ban on tobacco advertising shortly after the party received a £1-million donation (later returned) from Bernie Ecclestone, the man who in effect runs Formula One. The French government has repeatedly bailed out Crédit Lyonnais, a failed bank. The Bush administration has doled out all sorts of goodies to big oil companies. Worst of all, Silvio Berlusconi, who owns the private half of Italian television, is also, as Italy's prime minister, in charge of the public half. Then, of course, there is the Enron scandal, which is unfolding as I write.

Governments are clearly far from perfect. More urgently needs to be done to separate money and politics. Reform of the way political campaigns are financed is long overdue, especially in America. In 2000 unregulated 'soft-money' donations to US political parties *but pol. is important money!*

from unions, companies and individuals soared to $500 million. Greater government openness is also a must, so that politicians can be better held to account by parliament and the press.

Wherever you stand on globalisation, breaking the link between money and politics should be a priority. But even if politicians fail to deliver the much-needed reforms, the case for globalisation is not undermined. Globalisation is not to blame for the corruption of domestic politics. On the contrary, it can help clean it up: there are more opportunities for corruption in a closed economy, where lobbying for import curbs can provide companies with rich pickings, than in an open one, where global competition erodes profit margins. Nor is it true, for all the flaws of domestic politics, that rich-country governments always, or mostly, do big business's bidding. (Indeed, the very idea that 'big business' is a homogenous block with a single view on anything is a fallacy: companies typically have diverging and conflicting interests.) Consider the evidence.

Item one: competition policy. Cartels – which would allow companies to reap bumper profits by agreeing to raise prices – are illegal. Mergers that threaten competition are blocked. Companies that abuse their dominant position are slapped down.

In 2001 the European Commission stopped the world's biggest company, General Electric, from buying Honeywell. American businessmen and press vilified Mario Monti, Europe's competition commissioner, for the decision. Mr Monti took even more stick in France after he broke up a completed merger between Schneider and Legrand, two French electrical companies. In 2000 Time Warner, then the world's biggest media company, withdrew its proposed merger with EMI, a British music company, after the Commission objected. Microsoft was not allowed to buy Telewest, a British cable company; it had to settle for a minority stake instead. Vodafone, the world's biggest mobile-phone company, was only allowed to buy Mannesmann on the condition that it sold Orange, a Mannesmann subsidiary. One American telecoms giant, MCI WorldCom, was stopped from buying another, Sprint (a deal also blocked by American trustbusters). Volvo and Scania, two Swedish motor-vehicle makers, were prevented from merging in 2000, as were Airtours and First Choice, two British package-tour operators, in 1999. An aluminium deal, Alcan's bid for Pechiney, foundered following the Commission's objections. In 1998, the Commission vetoed a television alliance involving Deutsche Telekom and two German media giants, Bertelsmann and Kirch.

America's trustbusters have been equally active. Microsoft was nearly broken up; it is still being prosecuted by several US states and is also under investigation by the European Commission. Visa and Mastercard were found guilty of restricting competition between credit cards. Six European businessmen are in jail in America for conspiring to fix the vitamins market. Top executives at De Beers, the diamond cartel, face an outstanding warrant from a 1994 cartel investigation; they are, in effect, banned from America. Big mergers in defence (Lockheed Martin and Northrop Grumman), aluminium (Reynolds and Alcoa) and telecoms (MCI WorldCom and Sprint, and many cellular deals) have been blocked. American Airlines was prosecuted for predatory pricing. Many smaller deals were also blocked in areas such as bookselling (Barnes & Noble with Ingram), video rentals (Hollywood Entertainment and Blockbuster), helicopter making (Bell with Boeing), industrial gases (British Oxygen's acquisition by Air Liquide and Air Products) and initially cement (Lafarge with Blue Circle). Many mergers go through only with strings attached: for instance, Exxon Mobil and BP Amoco were forced to sell off many petrol stations; Diageo was made to sell Dewar's Scotch and Bombay Sapphire gin; Intel had to share chip technology acquired from Digital Equipment with Advanced Micro Devices and Samsung.

Item two: tax. In 1965, the heyday of Keynesianism and government meddling in the economy, corporate taxes accounted for 8.8 per cent of total tax revenues in rich OECD countries.[19] In 1999, in this terrible age of capitalist free-for-all, they still accounted for 8.8 per cent of the total tax take. Corporate tax rates have fallen in many countries, but revenues have not, because a widening of the tax base has offset the fall in rates. As a share of GDP, taxes on company profits have steadily risen: from 2.2 per cent in 1965, to 2.4 per cent in 1980, 2.7 per cent in 1990, and 3.3 per cent in 1999. So, as a share of national income, companies contribute 50 per cent more in tax to government coffers than they did a quarter-century ago. If businessmen are running the show, they are clearly masochists.

In 1980, at the start of Margaret Thatcher's rule, corporate taxes were 3.0 per cent of British GDP. By 1999, they had risen to 3.9 per cent. In 1997, moreover, the incoming Labour government imposed a windfall tax on privatised utilities. In France too, taxes on company profits have increased, from 2.1 per cent of GDP in 1980 to 2.9 per cent in 1999. In Germany, they have stayed stable, at 1.8 per cent of GDP. In the US, they dipped sharply after Ronald Reagan's early tax cuts, from 2.9 per cent of GDP in 1980 to 2 per cent in 1985, but they have since increased again, to 2.4 per cent of GDP. Same story, more or less, if we look at corporate taxes as a share of total tax revenues: up from 8.4 per cent in 1980 to 10.4 per cent in 1999 in Britain; up from 5.1 per cent to 6.4 per cent in France; down sharply in the US from 10.8 per cent in 1980 to 7.5 per cent in 1985, then up again to 8.3 per cent in 1999. In Germany, the figure dipped from 5.5 per cent in 1980 to 4.8 per cent in 1990 and 1999.

Item three: regulation. Companies' behaviour is regulated in all sorts of ways. They have to pay their employees a minimum wage, provide a healthy and safe work environment, and not discriminate against women or minorities. They generally have to recognise unions and give some notice and compensation to workers they want to fire. They have to comply with environmental standards on everything from how much they can pollute to how much they must recycle. Food and drugs have to be shown to be safe. Consumer-protection law sets out standards for advertising as well as customers' right to refunds. Product-liability laws make companies accountable for any harm their products may cause. A whole host of industries, such as water, electricity, telecoms, banking and broadcasting, are even more tightly regulated. And so on. The *Federal*

Register, which lists US government regulations, is 70,000 pages long. If anything, there is often too much regulation, not too little.

Item four: the courts. Where governments fear to tread, lawyers do not. Few people question that the justice system in most advanced countries is independent of company control. It would be hard to argue otherwise. In America, for instance, big tobacco companies paid out over $150 billion after successive class-action suits; car companies regularly shell out huge sums in product-liability cases; and McDonald's paid out a large sum because it sold scaldingly hot coffee. Each year people start almost 2 million lawsuits against American companies, which pay out damages of around $150 billion a year.[20] Whether or not you think lawsuits, rather than legislation, are the best way to curb corporate power, it is undeniable that they do.

All of this is pretty obvious. Which is why the charge that government is merely a big-business stooge is so fatuous. Clearly, business has an influence on government. But so do trade unions, campaign groups and ordinary voters. Ideas too are a powerful influence: the main reason Margaret Thatcher privatised Britain's state-owned industries was that she thought it made economic and political sense, not because she was taking handouts from big business. Even when governments do things that benefit business, these often benefit ordinary people too. Freeing trade, for instance, is good for consumers as well as competitive companies.

Companies do not run the world. But might globalisation nonetheless be eroding governments' powers? Money can move freely around the world. So, more or less, can skilled workers and rich people. Factories, even company headquarters, can be shifted abroad. If money, people and companies can no longer be tied down, how can governments tax and regulate them? If governments can no longer regulate, how will we protect workers and the environment? If they can no longer tax, how will we pay for the welfare state? *1984*'s nightmare was government everywhere; 2002's is government nowhere.

SIX

The Phantom Menace

Why government is not under threat

Globalisation has made it exceedingly difficult for governments to provide social insurance . . . international integration is taking place against the background of receding governments and diminished social obligations.

DANI RODRIK, *Has Globalisation Gone Too Far?*

Globalisation . . . has enabled companies to hold a gun to government's head: if it refuses to meet their demands, they threaten to disinvest, move their plant to Thailand, and damage its credibility by making thousands of workers redundant.

GEORGE MONBIOT, *Captive State*

Sovereign states are waging a war of competitive deregulation, forced on them by the global free market. A mechanism of downward harmonisation of market economies is already in operation . . . to imagine that the social market economies of the past can renew themselves

intact under the forces of downward harmonisation is the
most dangerous of the many illusions associated with the
global market. Instead, social market systems are being
compelled progressively to dismantle themselves, so that
they can compete on more equal terms with economies in
which environmental, social and labour costs are lowest . . .
If sources of revenue – capital, enterprises and people – are
free to migrate to low tax regimes, mutually agreed coercion
does not work as a means of paying for public goods . . . in
general terms the contradiction between social democracy
and global free markets seems irreconcilable.

JOHN GRAY, *False Dawn*

If the financial markets deem that a new national
healthcare scheme or a massive education reform will prove
too costly, they will respond with higher interest rates or a
collapsing currency. In this way global market forces not
only rule out the kind of compensation to losers that would
reduce the social costs of globalisation, they also seem to
challenge state sovereignty itself. The footloose, mobile
nature of global capital increasingly dictates what
governments can and cannot do . . . the levying of taxes,
arguably the most fundamental right of the nation state
and a potential means of redressing social and economic
inequality, is being squeezed by corporate pressure.

NOREENA HERTZ, *The Silent Takeover*

Nothing could demonstrate the power and hegemony of the
private economy better . . . but for the blackmail it exerts . . .
on the policies of developed countries so as to make them
fall into line, lower taxes, reduce public expenditure and
social welfare systems, regulate deregulation and 'free'
companies to lay off unimpeded, abolish the minimum
wage, make work more flexible, and so on.

VIVIANE FORRESTER, *The Economic Horror*

Impotent – that's what George Bush, Tony Blair, Gerhard Schröder and Jacques Chirac are, or near enough. Once, politicians could tax and spend with gay abandon, regulate at will and maybe even build a better world. No longer. Now, they have no choice but to cut taxes, pare back spending, deregulate. Global forces pen them in: when markets move, they quake. No wonder voters have no time for politicians.

The reasoning goes something like this. Globalisation is breaking down walls between national markets. Countries increasingly have to compete for footloose and fancy-free capital and workers. So if governments set high taxes to pay for socialised medicine or generous welfare schemes, people and firms will move elsewhere. If they try to borrow instead, markets mark interest rates up and the currency down. If they impose costly labour and environmental standards, jobs and investment flee to less regulated countries. The upshot is that globalisation is inexorably eroding governments' powers. It is stripping the 'social' out of the social market economy and taking the 'welfare' out of the welfare state. Higher taxes, redistributing money to the poor, socialised medicine, a minimum wage, a cleaner environment, full employment, you name it, are no longer possible in a 'global economy'. Governments are locked into a 'race to the bottom' as they lower taxes and regulations to stave off economic decline. Europe is being forced to reshape itself in America's image – and America in Mexico's.

That is the conventional wisdom. It unites right and left. Right-wingers exult in the death of their old foe, big government. Centre-left politicians wring their hands. Left-wingers despair: if government cannot deliver social justice, who can? For voters, it is either yet another reason for apathy – if voting can't change anything, why bother? – or else the spur to take to the streets to fight globalisation and reclaim democracy.

Even many supporters of globalisation seem to think that it severely restricts governments' options. In *The Lexus and the Olive Tree*, Thomas Friedman argues that once a country puts on the 'Golden Straitjacket' – his term for 'recognising the rules of the free market in today's global economy' – 'its political choices get reduced to Pepsi or Coke – to slight nuances of taste, slight alterations in design to account for local traditions, some loosening here or there, but never any deviation from its core golden rules. Governments – be they led by Democrats or Republicans, Conservatives or Labourites, Gaullists or Socialists, Christian Democrats or Social Democrats – that deviate too far from the core rules will see their investors stampede away.'

It is certainly true that many of the economic policies on offer from mainstream politicians are more alike than before. Class war is out of fashion. Lyndon Johnson's War on Poverty seems rather quaint. Faith in government's ability to cure every ill and micromanage the economy turned to cynicism amid the high inflation, rising unemployment and economic stagnation of the 1970s. Nationalising the 'commanding heights' of the economy has fallen out of favour; most governments now prefer to privatise. Many have cut tax rates and deregulated parts of the economy. There is a lot of talk about modernising and reforming government. But do the politicians we elect have a choice, or is globalisation forcing their hands?

Whatever you feel about government, you had better hope they do. Because if we are going to choose what kind of global future we want, we need to make a large part of that choice through our governments. True, one of the great things about globalisation is that it enhances individual freedom. We have more choice about where we work, where we take our holidays, what we buy, where we invest our savings and so on. But there are some things that people cannot do alone. You can help out a homeless person in the street, but you cannot reduce poverty. You can buy a cleaner car and drive it less, but you cannot curb air pollution. You may be able to afford adequate private health insurance, but many people cannot. Helping the poor, protecting the environment and guaranteeing good healthcare for all are only three of the many things that we can only do collectively.

Collectively does not necessarily mean through government.

Charities, trade unions, mutual societies and campaign groups can all have an impact. Shelter has helped many rough-sleepers in Britain; the United Steelworkers of America has won generous health insurance and pensions for its members; credit unions lend to those that banks ignore; international campaigns like Live Aid raise millions for starving Africans. Great. But only government has the democratic legitimacy to make decisions for society as a whole, and the power and resources to enforce them.

Some people disagree. Many right-wingers think governments oppress people rather than represent them. Government is part of the problem, not part of the solution, they claim. It should get off people's backs. They are sometimes right. Governments have been known to tax too much – to 'squeeze the rich till the pips squeak', as Denis Healey once said when he was Britain's Chancellor of the Exchequer in the 1970s, and to tax the poor pretty heavily too. They have all too often borrowed recklessly and squandered the money, wasted people's taxes and tied up the economy in harmful red tape. So a little bit of competition between governments might not be such a bad thing. The option of packing up and leaving is valuable: it may literally be a matter of life and death. Nazi Germany and the Soviet Union spring to mind, as do North Korea and Iraq now. But even libertarians see a need for government to provide law and order, as well as defence. Most people want governments to do much more on their behalf than this bare minimum.

That is certainly true in continental Europe. Fans of a night-watchman state are few and far between. It is also true in supposedly free-wheeling Britain. Most people think the government is right to temper markets with policies that aim to promote social justice. After all, the country's most treasured asset is not Vodafone or even the royal family, but the National Health Service. Even in America, where government is often a dirty word, there is broad support for public education, Medicare and Medicaid, and laws to protect workers and the environment. When the economy tanks or disaster strikes, people everywhere want governments to act. So we should all be worried if governments are no longer able to provide what people want.

At stake is not just governments' ability to intervene for the common good, but democracy and diversity too. Even if lower taxes and less government regulation boost the economy, there is more to life than maximising GDP growth. Europeans should be able to choose social democracy if they are willing to pay the price for it. Americans should be able to opt for bigger government if they don't mind shouldering the burden. People should not be prevented from having cleaner air if they are willing to pay more for petrol. Equally importantly, people in different countries ought to be able to make different choices about how much government they want. Europeans should not be denied the option of a national health service just because Americans make do without one. Swedes should be able to guarantee the poor a comfortable standard of living even if Britons choose to be less generous. Americans should be able to have cleaner air than Mexicans if they want. Democracy and diversity are not to be given up lightly. If globalisation stops governments from doing what people want, it is not such a good thing, however much it boosts economic growth.

Still alive and kicking

Fear not. Globalisation may constrain governments in some ways, but it does not seriously undermine their powers. Why? Because neither companies, nor people, nor even money are really footloose and fancy-free. All of them are still more or less tied to places, so governments still have sway over them.

For a start, as we have seen, the extent of globalisation is exaggerated. Despite fifty years of liberalisation, many barriers to trade remain – not least in agriculture and services, which together account for two-thirds of the world economy. New barriers, moreover, are forever cropping up – even in cyberspace. Witness the EU's data-privacy directive, which discriminates against foreign firms. More importantly, even if all trade barriers were abolished, differences in accounting rules, legal systems, language and culture would still segment markets, as the EU's experience with its single market shows. Besides, all sorts of things simply cannot be supplied from afar: haircuts, childcare, gym classes, restaurant meals, and so on. So even if globally mobile businesses move away, the tax base is not going to vanish.

Capital markets are not genuinely global either. Although rich countries (and many poor ones) now allow money in and out freely, most domestic investment is still financed by domestic savings. A Nissan car plant in Sunderland, a BMW factory in South Carolina or a Toyota facility in Valenciennes may grab the headlines, but such foreign investment is still the exception, not the rule. Inward investment in the US was 17.9 per cent of total US investment in 1999. In Britain it was 32.5 per cent, in France 17.5 per cent, in Germany 11.8 per cent. Portfolio investment – investment in bonds and shares, rather than factories and offices – is also overwhelmingly national. Of the $3.3 trillion of US government bonds (known as Treasuries) outstanding at the end of September 2001, only $1.2 trillion were in foreign hands.[1] Foreigners owned $1.5 trillion in US shares out of a total stockmarket value of $13.6 trillion.

Look at it another way. If capital were perfectly mobile, it would flow to wherever the returns were highest. Countries that are perceived to have attractive investment opportunities would lure huge flows of savings from around the world, while those with poor investment prospects would see a huge drain of cash. Since a country could draw on a global pool of savings to finance its investment needs, its domestic investment would not be correlated with its domestic savings. In practice, though, they remain tightly linked. The gap between a country's investment and savings, its capital-account surplus, which by definition is equal to its current-account deficit, rarely exceeds 5 per cent of GDP. Finance is still predominantly domestic too.

As for labour markets, although very rich people and many highly skilled workers can move around the world relatively freely,

[handwritten annotation: Those who are most hurt by glob., and who need youth most!]

most people cannot. Ordinary Britons can get only one-year visas to work in Australia. If you are fed up with France and have no qualifications, you cannot easily emigrate to America (although you can freely cross the Channel). Even if people were entirely free to move, few would. We are rooted to places by family, friends, language and culture. For every Bjorn Borg, who claims residence in Monte Carlo in order to avoid Sweden's high taxes, there are countless Svens who are still willing to fork out. Council-tax levels in London boroughs vary hugely, as do local income taxes in America, but is everyone fleeing high-tax Islington and New York? Of course not. There is more to life than a lower tax bill.

Besides, taxes are not simply costs: they generally bring benefits too. The French pay higher taxes than the British, but they don't have to wait a year for a hip transplant. The British pay higher taxes than the Americans, but they all have access to (almost) free public healthcare. Of course, some taxes are wasted, and some people get back less than they put in. But many people are net beneficiaries. Even those who are net losers don't lose out as much as the difference in tax burdens among countries suggests. Moreover, taxpayers may be happy to contribute if they feel a sense of solidarity with their fellow countrymen, if they worry that they might one day be poor or sick too, or if they would rather live safely in an open society than in fear in gated communities. Yes, some rich French professionals whose loathing for tax outweighs their love of cafés, warm baguettes and their desire to be near friends and family may move to America. But most won't. So the French government can continue to tax them heavily.

Companies too are rooted to places: by the investment sunk into a factory, by a local network of suppliers, by a skilled local workforce, by the need to be near their customers, or simply by the boss's desire to live near a good golf course. They are also tied down by culture and tradition. Few companies are genuinely 'transnational': Coca-Cola is still recognisably an American company, even though it operates across the globe. Boeing has moved its headquarters from Seattle to Chicago, but it is unlikely to move to

London. For sure, there are exceptions. Hoover shifted a factory
from France to Scotland in 1993 in order to take advantage of more
flexible working arrangements, a no-strike agreement and the
exclusion of new employees from pension rights for two years –
concessions that would have been illegal in France. Ericsson, a
Swedish electronics company, caused a big fuss when it sought to
avoid Sweden's high taxes by opening a big corporate headquarters
in London in 1999. But these cases grabbed the headlines precisely
because they are the exception, not the rule. For companies too,
there is more to the bottom line than low taxes, lax labour laws
and loose environmental controls.

Like people, companies derive benefits from taxes and regulations. They gain from good infrastructure, good schools, good
hospitals, low crime and clean air. High-tech companies, which are
more footloose than most, are flocking to high-tax, highly regulated economies like Sweden and Finland. Of course, taxes and
regulations can be a burden, and some companies suffer. But many
do not: they may find that higher standards cut costs – because
more secure workers work harder, for instance, or because cleaner
production methods enable them to charge a green premium –
and that they help them attract good staff, who want to live in a
clean and safe place. High taxes and costly regulations will drive
some companies away, but for most firms, the costs are tolerable.

Even so, surely France's high taxes, for instance, make it
'uncompetitive' and therefore condemn it to economic decline?
Not at all. If taxes are spent well, they boost an economy's productivity. Well-educated, healthy workers and trains that get them to
work on time are pluses. It is quite astonishing – and depressing –
that so many people on the left and centre-left, who presumably
believe in the benefits of government spending, seem to ignore
this, and fret that globalisation spells doom for government intervention. Even if people prefer policies that may actually reduce
productivity – if the French decided to work four-day weeks, for
instance, in order to spend more time enjoying life – this does not
spell a never-ending spiral of economic decline. It simply means

that they have to pay the one-off price of lower wages. They trade off more free time for less money. Presumably, since they are making this choice, this makes them better off: the increase in leisure time more than compensates for the loss of wages (although if the shorter working hours are stipulated by law rather than a matter of individual taste, some people who would have preferred to earn more may end up worse off).

The same is true of France's rigid labour laws, some of which may reduce productivity. They certainly impose costs on some French people, who are needlessly unemployed because of them. This may eventually make them politically unsustainable. But they are not unsustainable because of globalisation. If they raise the cost of hiring French workers, which increases the cost of producing a unit of output and so reduces companies' productivity and profitability, something will have to give. Managers might drive workers harder, and therefore restore the previous level of productivity. Otherwise, real wages will have to fall, either through a fall in the exchange rate, a rise in inflation or a direct cut in money wages. This adjustment may be painful, but once the one-off cut in wages has been made, and companies' profitability has been restored, that's it. The French economy will not carry on going down the tubes.

Admittedly, rigid labour laws can have another cost. They may make it harder for the economy to adjust to change. If there is less demand for steel and more for software, the steel industry needs to shrink and the computing industry expand. Strict labour laws may make it hard for steel companies to shed workers, and thus slow the growth of the software industry – and the growth of the economy as a whole. If globalisation increases the pace of economic change, it may exacerbate the costs of this failure to adjust. But, as we saw in chapter one, most economic change is due to domestic factors, not trade. Moreover, even this loss of flexibility is not the downward spiral that critics fear. It may ratchet up unemployment and slow economic growth somewhat, but it does not imply a continuous fall in living standards.

No sign of shrinking

If globalisation is forcing governments to slim, it is doing a pretty poor job. National economies have become much more open since 1980: trade barriers have fallen, capital controls have been abolished and foreign direct investment has soared. Yet governments are collecting more in tax than ever before.[2] Despite all the headlines about tax cuts, the average tax take in rich OECD economies has risen from 32.1 per cent of GDP in 1980 to 37.3 per cent in 1999. It is eleven and a half percentage points higher than in 1965.

Far from converging downwards, tax shares are diverging upwards. Back in 1965, the American government took 25 per cent of the country's national income in tax. Since then, it has taken steadily more: 27 per cent of GDP in 1980 and 28.9 per cent in 1999. Britain's tax burden has gone up even more, from 30.4 per cent in 1965 to 36.3 per cent in 1999. The trend in Germany is roughly the same: up from 31.6 per cent to 37.7 per cent. But France's tax take has really shot up: from 34.5 per cent to a whopping 45.8 per cent. So whereas the gap between the US and France was nine and a half percentage points in 1965, it is now nearly seventeen. Funnily enough, the countries with the biggest governments are among the most open: Denmark's tax burden was 50.4 per cent in 1999 and Sweden's 52.2 per cent.

Perhaps, though, the tax mix has changed. Mobile companies may be paying less tax, immobile workers more. Not a bit of it: taxes on company profits accounted for 9 per cent of the total tax take in OECD countries in 1999, the same share as in 1965. Revenues from personal income tax were 26 per cent of governments' total tax take in 1999, as they were in 1965. The US, Britain, France and Germany all raised a bigger share of GDP from personal income taxes in 1999 than in 1990. Moreover, there is a big spread among countries: Australia raises 14 per cent of its tax take from company profits, Austria only 4 per cent; Denmark raises 51 per cent of its revenues from personal income tax, Greece only 14

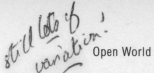

still lots of variation!

per cent. So there is plenty of scope for countries to raise more tax from companies and personal incomes if they want to.

Sceptics argue that this is about to change. The OECD has warned that the Internet could damage tax systems so much that it could 'lead to governments being unable to meet the legitimate demands of their citizens for public services'. Vito Tanzi, then at the IMF, has identified[3] eight tax 'termites' that he says are eating away at government's ability to tax. First, there is electronic commerce. Sales over the Internet are growing fast, and are starting to nibble away at US states' sales-tax revenues. According to Mr Tanzi, this raises three problems: politicians are reluctant to tax the Internet; tax authorities find it harder to trace electronic transactions than paper trails; and while physical objects, like books or CDs, can still be intercepted at customs, digital downloads – music, writing, photos, medical or financial advice – cannot. The spread of electronic money, the second termite, could make matters worse, by enabling people to make electronic transactions anonymously.

Third, an increasing share of world trade (now around 60 per cent) takes place within multinational companies. This allows them to shift profits from high-tax countries to low-tax ones by manipulating the prices that their foreign subsidiaries charge each other for cross-border transfers. Rupert Murdoch's News Corporation has made over £1.4 billion in profits in Britain since 1987 but paid no corporation tax in the country. Offshore financial centres and tax havens are also increasingly used to launder money and avoid tax. The UN estimates that $5 trillion, much of it dirty money, could be parked in them. Moreover, rich people can avoid tax by channelling their investments through unregulated 'hedge funds' based in offshore centres, as well as by using complex financial instruments like derivatives. Governments may also find it harder to tax footloose capital and individuals than before. Many professionals now earn income and invest their savings abroad and fail to declare this. Finally, people increasingly shop abroad to avoid local taxes and customs duties: think of all the British supermarkets in Calais or the stores in Tijuana across the border from San Diego.

It's a long list. Yet for the most part, these termites are not new. And as we have seen, tax revenues are so far holding up well. As for the Internet, its risk to tax revenues is probably exaggerated. Electronic commerce is still tiny: mail order accounts for a bigger share of retail sales. The predictions of its explosive growth made in the late 1990s now look overoptimistic, to put it kindly. Moreover, all sorts of things cannot be downloaded from the Internet: cars, food, fuel, clothes, most services and so on. In *Just Capital*, Adair Turner[111] calculates that, at most, the Internet could eventually erode 1 per cent of government revenues: significant, but hardly the end of government as we know it. Besides, ways could be found to tax most Internet sales. CDs bought from Amazon in Britain are taxed; so could those in America if there were the political will for it. Taxes on international sales could be enforced, if necessary, with the help of credit-card companies or parcel-delivery firms. → coöperation ! volition.

There is plenty that governments can do to limit tax erosion. America's tax authorities have set out guidelines, with severe penalties for non-compliance, on transfer pricing within multinationals. Another idea is a 'unitary tax', which involves taking a firm's total profits and allocating different slices of that total to individual countries on the basis of a formula that reflects the firm's relative economic presence in a country. The country can then tax that slice of profit at whatever rate it sees fit. Corporation tax could be abolished entirely, and shareholders taxed instead. (!) The OECD is cracking down on tax havens with a mixture of carrots and sticks, a move that has been given new impetus by the war against global terrorism. Hedge funds could be more tightly regulated. Governments could impose a so-called Tobin tax on international financial transactions. More countries could copy America's tax system: instead of taxing only US residents, the US taxes all Americans, wherever they live, on their global income, allowing them to offset income tax paid in the country where they live against their American tax liability. Tax authorities could also agree to share more information than before. They have so far been reluctant to do so, but that could change if they start losing revenues. A World Tax Organisation could even be set up one day if tax avoidance becomes a really serious problem. People are forever finding canny new ways of avoiding tax; governments always find new ways of closing loopholes and new things to tax. Computers may make it easier for people to avoid tax; but they may also make it easier for tax authorities to monitor their transactions. Last, but certainly not least, governments could shift the burden of taxes from labour and capital onto land or things that are detrimental to the environment, like carbon or road congestion. Governments' ability to tax is not seriously under threat.

Free to borrow

Taxes are still rolling in. So governments do not have to borrow to pay for their spending. But what if they want to? James Carville, who was an election adviser to Bill Clinton, once quipped that: 'I used to think that if there was reincarnation, I wanted to come back as the President or the Pope. But now I want to be the bond market: you can intimidate everyone.' International financial markets, it is said, disapprove of government borrowing, especially to pay for social programmes that do not directly contribute to future economic growth. Governments that try to borrow more than the market deems prudent are punished with higher interest rates and a weaker currency. Likewise, governments that try to borrow to boost the economy in a slump or maintain full employment will find their efforts undone by the markets.

There is an element of truth to this. International financial markets do make life difficult for many developing-country governments, an issue that will be discussed in chapter eleven. But rich-country governments have plenty of scope to borrow if they want to. Italy's has run up a debt that is bigger than the country's entire annual income. So has Japan's. In fact, governments find it easier to borrow in global markets than in domestic ones, because there is a wider pool of savings to draw from. The costs are lower too. Whereas in a closed economy, government borrowing soon bids up the cost of debt – interest rates – and so depresses companies' investment and consumer spending, in an open economy, it causes much smaller ripples in a bigger pond. In both cases, interest rates rise once lenders start to doubt a government's ability to repay its debts. So why have so many governments curbed their borrowing? Why does Gordon Brown, Britain's Chancellor of the Exchequer, drone on and on about prudence? For a purpose: profligate borrowing is simply not desirable. It means higher interest payments, which gobble up tax revenues that could have been spent elsewhere, and a bigger burden for future taxpayers, who have to repay the debt. Governments were not forced to limit their budget deficits; they chose to do so because they thought it was right. (The euro area's 'growth and stability pact', which commits governments to deficits of less than 3 per cent of GDP outside a deep recession, is a hairshirt that European governments have chosen to wear and one that they could take off if they wanted to.)

It is odd that people like John Gray and Noreena Hertz seem so wedded to government borrowing. There's nothing particularly left wing about going on a borrowing spree. Nor is there anything democratic about governments' continually spending more than people are willing to pay in tax. Gray and Hertz both seem to think that government borrowing is part and parcel of Keynesianism or social democracy. But it isn't. Keynes never said that governments should borrow recklessly: he said they should borrow when demand was slack in order to boost the economy. Governments are still perfectly capable of doing this. Social democracy means tax and spend, not borrow and borrow.

Where globalisation does make a difference is to how governments manage the economy. In a closed economy, both changes in the balance between taxation and government spending (fiscal policy) and changes in interest rates (monetary policy) can be used to try to smooth the economic cycle of boom and bust. In a fully open economy, where capital can flow in and out of the country freely, only one policy lever works. If the country's exchange rate is fixed, fiscal policy works, but monetary policy does not (because interest rates cannot diverge from those set on the global capital market). If the exchange rate floats, monetary policy works, but fiscal policy does not (because when increased government borrowing bids up interest rates, foreign capital flows into the economy, pushing the currency up and thus fully offsetting the fiscal stimulus).

In practice, although rich countries have abolished their capital controls, capital is not perfectly mobile. So both policy levers work somewhat, although fiscal policy works better with a fixed exchange rate and monetary policy better with a floating one. To complicate matters further, currencies tend to have a life of their own, so with floating rates, the economy's response to policy changes is particularly unpredictable. Most rich economies – the US, Japan, the euro area and Britain – now allow their currencies to move freely; but some, such as Sweden and Denmark, peg their currencies to another, in their case the euro. So most countries rely more on changes in interest rates to smooth the economic cycle than on changes in taxes and government spending. It is primarily to Alan Greenspan at the US Federal Reserve, Wim Duisenberg at the European Central Bank and Eddie George at the Bank of England that people turn for help when the economic outlook sours. (Many governments have contracted out monetary policy to independent central banks that operate outside politicians' day-to-day control. This limits governments' power, but they choose to tie their hands in this way because they think it delivers lower inflation – which is what voters say they want. More to the point, this curb on government power is unrelated to globalisation.) The upshot is that although they may use different policy tools to do so, governments – or the central bankers they have delegated monetary policy to – are still as capable (or incapable) of smoothing the economic cycle in an open economy as in a closed one.

Race to the top

What, then, of the 'race to the bottom'? There is not much evidence of a bonfire of environmental regulations. Environmental laws are generally much tougher than they were twenty years ago: petrol taxes are higher, cars are required to emit less pollution, companies have had to reduce their emissions of noxious chemicals into the air and water; many now have to recycle a lot of their waste too. Downward harmonisation? Tell that to the German and Scandinavian companies that every year are required to pollute less and recycle more. The gap between these eco-friendly countries and America is going up, not down.

Not only that, but there is little pressure on governments to loosen their environmental laws. Charles Oman of the OECD has compiled the most comprehensive review[5] to date of the impact of competition among governments for foreign direct investment (FDI). He finds that 'firms in modern manufacturing and service industries rarely move their operations to take advantage of lower environmental standards in another country; and ... efforts by national governments to compete for FDI in these industries through lax standards or lax enforcement of environmental protection are likely to be unsuccessful, perhaps even counterproductive'. Pollution havens are a myth. Even when companies threaten to move, this is often bluster. A big Dutch chemical company, for instance, threatened to relocate unless the government agreed to make concessions on environmental standards. 'When the Dutch government refused to concede, there were no further developments – the company had been bluffing, but it would readily have accepted relaxed regulations.'

In fact, competition for investment can actually raise environmental standards. One reason is that governments are increasingly keen to attract relatively clean knowledge-based industries, like computing or consulting – and managers and employees prefer to live in cleaner areas. Many companies find that higher

environmental standards reduce operating costs, such as water-fil-
tration costs, worker-health problems and the risk of incurring
clean-up costs. They also help attract highly qualified staff, as well
as boosting revenues by appealing to eco-conscious consumers. The
report's conclusion is unambiguous: 'Policy competition has raised
standards [of environmental protection] across much of Europe.'

What about labour laws? Admittedly, they have been liberalised
in many countries. But Margaret Thatcher did not try to smash
the unions because she wanted to attract foreign investment. Nor
did Ronald Reagan fire America's air-traffic controllers because he
was worried about foreign competition. They both did it primarily
for domestic reasons: because they thought unions had too much
power and that this was bad for the economy. More importantly,
recent history shows that globalisation does not prevent governments from tightening labour laws if they want to. America's legal
minimum wage has been raised from $3.35 to $5.15 since 1990. The
European Union has adopted a Social Chapter that beefs up worker
rights. In Britain, Tony Blair's government has introduced a minimum wage and forced companies to recognise a union where a
majority of workers want it to represent them. In France, Lionel
Jospin's administration imposed a thirty-five-hour working week
and raised the minimum wage. An OECD[6] study of seventy-five
countries that account for virtually all of world trade and investment found that, despite the explosion in overseas investment,
workers' union rights had not got significantly worse in any of seventy-five countries since the early 1980s. In seventeen – including
Brazil, South Korea and Turkey – they had markedly improved.

Richard Freeman, an American economist, has found[7] that,
rather than being dragged down to a common minimum, the differences between countries' labour markets are growing. He
compared changes in the unionisation rates and the extent of collective wage bargaining in a host of countries between 1980 and
the mid-1990s. Unionisation and collective bargaining fell in the
US, Britain, Japan, New Zealand and Australia. But in many
European countries the pattern was mixed. France, Germany, Italy

and the Netherlands witnessed falling unionisation but more collective bargaining. And in some European countries – Spain,
Finland and Sweden – unionisation and collective bargaining both
increased.

If foreign investment were mainly driven by a desire to escape
costly labour and environmental regulations, one would expect it
to flow mainly to developing countries, where rules are typically
laxer. But in fact, four-fifths of it goes to rich countries. In 2000
developing countries attracted only 19 per cent of global FDI
flows.[8] The poorest forty-nine countries, where standards are often
lowest, received only $4.4 billion of the $1,271 billion invested
abroad. Only $35 billion of America's stock of foreign investment is
in lower-standard Mexico; $116 billion is in higher-standard
Holland.[9]

What about fears that highly regulated countries face inexorable
economic decline? American free-marketeers are forever telling
Europeans that they must 'deregulate or die'. Buoyed by the
helium of the Internet boom, they boasted that America's productivity growth – which determines how fast an economy can grow in
the long run – was racing ahead while Europe's was flagging. Even
now that the Internet bubble has burst, many people seem convinced that America is in the ascendant and Europe in decline.
Admittedly, in the five years to 2000, GDP per hour worked rose by
2.1 per cent a year in America and 1.6 per cent in the euro area. But
America's GDP growth is inflated by the fact that it treats companies' software spending as investment, whereas in Europe it is
treated as intermediate consumption. One way to partially get
round this problem is to use net domestic product (NDP), which
subtracts capital depreciation, rather than GDP. Julian Callow, an
economist as CSFB, a Swiss investment bank, calculates that in the
five years to 2000 NDP per hour worked grew by 1.8 per cent in
America and 1.5 per cent in the euro area. But over any period
longer than the five years of America's boom, the euro area's productivity growth pulls well ahead. In the seven years to 2000, NDP
per hour rose by an average of 1.8 per cent in the euro area, but by

only 1.4 per cent in America. As Pam Woodall, the economics editor of *The Economist* points out,[10] these calculations also ignore the fact that American number-crunchers have done more than their European counterparts to take into account improvements in the quality of goods and services. So Europe's productivity growth is probably understated relative to America's. Despite its higher taxes and regulations, the euro area is doing at least as well as America.

what about the dev. world?

Bring back politics

It is a terrible irony that the left has lost faith in government. Governments are not impotent: they can still tax, spend and regulate. As economies have opened up over the past fifty years, government has grown, not shrunk. The biggest growth in government has been in small open economies like Sweden and Austria. Globalisation is not dragging everyone down to a common minimum. Countries are, in many respects, less alike than twenty years ago. The gap between high-tax and low-tax countries has grown. So have the differences between countries' labour and environmental laws. Diversity rules. The European model of social democracy – high taxes, a generous welfare state, tight labour and environmental laws – is not under threat from globalisation: Europe is not being forced to reshape itself in America's image. Nor is America's way of life imperilled: it is in no danger of becoming Mexico.

Rejoice: we are still free to choose. If globalisation does not stop Denmark taking half its citizens' income in tax, it certainly does not constrain Britain – or even France – from raising taxes if it wants to. If there is a constraint, it is political. People may not want to pay more tax. If so, persuasive politicians could change that. Tony Blair and Gordon Brown seem to have convinced Britons to cough up more to rescue their public services: they hiked taxes in the 2002 budget to fund better healthcare. Wherever you stand on taxation and spending, this is democracy at work.

The implications for conservative politics are clear. Those who favour tax cuts and small government have to argue their case on its merits. Spurious arguments about the need to compete in a global economy will not do – and progressives should point this out, forcefully. The same goes for privatisation, deregulation and all manner of liberalisation. Often, such policies may be a good idea. But they are not required by globalisation.

In fact, globalisation may call for more government, not less. When people are more exposed to the vagaries of global economic forces, they may be keener on social spending to insure against this increased risk. Dani Rodrik, an economist at Harvard University, has found[11] that government spending on social security and welfare is highest in countries that are very open to international trade *and* suffer from volatile prices for their exports. This suggests that globalisation increases the demand for social spending. Mr Rodrik frets that globalisation may prevent governments from meeting this increased demand for social insurance. But, as we have seen, this fear is misplaced. The challenge is actually a political one: to improve the welfare state both because it is right to help the poor and because it is necessary to buttress support for globalisation.

That is why, even if you are not a fan of government intervention, you should support generous social insurance. If people feel insecure, they may turn against globalisation. All its bounties could yet be lost – to everyone's eventual detriment. As globalisation progresses, we ought to see more social spending in many countries, not less, driven by the demand for a more protective social cushion and paid for by the increased economic growth that globalisation brings. This need not mean higher government spending overall, much less profligate borrowing. More could be spent on helping workers cope with change and less on subsidies to companies, for instance. Nor does it mean that government should not be reformed: it should. But the reason for reforming government is to make it deliver what people want, not to satisfy global capital.

The implications for progressive politics are liberating. Globalisation does not threaten the NHS, the Swedish model, the French state or American workers' rights. It strengthens the case for social spending. Nor does it mean that Europe has to deregulate its labour and product markets: perhaps it should, but it is not obliged to. All of the benefits of globalisation – faster economic growth, increased competition, a wider choice of cheaper imports, the faster transfer of technologies from abroad, the ability to specialise in what you do best and reap economies of scale – can be had without sacrificing governments' ability to intervene in domestic markets for the common good. If your priority is more spending on public services, that is not a reason to oppose globalisation. On the contrary. Progressive people should support globalisation, because it makes more resources available to fund social spending. Al Gore, Lionel Jospin, Gerhard Schröder, the *Guardian*, please note: attempting to embrace the anti-globalisation agenda is a dead-end for the centre-left.

Why, then, do politicians so often tell us that we don't have a choice any more? Are they simply mistaken, like Thomas Friedman and Noreena Hertz? Or do they just find it convenient to lie to us? The truth is probably a bit of both. The belief that globalisation limits governments' options is so pervasive that many politicians have doubtless come to believe it. But there is also a large element of deception. When politicians tell you that 'in a global economy', this or that policy has to change, take it with a bowl of salt. Like the EU or the WTO, globalisation is a helpful scapegoat for changes that are politically controversial. 'Whatever you do, blame globalisation' is the maxim of modern government.

Take Bill Clinton's decision to jettison the Democrats' commitment to big government. Clearly, he did it to woo 'Reagan Democrats' who had deserted his party to vote Republican. Doubtless, he no longer believed in big government either. But rather than confront traditional Democrats with this awkward repositioning, he found it easier to say that global markets had forced the change upon him. The Republicans collude in this lie because they think it reinforces their minimal-government agenda.

Same story in Britain. Tony Blair and Gordon Brown find it polit-ically expedient to claim that it is difficult to raise taxes 'in a global economy' because this reassures former Conservative voters and pacifies traditional Labour ones. Conservatives do not puncture this myth because it bolsters their case for lower taxes. Or consider Germany, where a social-democratic government is struggling to push through bitterly unpopular labour-market reforms to bring unemployment down. Rather than make the case for change on its merits, politicians prefer to claim that it is necessary to keep Germany globally 'competitive'.

In politics, the ends often justify the means. If the globalisation myth has helped centre-left parties win elections, then perhaps it is useful. But it would still be better to have a genuine debate about the scope and shape of government. There is still plenty of room for governments to pursue ambitious, and differing, social policies if politicians can convince voters that they are worthwhile. By pre-tending otherwise, politicians are taking a big risk. If they keep on telling people they don't have a choice, they cannot be surprised if many people eventually believe them. Democracy is diminished if people sit at home in apathy and threatened if people take to the streets in anger. Politicians will be largely to blame if people mis-takenly turn against globalisation and jeopardise all the opportunities that an open world has to offer.

SEVEN

Global Government

*How the world should
(and shouldn't) be run*

Many decisions affecting people's daily lives are being shifted away from our local and national governments and instead are being made by a group of unelected trade bureaucrats sitting behind closed doors in Geneva, Switzerland . . . At stake is the very basis of democracy and accountable decision-making that is the necessary undergirding of any citizen struggle for just distribution of wealth and adequate health, safety and environmental protections. The erosion of such democratic accountability, and the local, state and national sovereignty that is its embodiment, has taken place over the past several decades. The globalisation of commerce and finance has been shaped by multinational companies that, in the absence of global rules, simply conducted their business to suit their needs. Establishment of the WTO marks a landmark formalisation and strengthening of this heretofore *ad hoc* system.

RALPH NADER, *Whose Trade Organisation?*

By conflating the protection of human beings and the
environment with trade protectionism, by setting
maximum standards for world trade rather than minimum
ones, by overriding any national or international law with
which they conflict, trade agreements have become the
greatest threats to representative government on earth.

GEORGE MONBIOT, *Captive State*

Those who seek to design a free market on a worldwide scale
have always insisted that the legal framework which defines
and entrenches it must be placed beyond the reach of any
democratic legislature. Sovereign states may sign up to
membership of the World Trade Organisation; but it is that
organisation, not the legislature of any sovereign state,
which determines what is to count as free trade, and what
as a restraint of it. The rules of the game of the market must
be elevated beyond any possibility of revision through
democratic choice.

JOHN GRAY, *False Dawn*

Why should the global market escape the rule of
international law or human-rights conventions passed by
the UN? The WTO has arrogated the functions of legislature,
executive and judiciary solely for itself. In the eighteenth
century such an anti-democratic concentration of power
provoked the French revolution.

JOSÉ BOVÉ, French farmers' Leader

Bill Clinton once declared that globalisation needed a human face.
Meet Mike Moore, the bluff Kiwi who until September 2002 ran the
much-reviled World Trade Organisation (WTO). He's a big man
with a big heart, forever puffing on cigarettes and cracking jokes.
I've seen him charm the socks off Clare Short, Britain's development minister, and Rita Hayes, the old sourpuss who represented
the Clinton administration at the WTO in Geneva. He got on

famously well with José Bové, the French farmers' leader. Remarkably for a politician, he is honest and down-to-earth. Of course, he has his faults. He has a temper. He all too often gives people who don't deserve it the benefit of the doubt. His mind darts around erratically; and many of his ideas are flaky. Critics have even dubbed him 'Mad Mike'. His life suggests otherwise.

The New Zealand that Mike grew up in was an insular place. 'Even the humble spud was opposed by the merchants and church in its day. A church leader railed against the potato as being a dangerous narcotic, almost as bad as tea. The merchants and farmers wanted to protect their profits . . . against this dangerous, competitive new crop,' he writes in *A Brief History of the Future*. If New Zealand turned its back on the world, the world ignored New Zealand. Ideas did not flow into or out of it. It produced wool, not world leaders. Mike has changed that.

Born in poverty in Whakatane in 1949, Mike joined the Labour Party as a teenager. He left school at fifteen, and was unemployed for a while. After working as a printer, a meatpacker and a trade-union researcher, he became New Zealand's youngest-ever member of parliament, aged twenty-three, in 1972. But he lost his seat in 1975, and, having survived polio as a kid, almost lost his life to cancer. In those wilderness years, he read voraciously and wrote voluminously. In the process, he did one of the hardest things a politician can do: he changed his mind.

He realised that globalisation was happening, and that countries that resisted it would sink. What he saw going on around him, as much as the books he read, convinced him. 'It was absurd. We were importing TV sets, pulling them apart and reassembling them.' He came to see protectionism as the enemy of the poor, because it put up the price of basic necessities like food and clothing; and free trade as the natural corollary of the internationalism of the left. 'Why', he asks, 'is foreign aid good, but buying foreign products evil?'

In 1984 he got a chance to put his ideas into practice. Labour swept to power, and he became trade minister. The government embarked on one of the bravest economic and social experiments in recent times. Mike's job, to open the country's heavily protected markets to international competition, was at the core of its radicalism; and he was good at it. His political street-fighting skills and instinctive sense of when to compromise helped push change through; his erudite charm helped win over waverers.

The ideas behind Mike's agenda were gaining currency around the world, and New Zealand was in the vanguard of change. For the first time in history, the rest of the world turned to watch this distant little country. Delegations arrived. Economists wrote papers. Journalists came for interviews.

Despite the global adulation, Labour's policies did not go down quite as well at home. The government fell out of favour – but Mike didn't. In 1990, facing electoral annihilation, the party co-opted him to serve as prime minister for eight weeks. Labour still lost, but its reforms survived. Mike led the party in opposition until 1993.

His career looked finished. There was nowhere to go in New Zealand. But then the chance of running the organisation created to promote the ideas on which he had staked his career came up. He shuttled around the globe, running down his savings as he wooed WTO member governments. He secured the backing of a majority of them. But his rival, Thailand's Supachai Panichpakdi, would not admit defeat. There was a deadlock. Eventually, they agreed to share a six-year term. Mike started his job in September 1999, three months before the fiasco in Seattle. Since then, he has set the WTO back on track: a new round of world-trade talks was finally launched in Doha, the capital of Qatar, in November 2001.

Mike knows the problems that come with opening up, because he has lived through them. He sympathises with the fears of the unions, because he worked for one. He understands the language of the left, because he has spoken it. When he talks about ideas, they are not dry abstractions: he has lived them.

Mike Moore ought to be a hero for the left. Here is a man who has achieved so much off his own bat without abandoning his progressive principles. I think he is a genuinely good man. Yet such is some people's hatred for the WTO that he has been branded 'public enemy number one' and compared to Hitler.

Propelled to notoriety by the protesters who mobbed its summit in Seattle in 1999, the WTO has become the whipping boy for people's many fears about globalisation. Its rules are said to advance big companies' global ambitions at the expense of the poor, the environment and workers. That is bad enough. But the most explosive charge against the WTO is that it tramples on democracy. Critics claim that behind closed doors in Geneva unelected and unaccountable bureaucrats are taking decisions that affect our everyday lives. The future of our public schools and hospitals; the safety of our food and the protection of our environment; poor countries' access to life-saving medicines (see chapter nine) – all this, and much else besides, is no longer in our hands, it is claimed.

Most of these charges are untrue. The WTO is not a world government in embryo. It is simply a forum where governments hammer out trade rules and an umpire they can call on in disputes. But the controversy that surrounds the WTO highlights the crucial challenge of globalisation: how do we tackle global issues like trade or climate change when our democracy remains rooted in local communities and nation states? It is hard for governments and the other actors who increasingly demand a seat at the table – regional groupings, international organisations, pressure groups, companies – to work together internationally without leaving voters feeling out of touch. One day, perhaps, we might elect a world parliament and a world government to deal with global issues. But in the meanwhile, we have to muddle along in other ways. To see how tricky this can be, consider the WTO, which is possibly the most advanced example of international co-operation.

Hardly an ogre

The 550 faceless bureaucrats who allegedly run the world work in a rather drab building on the shores of Lake Geneva. Even Mike's office could do with freshening up. But this overstretched global colossus has a budget of only $80 million a year – less than the IMF's travel budget – so a new lick of paint will have to wait. The 144 squabbling governments that actually run the show deliberately keep the WTO on a short leash. They can veto anything and everything – and they do. Just to organise an innocuous seminar, Mike has to send the begging bowl round national capitals.

The WTO is still a fledgling. It was born in 1995, of seventy-eight quarrelsome parents. A further sixty-six have since adopted it. One hundred and forty-four guardians – what more could a child ask for? And yet often it still feels unloved. It gets tossed around as its parents bicker, and beaten up by other children who are envious of its fine pedigree. It has taken on the role – and much more besides – of its elder brother, the General Agreement on Tariffs and Trade (GATT), which had been around since 1948.

A hefty burden for one so young. But the WTO is popular in some quarters: with the thirty or so countries queueing up to join, notably. Momentously, after a long march that began in 1986, China became a member in January 2002, together with Taiwan. The world's biggest communist country has agreed to be bound by the rules of the top capitalist club. President Vladimir Putin has declared that Russia's accession to the WTO is a 'top priority'. One of Yugoslavia's first acts after the removal of Slobodan Milosevic was to apply to rejoin the WTO. Even Saudi Arabia – which has grown rich by restricting rather than expanding its exports – is clamouring for membership. Countries want a say in setting world-trade rules, as well as recourse to arbitration when they feel wronged. They want better access to export markets and the increased foreign investment that flows when investors know that domestic laws are bound by international agreement. In short, they want to avoid being left out of the ever-expanding global economy.

The WTO's main role is to help spread freer trade. In an ideal world, there would be no need for such an organisation. Each government would act in its country's best interests and adopt free trade unilaterally. It has happened, occasionally: Britain did so in the nineteenth century; Mexico scrapped many trade barriers on its own in the late 1980s; the tiny Baltic state of Estonia abolished all customs duties after it gained independence from the Soviet Union in 1991. But even though, as we've seen, the benefits of free trade far outweigh the costs, governments often find it hard to lower their trade barriers. Companies that fear foreign competitors tend to lobby governments harder than the disparate millions of consumers who benefit from cheaper imports. So in practice, governments tend to be mercantilist. They seek to pry open markets for their exporters, while protecting their domestic industries from import competition as far as possible.

The WTO helps to break this deadlock. Governments offer to open domestic markets in exchange for greater access to foreign ones. This galvanises exporters' support for liberalisation, which helps to overcome the opposition of import-competing industries. The second advantage of WTO agreements is that they tie governments' hands, making it harder for them to backtrack on liberalisation, as well as making their import rules transparent and predictable for business.

One reason, then, why the WTO is so unpopular is that it undermines sectoral lobbies. When the US steel industry protested at a rise in cheap imports in the wake of the world financial crisis in 1998, the Clinton administration responded by imposing anti-dumping duties on imports which it deemed 'unfairly' cheap. This did not satisfy the industry. So the administration offered a subsidy package involving $300 million in tax breaks, and promised to make it easier in future to get protection from import surges. But even that was not enough. The industry spent $4 million on a media blitz and lobbying campaign, urging the US to 'stand up for steel'. The House of Representatives rose to attention. In March 1999 it passed a bill to impose quotas on foreign steel producers. The administration said it would veto the bill: not because it was bad for Americans who would thus pay more for their cars, nor because it was bad for crisis-hit countries which needed to export to the US to escape depression, but because it would breach WTO law. Thankfully, Bill Clinton's mettle was not tested. The Senate stood up to steel and threw out the bill. But support for the WTO took another knock.

Freeing trade is a noble cause. Together, the WTO and the GATT have probably done more to better people's lives than any other government institutions. They have laid the foundations for our open world, where living standards have tripled since 1950. But the WTO's role now stretches beyond liberalising trade. It is also becoming a regulator of the would-be global economy. Its agreements span everything from agriculture, manufacturing and services to food safety, subsidies and intellectual property. They stipulate not only, for instance, how high a duty Switzerland can impose on steel imports, but also which kind of food-safety rules are acceptable and which are not, how countries must regulate their telecoms sector, as well as how long patents must be respected. But it is not the faceless bureaucrats of the WTO that set the rules. It is the 144 member governments, who make all their decisions by consensus. Even tiny Lesotho has a veto.

The WTO's core principle is non-discrimination: governments are not meant to treat products differently on the basis of where they are made. They are encouraged to lower their trade barriers, which discriminate between domestic and foreign products; and when they do so, they are meant to lower them equally to all WTO members. That way all foreign producers compete on a level playing field. So, for example, Switzerland should tax American and Japanese steel equally and eventually aim to eliminate its import duties altogether. Similarly, government regulations should not discriminate unnecessarily against foreigners. Non-discrimination is an essential condition of a genuinely global market.

Underlying that principle is the belief in a rules-based system. Rules that are clear for all to see; rules that apply equally to all, big and small, strong and weak; rules that are stable and predictable; rules that help defuse conflict; rules that are enforced by sanctions if all else fails. This is an ideal that even domestic legal systems fall short of. It is exceptionally ambitious for international law, where states are legally sovereign. States cannot easily be made to toe the line. Unlike people, they cannot be forced to pay fines, or thrown in jail. So the WTO relies mostly on countries agreeing to comply with the rules they have signed up to, in the belief that this will encourage others to do likewise, combined with a mixture of bribes and threats to keep recalcitrant members in line.

As a last resort, WTO rules are enforced by a dispute-settlement mechanism that is binding on all its members. It operates much like a commercial court. When a country feels that another is breaching an agreement, it can appeal to an independent panel of trade experts. The panel can authorise the imposition of trade sanctions if an obdurate loser refuses to abide by its verdict, but it cannot force a country to lift a restriction – like the EU's ban on hormone-treated beef – if it refuses to. The EU continues to thumb its nose at the WTO's rules.

The WTO's dispute-settlement mechanism is unique in international law. Unlike UN resolutions, which can be vetoed by the five big powers, WTO rulings apply to all – even the US. So governments – and pressure groups – are increasingly turning to the WTO to settle by legal means disputes that might often be best dealt with politically. They chastise it for being too powerful, but want to expand its remit by enforcing labour and environmental standards with trade sanctions. To many Americans, who view international institutions, such as the UN or the IMF, as sticks for disciplining foreigners but not themselves, the WTO smacks of world government. Others think the dispute-settlement mechanism is a tool for the rich and powerful, notably the US, to impose their writ on the poor.

World government? Nonsense. The WTO arbitrates in disputes only when asked to do so by a member government. Its panel verdicts, which are open to appeal, are based solely on rules to which all its member governments have previously signed up. The WTO does not prescribe what countries that breach world-trade rules must do to comply with them, nor can it impose trade sanctions if countries fail to amend their rules satisfactorily. Countries can at any time choose to withdraw a case and settle it politically instead.

Hats off to globalisation: in the late nineteenth century, the Japanese sought to emulate all things Western (*Hulton Archive*)

Jungle music: a European-style opera house opened in 1896 in Manaus, in the heart of the Brazilian Amazon, paid for by the proceeds from a global rubber boom (*Philippe Legrain*)

Men of steel: (from left to right) Gordon Jakubowski, Doc Iler, Chuck Swearingen, Phil Pack and Jerry Ernest of Bethlehem Steel (*Philippe Legrain*)

Not a pretty site: Sparrows Point, Bethlehem Steel's facility near Baltimore, Maryland (*Philippe Legrain*)

Building a better future: Samyang, a Nike contract factory near Ho Chi Minh City, Vietnam (*Philippe Legrain*)

Koreans do it better: Jack Lee, Samyang's boss (*Philippe Legrain*)

No Satanic mill: Samyang is bright, airy, clean and safe (*Philippe Legrain*)

The unbranded alternative: Husan, a locally owned shoe factory in Ho Chi Minh City (*Philippe Legrain*)

Sticking around: two-thirds of Samyang's workers have been with the company for over three years (*Philippe Legrain*)

Shattered: workers at Husan take a break (*Philippe Legrain*)

No rural idyll: farmers near Samyang's factory toil in the searing sun
(*Philippe Legrain*)

Scavenging through rubbish: the terrible poverty around the Husan
factory (*Philippe Legrain*)

Fifteen years ago this was marshland: the Pudong district of Shanghai (*Philippe Legrain*)

Everything for sale: along the Huangpu River in Shanghai (*Philippe Legrain*)

Cap in hand: Europe's protectionist Common Agricultural Policy (CAP) condemns Indian farmers to penury (*Hutchison Picture Library*)

Brave boy: aged eleven, Nkosi Johnson made a speech at the 13th International Aids Conference in Durban in July 2000 that shamed the world for ignoring the plight of the nearly five million South Africans infected with HIV. Eleven months later, he was dead (*PA Photos*)

International institutions were set up to manage the new international economy. The International Bank for Reconstruction and Development, known as the World Bank, would make loans to help rebuild war-torn economies and soon to finance development more generally. (It was complemented by America's Marshall Plan, launched in June 1947, which provided generous grants to help kick-start European recovery and stave off the threat of communism.) The Stabilisation Fund, now known as the International Monetary Fund (IMF), would lend money to countries that had temporary difficulties financing a balance-of-payments deficit and sanction an adjustment in their exchange rate if the problem seemed permanent.

The IMF's role has been transformed by the explosive growth of international financial markets. These have sprung from the offshore financial markets, known as the Eurocurrency markets, which developed in the 1960s out of the reach of American regulators and national capital controls. Financial markets got another boost when America suspended the dollar's convertibility in August 1971 and the world moved to floating exchange rates – markets, not governments, now mostly set currency rates. The oil-price shock in 1973 helped too: OPEC countries had vast sums to play with, which they invested in international financial markets. Finally, first rich countries (starting from the late 1970s), then poor ones (a decade or more later) lifted the controls they had placed on capital movements in order to tap the now vast international financial markets, which new technologies, such as computerisation, and new instruments, such as derivatives, have further bolstered. The IMF is now the guardian of the stability of the international financial system; a corollary of that primary aim is that it helps countries in financial distress.

An International Trade Organisation was to help lower trade barriers multilaterally, through reciprocal bargaining extended to all according to the most-favoured-nation principle. But the US Congress vetoed America's membership because of its dislike of this perceived intrusion on American sovereignty. Thankfully,

President Harry Truman used his executive authority to implement the provisions of the General Agreement on Tariffs and Trade (GATT) that had been signed in Havana in 1948. This stopgap provided a hugely successful framework for negotiating cuts in trade barriers. In manufacturing, where import duties have been slashed from an average of 40 per cent or 50 per cent to around 4 per cent, the volume of trade has risen forty-five-fold. In agriculture, where trade barriers have scarcely fallen, trade has risen only six-fold. A permanent institution saw the light of the day only in 1995, when the World Trade Organisation (WTO) replaced the GATT.

At first, only rich countries and a handful of Asian ones liberalised their trade. Until the 1980s, many developing countries chose to turn their backs on the international economy. In the 1950s, when the Argentine economist Raul Prebisch headed the United Nations Economic Committee for Latin America, it was fashionable to blame the underdevelopment of Latin America and of the Third World more generally on the global capitalist system. Prebisch argued that early developers in Europe and North America had structured the world economy in their favour and condemned those who came later to dependent positions as providers of raw materials. The prescribed solution – domestic industrialisation behind high trade barriers – was copied throughout the Third World. It proved a huge failure, as we discussed in chapter two. But its fate was sealed only with the demise of communism at the end of the 1980s. 'Between the fall of the Berlin Wall in 1989 and the collapse of the Soviet Union in 1991,' recalled one of the most senior economic officials in India, 'I felt as though I were awakening from a thirty-five-year dream. Everything I had believed about economic systems and had tried to implement was wrong.'[27]

Other mooted international bodies remain stillborn. Plans for a body that would help stabilise international commodity prices, and thus most developing countries' export earnings, were never enacted. Nor was a global body to maintain full employment ever created: this remains a task for national governments.

But if they do not, and a country fails to fall into line with WTO rules, the aggrieved government – not the WTO – is entitled to impose sanctions on the offender's exports. Alternatively, it can agree to compensation in the form of lower trade barriers in other areas. Countries are, of course, free to leave the WTO if they wish. The US Congress debated pulling out in 2000, but voted overwhelmingly against it.

At best, WTO arbitration helps defuse a trade war. Both countries end up better off. At worst, the two governments remain at loggerheads. The aggrieved party lashes out with trade sanctions, but it doubtless would have acted likewise had the WTO not existed. The only difference the WTO has made is that it has given those sanctions added legitimacy, by ruling that the aggrieved country had indeed been wronged. It has not imposed any sanctions of its own. Some world government! The WTO is in fact the piggy in the middle, desperately trying to referee in a quarrel between governments and getting punched about for its pains.

Critics ostensibly have the WTO in their sights because it is powerful, but they really target it because it is weak. The WTO cannot easily fight back. It has no votes to deliver, no lobbyists in national parliaments, no campaign contributions to splash around, no vast PR budget. Its total budget, over half of which is gobbled up on translating documents, amounts to less than a quarter of that of the World Wide Fund for Nature, one of its many critics.

The WTO's critics are abetted by governments, for which it is also a convenient scapegoat. They often blame job losses on 'unfair' competition from foreigners, while insisting that the WTO prevents them from taking protectionist measures. Attacking the WTO also deflects attention from domestic failings. The Clinton administration, whose trade policy was in hock to corporate lobbies, blasted the WTO for ignoring public opinion. EU governments, whose regulatory lapses have led to mad-cow disease and dioxin poisoning, claim that the WTO threatens food safety. Developing countries whose reforms falter argue that the WTO is biased against them.

Yet the WTO is far from a tool for the strong to oppress the weak. Listen to what Mike Moore had to say in 1998, before he ran the WTO: 'Far from weakening the integrity of a nation's state and allowing the great multinationals to ravage the world, I believe . . . the WTO do[es] the opposite. Each government must sign up and agree to the programmes. [The WTO] is a contract between nations to treat each other equally, with legal dispute mechanisms to resolve differences. It enhances the sovereignty of small and weak nations. Japan, or the United States, cannot ignore or push around small nations. They cannot do side deals and give each other preferences. For a generation, New Zealand trade ministers were humiliated by going to Brussels and Paris, not to negotiate for butter and sheepmeat access to Europe, but to lobby. Now we are independent; our trade rights are guaranteed by international law.'[1]

Consider the long-running banana battle between the US and EU, which was finally settled in February 2002. Critics claimed that the WTO was helping wicked US multinationals, such as Chiquita, drive Caribbean banana growers out of business. But that is bending the truth. The EU's banana regime mostly benefits European companies that market Caribbean bananas – such as Ireland's Fyffes – rather than Caribbean growers themselves. According to a study by Brent Borrell, an Australian economist, the EU's banana regime costs European consumers $2 billion a year in higher fruit prices. Over half that sum ends up as monopoly profits for fruit distributors. Banana growers in the poor countries gain only $150 million a year. The equally poor countries that the EU does not favour, such as Ecuador and hurricane-hit Honduras, lose. In short, the EU's rules are a rich man's racket, not a safety net for the poor.

The WTO is more a champion of the weak than a stooge of the strong. Ask Ecuador. Its annual income per person is about £1,000 – less than St Lucia's – but its banana growers are the most efficient in the world. Their problem is that the EU made it difficult for Ecuador to sell its fruit in Europe: the EU imposed strict limits on how many bananas it could export, and made it pay hefty import duties. This was no small matter for Ecuador. One in ten Ecuadorians depends on bananas for a livelihood; the fruit is the country's largest foreign-currency earner; and Ecuador's economy was in its worst crisis in decades.

Without the WTO, Ecuador would have been in even direr straits. It could have complained to the EU, but Ecuador doesn't have much clout in Brussels. Thankfully, it was able to appeal to the WTO, which ruled that the Europeans were breaching world-trade rules. Kicking and screaming, the EU has finally agreed to change its banana regime. Granted, American pressure was instrumental in bringing this about. But Ecuador – as well as Chiquita and other American producers – can now sell more of its bananas in Europe. Had the WTO not existed, the US and EU could have carved the Ecuadorians out. This need not deprive Caribbean banana growers of a living. So long as the EU gives better access to bananas from the rest of the world, it can continue to give preferential access to Caribbean fruit.

This is not the first time that the WTO has helped a small poor country fight its corner against a big rich one. The US lifted its restrictions on imports of Costa Rican underwear after the WTO ruled that it was in the wrong. True, the dispute-settlement mechanism is not as fair as it could be. The US can marshall a battery of top lawyers to fight its cases; poor countries have to scrimp. But efforts are being made to remedy this; and a legal-aid centre for poor countries has been set up. In a world of unequal power, the WTO's dispute-settlement mechanism is much fairer than the alternative: the law of the jungle, where might equals right. That is why even Fidel Castro is a fan of the WTO: he sees it as a bulwark against American imperialism.

Delicate matters

The WTO also attracts controversy because trade quarrels now touch on sensitive issues like food safety and the environment, which were once exclusively a matter for domestic policy. Why? Because countries' economies are now so closely intertwined that almost any government policy can have a discriminatory impact on foreign companies. Rows about things like hormone-treated beef, GM foods, dolphin-safe tuna and turtle-friendly shrimp are particularly tricky, not least because they mobilise all sorts of people who were previously uninterested in trade and because governments are reluctant to compromise their ability to pursue other aims for the sake of free trade.

The multilateral trading system, founded in 1948 when memories of the 1930s were still fresh, recognises that governments have legitimate aims other than free trade. Governments were keen to liberalise international trade, but were wary of giving up policy tools that might help them prevent another slump. So a delicate compromise was struck. Governments agreed to be bound by multilateral rules in order to trade freely internationally, but retained the right to set their own policies domestically.

In the 1950s and 1960s, the compromise worked well. Countries agreed to lower their most blatant barriers to trade – such as import tariffs or quotas imposed at the border – while intervening at will, with taxes, subsidies and regulations, in their domestic economies. But by the 1970s, problems began to emerge. As border barriers fell, it became clear that domestic regulations were also a serious impediment to trade: a subsidy or a discriminatory rule could shut out imports just as effectively as a tariff. Moreover, governments began to abuse these loopholes for protectionist ends: anti-dumping cases and import-restricting regulations proliferated. So the focus of trade policy turned to limiting such abuses.

Now, the compromise is in tatters. The problem is how to craft a new one that secures the huge benefits of free trade while respecting countries' different cultural traditions. This is a delicate balancing act. Trample too much on domestic sovereignty and popular support for free trade will evaporate. Tread too lightly and it will be open season for protectionism. Broadly, the solution is for governments to pursue their political aims in ways that harm the rest of the world as little as possible. But that is often tough to achieve in practice.

Consider the battle between the US and the EU over beef hormones, which I will discuss further in the next chapter. It is very different from a traditional trade quarrel such as a row over restrictions on steel imports. Traditional disputes are quite simple. They are usually about explicitly protectionist measures such as import tariffs or quotas, which keep out foreign goods at the border. The costs of such measures (higher prices and less choice for consumers) are reasonably easy to quantify; they typically outweigh the benefits (fatter company profits and tariff revenues for governments). Even mercantilist governments should be able to resolve such narrowly economic disputes. One way is to buy off steel companies and unions. Another is to exchange access to domestic markets for access to foreign ones.

The new trade disputes are more complicated. They are not just about economics but about social and cultural issues, too. They are about domestic regulations that have international effects, rather than about border controls: Europe has banned all hormone-treated beef, not just America's. Such regulations are not wholly protectionist. Although Europe's ban does keep out American imports and is partly motivated by a desire to protect inefficient European farmers, it is also a response to public fears about food safety.

The costs of the ban (higher beef prices, less choice) are quite easy to establish. But the benefits are not: the value of safer food is hard to quantify and reasonable people may put widely different prices on it. Indeed, some of the new actors in such disputes, such as consumer-rights activists and environmental groups, may not be susceptible to economic reasoning. So even liberal governments may have trouble resolving such quarrels. They may be particularly wary of setting precedents that they may later regret: the beef war is widely seen as a forerunner to a larger battle about GM crops. Many may feel that such disputes intrude too far on national sovereignty, and thus refuse to accept that international trade rules should trump domestic political considerations. Yet such disputes are not intractable. The best solution, as I will argue in the next chapter, is labelling. This should satisfy Europeans' concerns about food safety while allowing America to trade freely. Nor is it true that the WTO always puts free trade first. When Canada complained that France's ban on white asbestos was an unfair restriction on trade, the WTO sided with the French: the measure was justified, it said, to protect people's health.

Scares about services

Another scare story about the WTO is that it threatens public (state-funded) schools and hospitals. Critics claim that the WTO's services agreement, known as the GATS (General Agreement on Trade in Services), undermines governments' ability to provide public services, their right to regulate and their scope to impose restrictions on foreign investment.

Not so. There are very good reasons for trying to open up trade in commercial services, which include construction, tourism, transport, telecoms, finance, accounting, advertising, computer services, environmental services, and private health and education. Services make up three-fifths of the world economy, but only a fifth of world trade. So there is huge scope to expand services trade. Allowing foreign suppliers to compete with domestic ones lowers prices, improves quality and increases choice. Foreign competition has made a huge difference to telephone services in Europe; America's airlines would have to shape up much more if they faced foreign competition at home. An efficient service sector is the backbone of a successful economy. If your banks, your phones and your planes aren't up to scratch, you'll find it hard to produce anything competitively, whether it is T-shirts, tomatoes or Testarossas.

The GATS is an agreement to free up trade in services. It is not an agreement to privatise or deregulate them. Moreover, it explicitly excludes services provided by governments. So it poses no threat to public schools and hospitals. If it wants to, a government may choose to allow foreign companies to provide private healthcare or education, but that is hardly privatising public services. If you are worried about the privatisation of the National Health Service, direct your anger at the British government, not the WTO. Nor does opening up your market to foreigners imply compromising standards: governments can enforce the same standards on foreign suppliers as on nationals. They can even impose additional requirements on foreigners if they want to.

The GATS is an incredibly flexible agreement. It spells out a few general obligations, notably that countries must not discriminate between foreign suppliers (and they can request an exemption, in principle limited to ten years, from even this obligation). But otherwise, governments can do pretty much what they want. They can choose which sectors they want to open up to foreigners. Where they choose to make commitments, governments can set limits on how far they want to open their markets to foreigners and the extent to which they treat foreign suppliers like domestic ones. Governments can also limit their commitments to one or more of the four ways in which services are traded. For instance, they might allow cross-border software trade, but prevent a foreign software company from setting up shop in their domestic market. Or they might encourage tourists to visit, but prevent foreign tourist guides from coming to work.

The GATS is not a set of rules about foreign direct investment (FDI). True, governments can, if they want to, use the GATS to attract FDI by guaranteeing potential investors that they will not suddenly change the rules of the game. But multinationals or other service suppliers cannot simply go into any WTO member country and buy anything and everything. Member governments decide which services foreigners are allowed to provide and under what conditions. Nothing stops governments from favouring domestic suppliers of a service over foreign ones if they want to. Of course, most governments now welcome FDI with open arms rather than trying to protect themselves from it. (It's the lack of investment that's the problem for many countries: Singapore gets more investment than all of Africa.) But the GATS allows governments to do as they see fit.

Regional riles

One of the WTO's biggest flaws is what it doesn't do rather than what it does. It turns a blind eye to regional trade agreements, like the EU, NAFTA, Mercosur and a plethora of less ambitious groupings. Over 170 of them are in force around the world, half of them concluded since 1990. A further seventy or so are in the making. Nearly every WTO member is part of one. These criss-crossing regional deals make a mockery of the notion of a single global economy.

Regional agreements come in many shapes and sizes. They may involve two countries or more, encompass all trade or just some, be between neighbours or span continents. Some are customs unions, like the EU, with a common external tariff; others are free-trade areas, like NAFTA, where each member has its own customs duties on imports from the rest of the world. They may have common institutions, like the European Commission or the North American Development Bank. They may also have a mechanism for settling intra-regional trade disputes, as do both the EU and NAFTA. But what they all have in common is that trade within them is freer than trade with the rest of the world. This preferential treatment encourages regional trade at the expense of global trade.

Take the EU. Meshing Europe's markets together has skewed its pattern of trade. Trade within the EU's single market, which is relatively cheap and easy, has grown much faster than trade with the rest of the world, where firms still have to contend with a thicket of tariffs and regulations. That is a big reason why Britain now sends 58.5 per cent of its merchandise exports to the rest of the EU, up from 35 per cent when it joined in 1973.

A single currency tilts the playing field even further. Jeffrey Frankel and Andrew Rose estimate that belonging to a currency union more than triples trade with other members of the zone. That helps explain why Spain imports more from far-off Finland than from neighbouring Morocco. This regional bias, in turn, reinforces the rationale for closer economic and political integration.

A similar process is happening in NAFTA. Mexico has replaced Japan as America's second-biggest export market, behind Canada. Its two NAFTA partners now account for 36 per cent of US exports, up from 28 per cent in 1990. Since 1997 US exports to non-NAFTA countries have actually been falling.[2] As for Canada and Mexico, nearly nine-tenths of their exports are now within NAFTA.

These closer links have spurred demands, at least on the Mexican side, for deeper integration. President Vicente Fox has mused about Mexico's adopting the dollar. He has repeatedly called for a 'NAFTA-plus', a club more like the EU. The US is less keen, especially since September 11th. Even so, cross-border co-operation is growing, and the US will be drawn ever closer to Mexico as Latinos' political weight in America increases.

Regionalism drives a coach and horses through the WTO's core principle of non-discrimination. Preferences granted to some are handicaps imposed on others. Admittedly, WTO rules do allow regional agreements, but only if they meet certain conditions: they must cover 'substantially all trade', eliminate internal trade barriers, and 'not on the whole' raise protection against excluded countries. Few regional deals meet these criteria. Yet since all its members are rushing to conclude them, the WTO is helpless. No country has challenged the legality of all these discriminatory deals – and none is likely to.

To be fair, some regional agreements do a lot of good. NAFTA has locked in Mexico's economic and political reforms. From a US perspective, it has helped stabilise a volatile neighbour with which

America shares a 2,000-mile border. The EU has cemented peace in Europe. It is building a single market with a single currency that promises huge economies of scale for companies and the benefits of increased competition, such as lower prices, for consumers. It has helped poorer countries, like Ireland and Spain, catch up with France and Germany. It is a testbed and model for other countries that want to co-operate regionally. Better still, the lure of EU membership helps keep most of eastern Europe on the straight and narrow.

Together, Europeans also have more clout, not least when the Commission negotiates at the WTO or vets mergers, such as that between General Electric and Honeywell, which might otherwise harm European consumers. They can stand up to the US – over beef, steel, tax, planes, Cuba, data privacy and much else. The EU gives Europeans more policy options. If 'sovereignty' means the scope to determine one's destiny, then far from surrendering it to Brussels, Europeans are enhancing it within the EU. Like Americans, they are freer to choose. That is a huge bonus – even if one wishes that they would sometimes choose differently: fewer handouts to farmers, for starters. But this added discretion comes at a cost, insofar as some Europeans' interests diverge from others'. Acting alone, for instance, Britain might subsidise its farmers less.

All in all, the EU is a good thing, but its huge network of preferential pacts is not. The EU has partnership agreements with all other European countries except Albania, Bosnia, Croatia and Yugoslavia. It also has deals with Turkey, Israel and Morocco. It is negotiating agreements with most other Arab countries. By 2005, the only countries in its vicinity with which it is unlikely to have sweetheart deals are Libya, Iraq and Yemen.

Further afield, the EU has struck deals with Mexico and South Africa. It is pursuing agreements with Chile and the four Mercosur countries (Argentina, Brazil, Paraguay and Uruguay). It is also pressing seventy-one poor African, Caribbean and Pacific (ACP) countries, mostly ex-colonies, to sign up to new regional arrangements. Taking into account the hundred or so other poor countries covered by the Generalised System of Preferences, the EU's network of preferences already covers most of the world. In fact there are only six countries – Australia, Canada, Japan, New Zealand, Taiwan and the US – with which it trades on a 'normal' basis.

The EU's fondness for all these preferential pacts is partly political. The European Commission is keen on them because they are, in the words of Patrick Messerlin of the Institut d'Etudes Politiques in Paris, a 'proxy for a foreign policy', which is otherwise the remit of EU governments. Bilateral deals are seen as strengthening EU member states' influence abroad. The Europe and Euro-Med agreements, for example, help to anchor eastern Europe and North Africa in the EU's sphere of influence. They may also help to keep neighbour governments stable and potential migrants at home. And they stir up less controversy with anti-globalisation protesters than negotiations at the WTO.

Economics is a bigger spur, however. Thanks to its bilateral deals, the EU is an export and investment hub with preferential access to markets in very many spokes. This helps European exporters corner foreign markets. They have an edge not only over the Americans and the Japanese, but also over firms from spoke countries, since, for example, South Africa and Mexico do not enjoy privileged access to each other's markets.

What, then, do the spoke countries gain? There are political benefits to cosying up to the EU. The east Europeans were anxious to escape Russia's embrace; Latin America would like to emerge from the US's shadow. A deal with the EU may also help lock in free-market reforms. But international capital markets surely do more to keep, say, Mexico prudent than the EU ever will. Often the EU has actually set back economic reform. For instance, it insisted that the east Europeans raise their import tariffs to the rest of the world in order to help EU firms gain market share. Estonia is no longer the bastion of free trade I described: it has had to erect some tariff walls in preparation for joining the EU.

Poor countries often lose economically from their deals with the EU. Consider the South African agreement. Undeniably, some South African firms can now sell their goods more easily in the EU. But their farmers, who are highly competitive, cannot, since politically 'sensitive' agricultural products, such as cereals, are excluded. This gives them a perverse incentive to switch to making goods that the EU allows in more freely.

South African consumers get a raw deal too. Import prices are unlikely to fall, since South Africa is only lowering its tariffs to EU firms. They may well respond by raising their prices, so consumers will see little benefit. But the Europeans will gain market share from the Americans – and Africans for that matter – who still have to pay high import tariffs. And they have stamped out some local competition by insisting that South Africa stop describing some of its products as 'grappa' and 'ouzo', spirits that the EU says can be made only in Italy and Greece.

Nor is the deal likely to attract much foreign investment to South Africa. Devilishly complicated 'rules of origin', which define how much local content is required before goods are considered South African and thus eligible for preferential access to the EU, entangle investors in red tape and deter many from setting up shop in South Africa.

The biggest losers from all these sweetheart deals are the countries they exclude. Yet the deals create their own infernal logic, whereby those who are discriminated against seek their own preferential deal. The EU is well aware of this: it sought a deal with Mexico because its exports to that country have slumped since Mexico joined NAFTA.

The US has suddenly woken up to this European attempt to carve up world markets. The Business Roundtable, a big-business lobby group, warned in February 2001 that the US was 'falling behind' in the race to sign new preferential deals. The new administration took note. President George Bush gave new impetus to plans to extend NAFTA throughout the Americas. He aimed to conclude the Free Trade Area of the Americas (FTAA) by January 2005. But he has scaled back his ambitions since September 11th:

the talk is now of a much more modest deal with Central America.

Latin America is still to play for. Brazil sought to mimic – and counterbalance – NAFTA by creating its own regional club, Mercosur, with Argentina, Paraguay and Uruguay. But although trade between Mercosur's members has quadrupled since its creation, it has fallen since 1998 and amounts to only around a fifth of their total trade. More importantly, the pressures dragging them apart – such as Argentina's default on its debts in December 2001 – seem stronger than those pulling them together. That gives the Europeans and Americans an opportunity to scrap over the spoils. The EU boasts that its talks with Chile and Mercosur put it in 'pole position' in the race for business in South America, ahead of the US, whose efforts to establish a free-trade area of the Americas were stalled for years.

The scramble for Asia is now on. The US staked an early claim to it in 1989 by setting up the Asia-Pacific Economic Co-operation forum (APEC), a twenty-one-member group that includes most of East Asia, Russia, Australia, New Zealand, Chile, Peru and the NAFTA-three. But so far APEC has remained largely a talking shop.

The big question is whether East Asia will manage to cobble together a regional hub of its own. A group that included China, Japan and South Korea plus the ten members of the Association of South-East Asian Nations (ASEAN), among them Singapore, Thailand, Indonesia and Malaysia, would be a heavyweight in international trade.

The creation of such a regional hub is no longer inconceivable. East Asians are still smarting from the high-handed way they feel they were treated during the world financial crisis that started in Asia in 1997. They are offended by Westerners' crowing at the demise of the once lauded Asian model. They are furious that the US slapped down proposals for an Asian Monetary Fund. So they have reacted by setting up a regional system of currency repurchase agreements to help them deal with future Asian crises. And they have made tentative steps on the trade front too.

Until recently, Japan had been a stalwart supporter of the multilateral trading system. It had stood aloof from the rush towards regionalism, preferring to pursue its trade aims through the WTO. But in the aftermath of the failure to launch a new round of WTO talks in Seattle in late 1999, Japan announced that it too was going regional. So did South Korea, which had also eschewed preferential pacts in the past. Suddenly, an East Asian Free-Trade Area is being talked about. Already, Japan has struck a deal with Singapore and is talking to South Korea among others. South Korea is in talks with New Zealand and Chile. A link-up between Japan, South Korea and China is being studied. They could then hook up with ASEAN, which is also negotiating with Australia and New Zealand.

To be sure, powerful obstacles remain. There is immense antipathy among many East Asian countries. Many see their neighbours as rivals rather than partners. Just as the EU would find it hard to admit Russia, so China's neighbours would find it difficult to throw in their lot in with such a giant. Clearly, there is still an opportunity for the US, on which most of the region relies for its security, to carve up markets for itself in East Asia, as the EU is doing in eastern Europe, the Middle East and Africa.

This headlong rush for advantage is unlikely to lead to outright hostility between rival trade blocs. Fears about a Fortress Europe, for instance, have so far proved unfounded. But regionalism does end up making everyone worse off. A maze of preferential agreements, with differing tariff rates, rules-of-origin requirements and industrial and health regulations, distorts trade and creates huge new administrative burdens, not to mention opportunities for corruption. It is a lawyer's heaven, and an economist's hell.

The spread of regionalism would not be so worrying if global trade were getting freer. Privileges granted to a few would soon be eroded by better access for all. Regional hubs might turn out to be building blocks of a genuinely global economy. But since 1997, moves towards freer global trade have stalled. With luck, the new round of WTO talks launched in Doha in November 2001 will change this. They aim to conclude by January 2005, but trade negotiations have a habit of dragging on. The Uruguay Round, which gave birth to the WTO, lasted eight years. We look set to continue living in a not-so-global economy for quite a while yet.

Democracy in a global age

The Marrakesh treaty is rather less eloquent than the US Constitution. 'The Parties to this Agreement . . . Agree as follows: The World Trade Organisation is hereby established' does not have quite the same ring as 'We the people'. This stylistic difference points to a more deep-seated problem. The WTO and its member governments have been slow to recognise that the WTO is now judged not only on what it achieves, but also on how it achieves it. It can seem detached from the cut and thrust of domestic politics through which people scrutinise what governments do in their name. This remoteness undermines the perceived legitimacy of the usually good work governments do at the WTO. 'We the people' may feel we are not parties to agreements at the WTO.

Strictly speaking, this is not true. All WTO agreements are agreed by a consensus of its 144 member governments. Every government has a veto. In most countries, the deals are then ratified by democratically elected national parliaments. In that very real sense, the people's chosen representatives approve all WTO rules. Admittedly, parliaments may not scrutinise WTO agreements as carefully as they ought to, but that is hardly the WTO's fault.

Even so, for many people, that is not democratic enough. They view the WTO as a closed club that they can scarcely influence. Now that governments' work at the WTO deals with sensitive issues that affect people directly, such as what they eat and how clean the air they breathe is, people want to know more about what their representatives are up to. They also want more opportunities to make their views known. In short, they want international politics to be more like domestic politics.

The WTO is indeed too secretive (at the insistence of member governments). It is also not accountable enough (except to member governments, who want it to stay that way). But more fundamentally, there is an inevitable tension between the need to tackle global issues, like trade or climate change, and the demands of national democracy. Globally, these strains are most apparent at the WTO, where co-operation has gone furthest, but they are obvious at a regional level within the EU too. They will also apply if and when a proper World Environment Organisation sees the light of day.

International politics is fundamentally different from domestic politics. 'The world as a whole lacks a coherent public, a corresponding public space for discussion, and institutions linking the public, through elections, to governing organisations,'[3] point out Robert Keohane of Duke University and Joseph Nye, the dean of Harvard's Kennedy School of Government. Globally, although some groups – such as multinational companies, non-governmental organisations (NGOs), and the Socialist International – operate across borders, there is no such thing as a world electorate. Three hundred million Americans and 350 million Europeans would not accept 1,300 million Chinese outvoting them. So we cannot treat the world as if it were a nation state writ large. One day, perhaps, there may be world elections to a world parliament and even a world government. But for the foreseeable future, this is a non-starter. Even in the EU, where cross-border co-operation is uniquely advanced, we are nowhere near such a state of affairs.

George Monbiot, a British anti-corporate campaigner, disagrees. In response to an article I wrote in the *Guardian* on why the left should love the WTO,[4] Mr Monbiot replied:[5]

> Philippe Legrain . . . argued that world elections to a world parliament are not realistic . . . [He] has, unintentionally, presented the anti-globalisation movement with its central challenge. If those of us in the rich world who are protesting

against the inordinate powers of the G8, the World Bank or the WTO are serious about overthrowing unaccountable power, then we must rise to his bait . . . we in the rich world live in comparative comfort only because of the inordinate power our governments wield, and the inordinate wealth which flows from that power . . . Accepting the need for global democracy means accepting the loss of our own nations' power to ensure that the world is run for our benefit . . . Global democracy is meaningless unless ultimate power resides in a directly elected assembly. This means, of course, that a resident of Kensington would have no greater influence than a resident of Kinshasa . . . The people of China would, collectively, be twenty-two times as powerful as the people of the United Kingdom. In a truly democratic world, the people's assembly would . . . be sovereign. All other global bodies would report to it and act on its instructions. The danger, of course, is that the world parliament might make decisions we don't like very much . . . But the democratisation which may or may not result in such changes cannot even be widely discussed until we, the new world order's prosperous dissidents, are prepared to take our arguments to their logical conclusion . . . I hope that we, unlike Orwell's bourgeois socialists, are ready for this challenge. If not, we may as well as cancel our tickets to Genoa and stay at home eating strawberries and cream.

Quite. I have quoted Mr Monbiot at length so that you can see how deluded he is. The first decision that his sovereign world parliament would take is to tax away – confiscate, if you prefer – not only his income but also his assets. Not only Mr Monbiot's, but everyone's in rich countries. I doubt even the self-styled 'new world order's prosperous dissidents' are prepared to make that sacrifice. It would be like turkeys voting for Christmas.

At the other extreme, some people think we should do away with international institutions altogether. The black-helicopter brigade of right-wing nuts think even the existence of the US federal government is a demonic curtailment of their God-given freedom. Slightly less extreme right-wingers feel the same about the WTO. Here's Pat Buchanan, eternal failed candidate for the US presidency:

> The World Trade Organisation was erected on ideas
> American patriots must reject. It subordinates everything to
> the demands of trade. It exercises a supranational authority
> in conflict with our forefathers' vision of an America forever
> sovereign and independent. Its dispute-resolution
> procedures shift to Geneva decisions that ought to be made
> in Washington. And if we refuse to abide by the WTO's
> edicts, America can be chastised and fined. Run by
> nameless, faceless, foreign bureaucrats, the WTO is the
> embryonic trade ministry of a world government. There is
> no place for such an institution in a world where free
> nations negotiate their trade agreements in good faith and
> themselves oversee the execution of those agreements.[6]

If each country set its laws in isolation, we would not need to worry about the imperfections of international democracy. It is certainly a more realistic option than Mr Monbiot's: the world did without the UN, the IMF, the World Bank and the WTO in the nineteenth century. But a retreat into isolationism or unilateralism would make all of us – even Americans – worse off. There would be less trade, no action to combat global warming, no alliance against terrorism, none of the benefits of the EU. We have been down that road before in the 1930s. International institutions are far from perfect: I know, I worked for one. But they are still better than nothing. The best way forward is to reform them, not scrap them.

Here are some of the ways we could reconnect them with voters. The WTO needs to do away with its culture of secrecy: in a democratic age, it is simply unacceptable. Even when the WTO does good, it is treated with suspicion because decisions are taken in private. True, the WTO is already more open than most government bodies – more open than the IMF or the British government, for instance. Nearly all WTO documents are published on its website within days. WTO rules are all publicly available, as are dispute-settlement-panel rulings, but trade negotiations are conducted behind closed doors. The arguments and reasoning that lie behind WTO rules – or to be more exact, the haggling and horse-trading between governments and lobby groups – are never made public. Dispute-settlement hearings are held in private. All of this has to change.

Defenders of the status quo object that the WTO will grind to a halt if it becomes more open. But that is not a valid defence. Our parliaments meet in public so that we can see what is being decided in our name. Our courts operate in public so that we trust that justice is being done. Trade policy is now too important to people's lives to take place in private. If that forces governments and lobbyists to behave more respectably, all the better. Sunlight is indeed the best disinfectant. It may even make trade negotiations easier, not harder, because governments might be too ashamed to face the public with their brazen defence of sectional lobbies at the expense of the national interest. It would also dispel fears that the WTO is conspiring to take over the world.

Greater openness is one requirement, but the WTO also needs to be more accountable. It is a government-to-government organisation, so it is mostly held to account through its member governments. The WTO also has contacts with trade unions, companies, NGOs and churches. But who holds governments accountable for the decisions they take at the WTO? The media, in part. Yet governments also need to develop better procedures for informing parliaments and voters about their work at the WTO, just as some EU members have done about their work in Brussels. The US is a model in this respect. National parliaments (as well as the European one) should also become involved in the WTO's work. Parliamentarians could hold hearings before or after meetings, and could themselves become national delegates to WTO meetings. MPs could do more to bridge the gap between the WTO and voters in other ways too. Mike Moore made a point of testifying before parliamentary committees as often as possible. His successor, Mr Supachai, ought to do the same.

The public could also participate more at the WTO. Let people visit the WTO headquarters if they want to. The WTO is already reaching out more to people through discussion groups and questionnaires on its website. Mike Moore has responded to people's questions online. This could develop into more formal and frequent public hearings. And so on. To those who say all of this would make the WTO ineffective, I say: nonsense. A WTO that is seen to be open and accountable will have more legitimacy. A more legitimate WTO will be more effective. The WTO deals with intrinsically political issues. It cannot escape from politics. It has to become more political, not less.

Pressure for change

What about the pressure groups, or NGOs as they are sometimes known, that now demand a seat at the table? International NGOs have exploded in size and number over the past decade. There are more than 38,000 international NGOs, up from 6,000 in 1990.[7] The World Wide Fund for Nature (WWF) now has around 5 million regular supporters, up from 570,000 in 1985. Globalisation has given them not only a growing set of global issues to campaign about, but also the technology – email and the Internet – to operate cheaply and quickly around the world. They played a big part in pushing through agreements on controlling greenhouse gases at the Earth Summit in Rio de Janeiro in 1992. They disrupted the World Bank's anniversary meeting in 1994 with a 'Fifty Years is Enough' campaign that forced the Bank to rethink its goals and methods. In 1998, they helped undermine negotiations on a

Multilateral Agreement on Investment (MAI) that aimed to harmonise rules on foreign investment. They brought Seattle to a standstill during the WTO's summit in 1999. Since then, they have disrupted every big international meeting.

In their favour, many NGOs operate across borders. Friends of the Earth mobilises worldwide against global warming; Jubilee Plus campaigns internationally for Third World debt relief the Malaysia-based Third World Network, which has offices on four continents, fights for WTO reform. These NGOs are the stirrings of a global politics. But they also have big flaws. They are self-selected, not democratically elected. They are largely unaccountable. And they are unrepresentative: most of them are left-wing or green and come from rich countries. It is far from clear why the WTO should answer to Greenpeace, which is scarcely accountable to its 2.5 million members, rather than to the Indian parliament, which 600 million voters elect. And if to Greenpeace, why not to the Road Haulage Association or the National Front too?

Michael Edwards of the Ford Foundation in New York has proposed that NGOs be given 'a voice, but not a vote'.[8] Only NGOs that were sufficiently open, accountable and democratic, as well as having relevant knowledge, would qualify. Quite right too. People need to know who NGOs' members are, how they answer to them, who funds them, and so on. NGOs should also have to reject violence, and meet the standards that they demand of others. They should be monitored, perhaps by Transparency International, another NGO. Mr Edwards also argues that more needs to be done to encourage a more representative range of NGOs. Foreign-aid budgets could be used to fund more NGOs in poor countries, for instance.

If NGOs are to play an official role, it must be a constructive one. It is hard to see how people like Lori Wallach, the head of Public Citizen's Global Trade Watch, who wants to 'nix the WTO' (and turned down repeated invitations to visit the WTO in Geneva) can be anything other than destructive. Nor do the Peoples' Global

Action – slogan: 'The WTO kills people. Kill the WTO' – and a group called "Alien Hand Signals" that was also in Seattle seem to have much to contribute.

NGOs already provide international institutions with analysis and information. When I worked at the WTO, I often found the International Centre for Trade and Sustainable Development's research useful. More importantly, these technical (rather than campaigning) NGOs help train delegates from poor countries in WTO law. At the World Bank, NGOs play a much bigger role.[9] James Wolfensohn, the Bank's boss, has put 'dialogue' with NGOs at the heart of the organisation's work. More than seventy NGO specialists work in the Bank's field offices. NGOs are involved in most of its projects. 'From environmental policy to debt relief, NGOs are at the centre of World Bank policy. Often they determine it.' But, as Zanny Minton-Beddoes of *The Economist* rightly points out: 'The new World Bank is more transparent, but it is also more beholden to a new set of special interests.'

The WTO should reach out to NGOs, as it does to trade unions or universities. It should aim to co-opt the more reasonable ones and sideline the extremists. Talk yes, listen certainly, but give them a seat at the table, certainly not. Unelected NGOs have no place at the negotiating table with elected governments. Nor should they be a party to dispute-settlement cases, except to submit evidence to national governments. Let them lobby governments all they want: that is their right. But they do not have a right to bypass democratic governments that fail to listen to them. A world run by a cabal of NGOs would not be a more democratic one.

Corporate claptrap

Another approach to global governance focuses on corporations. Multinational companies are under increasing pressure to adopt 'corporate social responsibility' (CSR) programmes. In essence, what this means is that companies should aim to do more than just make profits; they should also contribute to society in other ways, by promoting economic, social and environmental progress more broadly. They should be 'good citizens', 'give something back to the community', promote 'sustainable development'. So, for instance, Shell, the Anglo-Dutch oil giant, aims to employ local people and local contractors wherever it invests; is shelling out $50 million a year on a community-development programme in Nigeria; and is paying for forest conservation in Brazil. More generally, fans of CSR argue that multinationals should work together to build a better world: stamp out child labour, curb greenhouse-gas emissions, pay for schools and hospitals in the Third World. In short, big companies should use their money, power and global reach to step in where governments fail to act.

CSR has found favour in many quarters. Pundits and politicians praise this attempt to give capitalism a 'human face'. Companies latch onto it as the perfect foil for all those pesky protesters. Look, they can say, we are doing good: we put people before profits – although in fact, CSR is seen as enhancing their reputation and hence their profits. Consultants rack up huge fees for helping companies pursue their new aims. Pressure groups are all too eager to co-operate: CSR gives them a seat at the table and a vehicle for furthering their private agendas. International organisations are keen on the idea too: it gives them a piece of the action and makes them feel as if they are doing good. Thus Kofi Annan, the secretary-general of the United Nations, has proposed a Global Compact between business, governments, NGOs and the UN to raise standards across the world. 'The Global Compact is not a regulatory instrument or code of conduct, but a value-based platform designed to promote institutional learning. It utilises the power of transparency and dialogue to identify and disseminate good practices based on universal principles,' its website[126] declares. The OECD and the EU have also jumped on the bandwagon.

Nobody wants companies to behave irresponsibly or anti-socially. Yet CSR is not the force for good it is made out to be. One criticism is that it is a load of waffle. Signing up to grand declarations is good PR, but it does little to tackle genuine economic or social problems. Corporate codes of conduct or global compacts are vague and cannot easily be enforced. But even if CSR does only a little good, surely that is better than nothing? What could possibly be wrong with spreading 'good practices' based on 'universal principles'?

Well, for a start, it is undemocratic. Who decides what those 'good practices' and 'universal principles' are? If everyone agreed on the solution to the world's problems, there would be no need for politics. We could just appoint administrators and let them get on with the job. But in fact, people disagree on just about everything. That is why we have elections, governments and political debate. It is a messy, rough-and-ready way of deciding society's priorities, but it is less bad than all the alternatives – not least CSR.

'The picture of reality that CSR presents is at fault in several respects,' argues David Henderson, a former chief economist at the OECD. 'For one thing, it greatly oversimplifies issues, problems and choices. Its supporters characteristically take it for granted that the problems of today have known and agreed "solutions". In particular, they speak and write as though the objective of sustainable development, and the means to achieving it, were well defined and universally agreed. This is not the case.'[9]

Exactly. CSR has not come out of nowhere. It is companies' response to anti-corporate campaigns. Activists have picked off companies, like Nike, McDonald's and Shell, and tried to bend them to their will. This approach has a double appeal: companies are rich, powerful and global enough to make a difference, but vulnerable enough to cave into protesters' pressure. On its own narrow terms, it works. 'People are beginning to fight the big global economic battles by focusing on one or two brand-name corporations and turning them into large-scale political metaphors,' says Naomi Klein. 'They are having more luck with this strategy than they had with decades of fighting these battles on a policy level with governments.'[10]

Shell was hit with a double whammy in 1995. Greenpeace attacked it for trying to dispose of the Brent Spar oil rig at sea, as well as for failing to oppose the Nigerian government's execution of Ken Saro-Wiwa, a human-rights activist in a part of Nigeria where it had extensive operations. Shell reacted by rewriting its business principles, putting in place a new reporting system to make sure they were implemented, and engaging more with NGOs. Robin Aram, the company's head of external relations and policy development, explains: 'Clearly, we are not a charity, we are not a government, we are not a social agency, we are still a business, but we feel we have some responsibilities to our customers, our employees and our neighbours.'

Fair enough. Yet even by activists' own standards, gunning for Shell is a poor second-best. As Klein admits, campaigns typically concentrate on populist issues and target their fire at a handful of prominent companies. 'The companies being targeted – Disney, Mattel, The Gap and so on – may not always be the worst offenders, but they do tend to be the ones who flash their logos in bright lights on the global marquee,'[11] she says. Moreover, whereas a recycling law might apply uniformly to all companies and all forms of industrial waste, a consumer campaign may target only, say, McDonald's disposal of hamburger packaging. Clearly, that is not the best way to protect the environment.

What a terrible irony! The critics of corporate power are urging companies to take over tasks that were previously the stuff of elected representatives. Certainly, theirs is partly a counsel of despair – governments are impotent, they rail, so let's try to tame the beasts ourselves – but it is also remarkably self-serving. Critics hope to harness those nasty companies to their own ends. It is far from obvious that campaigners' agendas are popular, let alone sensible. Who exactly do Naomi Klein and her ilk represent? Ralph Nader, whose views closely mirror hers, scored 3 per cent in the US presidential election in 2000. So rather than fight their corner in elections, they prefer to bypass them. Bludgeon companies with consumer boycotts, threaten to besmirch their precious brands, then exact your price: we'll lay off if you forward some of our agenda. How could companies resist this Faustian bargain? Now, like rats conditioned by electro-shock treatment, companies no longer need prompting. They know what is expected of them, nay, they can use CSR to their advantage. 'The next big thing in brands is social responsibility,' says Wally Olins, a corporate-identity consultant. 'It will be clever to say there is nothing different about our product or price, but we behave well.'[12] We have come full circle. Except that the people who matter – voters – have been left out.

Not only that. As we have seen, the protesters are wrong on nearly every count. Globalisation is helping poor countries, not harming them. Companies do not rule the world. Governments are not powerless. The protesters' mistaken views do not matter too much, so long as they are just the opinions of a small, albeit vocal, minority. But if they manage to impose their will on society by hijacking companies to their own ends, we all need to worry.

Globally, CSR applies the tastes and values of an anti-capitalist minority in Europe and North America to the whole world. This not only has echoes of imperialism, it can also harm the people it purports to help. Ask Antonia Cordoba, a seamstress in a Nicaraguan jeans factory run by a Taiwanese company called Chentex. After some workers were dismissed for calling a strike, American congressmen and labour activists sued the plant in a US court for labour violations. Yet Ms Cordoba and other workers at the 'sweatshop' factory have protested that they want the suit dropped. They fear for their jobs because the bad publicity has caused orders from the US to slump. 'This boycott is a threat to our livelihood. I do not live like a queen, but my family eats. It is the only job I will get that pays a decent rate,' she said.

Moreover, once big companies have accepted the CSR agenda, they have an incentive to burden their competitors with the extra costs too. Chris Helzer, Nike's head of external relations in south-east Asia, is open about it. 'We are in favour of enforcing minimum labour and environment standards at the WTO,' he says. 'If we have to pay the costs, we don't see why our competitors shouldn't have to too.' There you have it: undesirable aims achieved by undesirable means. Poor people in poor countries will end up poorer as a result.

Of course, consumers have every right to spend their money as they see fit. Forward-thinking companies are also right to respond to their customers' preferences. They should act responsibly and be seen to do so. A few community schemes here and there are fine, but a cabal of self-selected campaigners and self-interested companies should not be in the business of setting social standards – that should be for elected parliaments. 'Change the world: burn your Nikes!' is a catchy slogan. But it is not a good way to set public policy.

Companies' social responsibility is to make profits, not to decide how, or how much, the environment should be protected. It is a duty that they have to their shareholders who have entrusted their savings to them. Workers' jobs depend on it, as does a country's prosperity: scarce resources should be tied up in a company only if it is adding value. Profit is not a dirty word. Profits help pay for schools, hospitals and pensions.

Certainly, people have aims besides getting richer. They care about how the pie is shared out, as well as its size. They also care about how the pie is produced: whether corporate activity damages the environment or compromises workers' safety and dignity. These plural aims do not always conflict: companies with happy workers are often profitable, and vice versa. But sometimes they do. That is where there is a role for governments: to draft and enforce laws that express society's collective view about how, say, the balance between economic growth and environmental protection should be struck.

This traditional model of governance has many advantages. The lines of responsibility are clear: governments set the rules of the game, companies then aim to make profits subject to those constraints. This is not only democratic. It is also fair: laws are transparent, apply equally to all companies, and are impartially enforced by the courts. And it is flexible: laws can vary according to local conditions and preferences. The best way to help workers and the environment is generally through national laws drafted on the basis of democratic participation and consultation. Governments are more than capable, either individually or collectively, of achieving social aims through legislation.

↳ *Clear inconsistent and incomplete application achieved by protests advocating corporate social responsibility.*

EIGHT

Food for Thought

Why farm trade should be freed

Malbouffe is completely uniform; it's food from nowhere, not even a degeneration of American culture. Everywhere the same labels, the same way of running the 'restaurants'. We did not want McDonald's to be seen as a prime target. It's merely a symbol of economic imperialism. It represents anonymous globalisation, with little relevance to real food . . . For me, *malbouffe* means both the standardisation of food – the same taste from one end of the world to the other – and the choice of food associated with the use of hormones and GMOs, as well as the residue of pesticides and other things that can endanger health. It also involves industrialised agriculture, that is to say mass-produced food in the sense of industrialised pig-rearing, battery chickens and the like . . . Today the production of food is determined by the global market. Means of transport and communications ensure that today's market is genuinely worldwide. As far as world leaders are concerned, the entire planet should submit to market laws. Our struggle is based

on resistance to this development. Health, education,
culture, food – these are all issues that are close to
everyone's heart. Today they are in danger of becoming
commodities . . . Agriculture should not be reduced to mere
trade. People have the right to be able to feed themselves
and take precautionary measures on food as they see fit.
>   José Bové and Francois Dufour, *The World Is Not for Sale:*
>   *Farmers against Junk Food*

Europe's leaders and the WTO need to rethink the need for
ever more international food trade. This is crucial not just
because the trade forces down food and animal-welfare
standards, reduces food security for many of the world's
poor and contributes to such disasters as foot-and-mouth
and BSE but also because it exacerbates climate change . . .
European leaders should begin by replacing the Common
Agricultural Policy with a localist rural and food policy. Its
goal would be to keep production closer to the point of
consumption and help protect and rebuild local economies
around the world.
>   Caroline Lucas, Green member of the European Parliament

The right to trade freely on a global scale is being
established as the highest right. People's right to safe and
adequate food is being treated as a non-tariff trade barrier,
to be dismantled and destroyed.
>   Vandana Shiva, Indian environmental activist [1]

Outside a vandalised McDonald's in Seattle, José Bové is handing
out Roquefort cheese. With his trademark moustache, he looks
like Asterix, another plucky Frenchman who enjoyed taking a pop
at authority. This self-styled peasant revolutionary shot to global
fame by driving a tractor into a McDonald's in Millau, in south-west
France, in protest at the spread of what he considers *malbouffe* ('bad
food'). A few months later, in early December 1999, he is in Seattle

to strike a blow against the WTO, which is meeting to try to launch a new push to free world trade. Amid a throng of journalists and television cameras, he makes a show of trying to educate Americans about the superior pleasures of French cheese. But aside from this media circus, a handful of real people are making a different kind of protest. 'Why is McDonald's shut?' says one of the girls as she bangs on the cracked door pane. 'Let me in, all I want is a burger.'

The world's most famous farmer is actually not much of a farmer at all. In the early 1970s, when he was a peace activist campaigning against the expansion of a military base in the Larzac region of southern France, he squatted a farm that the army had bought and started raising a few sheep and making cheese. In 1987, he set up Confédération Paysanne, a radical farmers union, to fight against the industrialisation of French farming. But his big break came on 12 August 1999, when he took on Ronald McDonald in Millau. The publicity stunt paid off: he was arrested and sent to jail for criminal damage, which instantly made him a martyr and a media star. Now Bové has gone global. Indeed, he is so busy jet-setting around the world campaigning against globalisation – marching with the Zapatista rebels in Mexico, protesting against genetically modified (GM) foods in India, or addressing the World Social Forum in Porto Alegre, Brazil – that he scarcely has any time for farming. Being a media star, it seems, is more alluring than tending sheep in the rain.

José Bové may be a fake, but this pipe-puffing pseudo-peasant plays well with many people. Globaphobes mob him; politicians court him; the media lionises him. 'We want a serious change in agricultural policy,' he says. 'Yes, we want to protect small farms, but we also want to rejuvenate agriculture, and attract new people into farming. We also want to ensure that agriculture and environment work in harmony. Finally, we want Europe to concentrate on small farming, peasant farming, feeding its people, rather than on destructive industrial agriculture. We want to modify the

Common Agricultural Policy and the WTO to achieve these aims.'[2]

The European Union's Common Agricultural Policy (CAP) certainly needs modifying. It eats up half the EU's budget, hikes up food prices, piles up wasteful food mountains, harms the environment, undermines food safety, and stuffs the pockets of crooks, middlemen and big agri-companies while failing to do much for small farmers. And that's not all: it also denies farmers in poor countries a living.

This is criminal. As Alan Winters of Sussex University points out: 'Agriculture is vital for income generation and poverty alleviation in most developing countries. Three-quarters of the poor live and work in rural areas; agriculture is their major source of income; farm incomes have large spillovers to others in the rural economy; and food accounts for a major share of all poor people's expenditure.' Rich-country farm protectionism costs poor countries over three times what they receive in overseas aid.[3]

The CAP does not come cheap. The OECD[4] reckons it cost Europeans $103.5 billion in higher taxes and food prices in 2000 – $276 per person, $1,100 for every family of four. Europeans pay over two and a half times the world price for their sugar; over twice the world price for lamb and butter; double what they should be paying for their beef; over 80 per cent more for their bananas; and 50 per cent too much for their corn.

It is not only European farmers who have their snouts in the subsidy trough. Total support to agriculture in rich OECD countries came to $327 billion in 2000 – more than the entire GDP of sub-Saharan Africa. The US doled out $92.3 billion in 2000 – $338 per person. Next is Japan, which gave $73.3 billion ($578 per person) followed by South Korea, which shelled out $24.3 billion ($518). But the most munificent are the Swiss, where each citizen coughed up $671 for their farmers, followed by the Japanese, the Icelanders ($576) and the Norwegians ($543).

This largesse is spread among remarkably few people. Despite all the handouts, farmers are a dying breed in rich countries. What is true for manufacturing is true for agriculture in spades: rising productivity means that fewer and fewer farmers can produce ever more food. In 1960 America had 5.6 million farmers; by 2000 it had only 3.5 million. Japan has lost over three in four of its farmers over the past forty years: they number only 3.1 million, down from 12.8 million. France has seen a similar decline: down from 4.3 million to fewer than a million. West Germany had 3.6 million farmers in 1960; unified Germany had only a million in 1999. Britain had fewer than half a million farmers in 2000, compared with 1.1 million in 1960. Only one in twenty Japanese (4.9 per cent) are farmers; one in twenty-four Frenchmen (4.2 per cent); one in thirty-six Germans (2.8 per cent); one in thirty-eight Americans (2.6 per cent); and a mere one in fifty-nine Britons (1.7 per cent).[5] In the EU as a whole, one in twenty-one (4.7 per cent) are farmers. Only in South Korea are there still many farmers: one in eight (11.8 per cent) work on the land.

With so much money split between so few people, the average handouts are truly astronomical. European farmers get the equivalent of $14,000 each – enough for two round-trip tickets on Concorde from Paris to New York. American farmers do even better: they get $20,000 a head – more than double the federal pension a poor war veteran receives. South Korean farmers get $26,000, the Japanese $28,000; the Norwegians and the Swiss $29,000 – enough to buy a new Mercedes C-Class every year.

Agriculture contributes very little to rich-country economies. US farmers produce 1.5 per cent of the country's GDP, but they receive subsidies worth 0.9 per cent of GDP, so their net contribution is a measly 0.6 per cent of national income. Japanese farmers are even worse: they produce 1.7 per cent of GDP but receive 1.6 per cent of GDP in handouts, which makes a net contribution of just 0.1 per cent of national income. European farmers add value worth 2.2 per cent of EU GDP but get 1.3 per cent of GDP in subsidies: a net contribution of 0.9 per cent of national income. Korean farmers actually destroy value: they contribute 5.1 per cent of GDP but receive subventions worth 5.3 per cent of GDP. These figures ignore much of the damage that farm subsidies do: the pure waste, the harm to the environment, the impact on food safety and the stunting of poor-country exports. The world would be much better off with free trade in food, combined with suitable regulation to protect the environment and keep food safe.

Trade in food is anything but free. For a start, farmers receive price-related subsidies. So if, for instance, the world price of sugar falls, rich-country farmers get a bigger top-up from taxpayers: this allows them to fend off cheaper imports and sell more abroad too. Next, they get 'emergency' help to compensate for lower revenues or higher costs. America doled out $8.7 billion in such aid to farmers hit by low prices in 1999, a further $7.6 billion in 2000 and $5.5 billion in 2001. The EU gave $850 million in compensation to farmers that had to destroy their herds because of BSE. Then, European farmers get export subsidies – and Americans export credits – that lower the cost of selling abroad. What's more, farmers are protected by high import tariffs. Whereas the average import duty on manufactures is around 4 per cent, it is around 40 to 50 per cent on agricultural produce. The US tax on foreign sugar reaches 129 per cent. Canada's import tariff on butter rises as high as 343 per cent. The EU's duty on offal imports peaks at 826 per cent. Japan's tax on foreign rice is nearly 1,000 per cent. Worse, import tariffs typically rise with the level of processing. In Japan and the EU, fully processed food products face tariffs twice as high as unprocessed ones; in Canada tariffs are twelve times higher for processed foods. This makes it hard for poor countries to industrialise: Kenya can easily sell bulk coffee beans, but not instant coffee in jars. So Western companies capture most of the value-added.

There are also quotas, 'anti-dumping' duties on imports that are deemed too cheap, 'safeguard' measures to protect against import surges, unduly restrictive quality standards, and more. One EU regulation that is estimated to save not even one life a year is reckoned to cost poor African countries $700 million in lost exports. The EU's insistence on levels of aflatoxins, which have been linked to liver cancer, lower than the World Health Organisation deems necessary is expected to save two lives for every billion people. But the tighter standard, which came into force in 2001, will cut exports of cereals, dried fruit and nuts from nine poor African countries that are reliant on the European market – Chad, Egypt, Mali, Nigeria, Senegal, South Africa and Zimbabwe – by two-thirds, or $700 million.[6]

All of this stunts farm trade. The volume of trade in manufactures in 2000 was forty-two times what it was in 1950; world GDP was over six times greater; but the volume of farm trade was less than six times higher. It is nonsense to blame globalisation for all the problems in modern farming: the barriers to farm trade are as high now as those in manufacturing were fifty years ago. A more likely culprit is protectionism. Farmers don't need to worry much about what consumers want because governments guarantee them a livelihood whatever they do. In the realm of food, our world is still far from open.

Nonsense on stilts

The CAP and its equivalents in other rich countries are ripe for root-and-branch reform – or even outright abolition. But the EU's farm commissioner, Franz Fischler, disagrees. As well as propping up farmers' income and ensuring Europe can feed itself, European agriculture, he says,

> provides many services: maintaining a living countryside; preserving family farming or undertaking essential environmental services, to name but three. This multifunctional characteristic makes it clear that measuring EU agriculture with a purely economic yardstick is inadequate and inappropriate . . . No CAP would mean enormous social and environmental costs, once farmers no longer render their additional services to society: who but the taxpayer would pay for natural disasters like avalanches,

landslides and desertification that would result from a
reduction in farmers' ranks?[7]

That is simply not true. For a start, 60 per cent of the cost of the
CAP to consumers and taxpayers goes on administration, storage,
export subsidies and fraud. (Crooks are reckoned to embezzle
around $4 billion a year.)[8] Of the remaining 40 per cent that goes
to farmers, around half goes on extra farming inputs, 45 per cent
on higher land rents or land values and only 5 per cent ends up in
farmers' pockets. The upshot is that although some farmers are
raking it in – the largest 25 per cent of farms receive almost 70 per
cent of the subsidies – the average farmer's income has fallen by 30
per cent over the past ten years. Over 200,000 farmers leave the
land each year. Nor does the countryside benefit much from the
CAP. Only a tenth of CAP spending goes on rural development;
rural unemployment is much higher than in cities. So much for
'maintaining a living countryside' and 'preserving family farming'.

The CAP also does huge damage to the environment. Over half of
Europe's rivers are heavily polluted with fertilisers. While the EU is
aiding the clean-up of industrial waste and sewage from European
rivers, it is encouraging farmers to pollute surface and underground freshwater. In Austria, where Mr Fischler is from, most
groundwater is unsafe to drink before it is treated because it is full
of nitrates and pesticides from farming. The CAP subsidises crops
that require irrigation, like maize, tobacco and sugar beet, in
Mediterranean countries like Spain where water is in short supply.
It has also encouraged over-intensive agriculture: British hedgerows
have been cut down, Belgian wetlands drained, French wildlife
habitats invaded by crops and livestock, soil eroded by massive
overgrazing. Pesticide use in some areas is ten times what it is in
Australia or Argentina. Until recently, countries could not place
any environmental conditions on the payment of CAP funds.
'Incredibly, farmers could previously flout every environmental
law on the European statute book and continue to receive their

farm subsidies,' says Tony Long of the World Wide Fund for Nature.[9] 'For example, there are many areas in Europe where nitrogen and pesticide levels are above those specified in EU legislation as a result of farming practice.'

Europe's myth is that farmers bind us to an idyllic rural past. America's is that farmers are rugged individualists and frontier-settlers. Hence Congress's 1996 'Freedom to Farm' Act, which doled out $36 billion to farmers with no strings attached. It was touted as one-off aid to farmers in distress, which they could use as they saw fit to get back on their feet. Yeah right. American farmers were soon clamouring for – and receiving – more pork: 'emergency' aid year after year. One American farmer, Victor Davis Hanson, was scathing: 'Some farmers in the Midwest are to receive money because there are too many harvests, others in the east because there are too few. By this strange rationale, farmers are to be paid whether they lose their crops to drought, or produce to surfeit and thus help saturate the market.'[10] Worse, in May 2002 President Bush approved a new subsidy package that could be worth more than $190 billion over ten years. Politicians claim such largesse is needed to help small family farmers. Yet hardly any small farmers are still in business. So most of the money goes to big agri-business. One per cent of American farmers account for over half of farm income; nine out of ten earn less than $20,000. Five per cent of American landowners own three-quarters of the land; the bottom four-fifths just 3 per cent. American farmers also get goodies such as cheap water, which makes it economical to irrigate the Californian desert to grow fruit and causes a water shortage for other Californians.

Thankfully, there is growing pressure for reform. America and other big agricultural exporters, such as Canada, Australia, Brazil and Argentina, are gunning for Europe's CAP. The aim of freeing farm trade is at the heart of the new round of WTO negotiations that were launched in Doha in November 2001, and are supposed to conclude by January 2005. The proposed enlargement of the EU to the east could also be a catalyst for change. Subsidising eastern farmers could raise the costs of the CAP by two-thirds; west European taxpayers are likely to baulk at footing the bill for huge handouts to Poland's 2 million inefficient farms. But perhaps the most potent force for change now comes from Europeans themselves. They are sick of seeing tottering cows foaming at the mouth and burning pyres of animals in the British countryside. Britain's ministry of agriculture has been remodelled as a ministry of food and rural affairs. Germany's is now a ministry of food and consumer protection, headed by a Green politician, Renate Künast, who is pushing for a more consumer- and eco-friendly approach to farm policy. 'The BSE scandal marks the end of agriculture policy of the old style,' she said in her maiden address in 2000. If all of this convinces the EU that it has to cut back on its harmful farm subsidies, it could bring about freer farm trade worldwide. If the EU embraces reform, it is sure to demand sweeping changes elsewhere too, especially in America, as part of any WTO deal.

But don't rejoice too soon. The EU is a past master at dodging farm reform. The previous round of world-trade negotiations dragged on for eight years, largely because of the EU's refusal to countenance agricultural liberalisation. It eventually signed up to the WTO's Agreement on Agriculture, but this has not changed much. The agreement made support to farmers more open and transparent, and provided a framework for future liberalisation, but it did little to curb farm protectionism, which has actually been rising in recent years. Any new WTO agreement may prove equally hard to come by and ultimately toothless. Nor is enlargement an insuperable problem for opponents of reform. Already, Brussels is coming up with clever new ways of resisting change – for instance, by paying Polish farmers less than French ones over a ten-year phase-in period after Poland joins the EU. As for pressure from voters, it is all too easily manipulated. José Bové, for instance, has cleverly positioned himself as a friend of the people and enemy of the CAP – all the better to urge ways to prolong Europe's obscene farm protectionism in a new guise. The changes that he and many Greens have in mind would actually make matters worse.

A medieval charter

Mr Bové's priority is 'food security', nationally and locally. Countries and regions should trade food only if they can feed their own people. He also wants food to be produced by small peasant farmers rather than big agricultural companies. That means redirecting taxes and subsidies, not scrapping them. 'We are all small farmers against globalisation and the corporate destruction of farming,' he says. 'We all believe that our countries should be able to feed their own people in their own way. This does not mean no trade, but it means countries should be able to protect their own ways of farming and eating. That is a global principle.'[11] He calls this a new direction for farming. In fact, it would spell a return to the Middle Ages.

Take the case for food security first. It is analogous to Hank Barnette's national-security argument for protecting America's steel industry: food is so vital that we cannot depend on foreigners for it. But consider the huge cost that trying to be self-sufficient in food implies and set it against the tiny risk that we will not be able to import enough food to feed ourselves (and be unable to start growing enough food again were such a catastrophe to occur), and you see how ludicrous an argument this is. It is as ridiculous as if all city-dwellers tried to grow their own food in their back garden, and raised a cow in the shed for good measure, so as not to be vulnerable to a peasants' revolt that might cut off food supplies to supermarkets.

Mr Bové thinks there are also national ways of eating that need to be protected – that the French should eat their traditional food, made in the traditional way, and so on. But nobody is stopping them doing so if they want to. Any visitor to France knows that there are plenty of traditional French restaurants. What really rankles with Mr Bové is that some people don't share his tastes. Some French people sometimes prefer a McDonald's, a Chinese meal or Australian wine. Who is Mr Bové to deny them this option?

Think of the loss of choice that national production implies. Britons would forgo claret and Australian wine, and make do with more expensive, inferior stuff from Kent. The French would say *non* to basmati and jasmine rice and eat only local varieties. The Swedes would try to grow oranges in greenhouses at vast expense. Americans would settle for Californian fizzy wine rather than champagne, Monterrey Jack rather than Roquefort, baloney rather than Parma ham. This does not bother some Greens. On the contrary. Caroline Lucas, a Green member of the European Parliament for south-east England, argues that 'it is not necessary or healthy to consume some products in such quantities e.g. sugar, and livestock products'.[12] Ms Lucas clearly feels she has a right to decide what we can eat. And if, perish the thought, the idea of 'food security' were pushed to its logical extreme, we would all have to make do with local produce. What thin gruel our diet would then consist of!

In fact, this crazy idea is exactly what some Greens propose. In his book, *Localisation: A Global Manifesto*,[13] Colin Hines, who used to run Greenpeace International's economics unit, argues that local areas should aim to be self-sufficient. He defines a local area as the circulation area for a local newspaper; a radius of 10 to 15 miles around local towns of 1,500 to 10,000 people; or, within cities, the area bounded by the nearest supermarket, shopping centre and school. What Mr Hines's plans imply is not far from a return to subsistence farming. Presumably, to enforce these draconian curbs on trade, an army of inspectors would have to check shoppers' bags to make sure they were not illegally transporting food from one locality to another. Or perhaps the authorities could set up customs points around each locality to slap whopping duties, say, on Taunton apples sold in Bristol. And what would happen if the local harvest failed or was destroyed by pest or flood? Could an exception to localist dogma be made to stop people starving?

Such lunacy was not even tried in the Depression years of the 1930s, when countries, not localities, pursued autarky. A forced return to small-scale peasant farming would compound the misery. Such farms still survive – just – in parts of France, like the dirt-poor *département* of the Lot. As a child, I spent several summers on one of them, where my father had spent much of the Second World War away from Nazi-occupied Paris. Mimie and Lucien Bardes, who have since retired, owned 40 hectares of hilly land on which they raised sheep and grew corn, beans and other vegetables, as well as some tobacco. They also had some chickens, a few rabbits and some walnut and plum trees. This is the rural idyll, *la France profonde*, to which José Bové harks back.

Yet it was no such thing. The Bardes were desperately poor. They eked out a miserable living, never took a holiday together and barely travelled, although Lucien dreamt of seeing the world. It was hard work in the boiling summer sun and the biting winter wind; Lucien got terrible back pains. Yes, they ate good, hearty food, but there was little variety. They preferred to spend some of their meagre income on foreign produce from the supermarket in nearby Souillac rather than rely solely on local farmers' markets. When they retired, nobody in the family or locally wanted to continue farming their land. It is fanciful to think that such small peasant farms, organic or otherwise, are a viable way of feeding Europeans. They are so inefficient that it would require many more farmers, much more land under cultivation and even higher subsidies. It would also lead to much higher food prices. Since food accounts for a much bigger share of poor people's budgets than rich people's, such a policy would hit the poor hardest.

But what could possibly be the benefits of small-scale local farming? In a report[14] co-authored with Mr Hines, Ms Lucas points to four: to the environment; to animal welfare; to rural communities; and to animal and human health. First, she claims transporting less food around would reduce air pollution and greenhouse-gas emissions. That may be true. Food distribution, especially air freight, does use up lots of fuel. But growing kiwi fruit in heated greenhouses in England gobbles up more energy that transporting them from New Zealand. Keeping cows in heated barns over a long, freezing-cold Finnish winter burns more fossil fuels than raising them in Brazil, where they can spend the whole year outdoors, and then shipping the meat to Finland. So localised production is not necessarily better for the environment. More importantly, there is a better way of ensuring that only trade whose economic benefits outweigh the environmental costs takes place: tax carbon use and then let the market decide the pattern of production.

Next, Ms Lucas claims that farm trade harms animal welfare, in particular because so many animals are shifted around in poor conditions. Certainly, some animals are badly treated. Governments should clamp down on such sharp practices if that is what voters want. But that is an argument for tougher regulation, not stopping farm trade. It is perfectly possible to ship animals decently. Nor is animals' welfare guaranteed if they stay put. Battery hens don't move around much. To make *foie gras*, French farmers literally stuff food down geese's throats to fatten them up and make their livers expand. Moreover, freer trade would improve animal welfare in many cases. In countries with wide-open spaces such as Argentina and Australia, livestock are not cooped up or penned in as they are on cramped European farms. Animal welfare would improve if we ate New Zealand lamb or Argentine beef.

What about the impact on rural communities? No question, freer trade would harm uncompetitive farmers: people like the Bardes. Unless they could find a niche for themselves as producers of speciality meats, like Parma ham, or cheeses, like Cheddar, most would go out of business. But that need not mean rural decline. Tourism is now a bigger earner than farming for much of the countryside. The Bardes used to rent out a house to holidaymakers from the city. Nor would small-scale local farming improve matters. That is what the Bardes practised, and they were dirt poor. Just think of the chilling impact on the rural economy that redirecting people's efforts from productive employment to unproductive farming would have. Local spending power would collapse.

Finally, Ms Lucas argues that farm trade spreads diseases that harm animals and people, such as foot-and-mouth and bovine spongiform encephalitis (BSE). That is an odd argument. Start with foot-and-mouth disease. It was endemic in Britain in the nine-teenth century, when farming was overwhelmingly local, but was then eradicated in the more internationalised twentieth century. It is still endemic in many parts of Asia. The outbreak that swept through Britain in 2001 and led to isolated cases in parts of Europe and elsewhere might well have been caused by illegal imports from Asia, but that is hardly the fault of legal farm trade. It is perfectly possible to combine international trade with strict sanitary regu-lations: countries that are free of foot-and-mouth already ban imports from infected areas. Besides, even if all international food trade was banned, or curbed by massive import duties, there would still be illegal trade. In fact, there would probably be much more, because the profits from smuggling would be so much greater. Banning cocaine imports has hardly stopped the global trade in it.

Ms Lucas is on even shakier ground with mad-cow disease. It is a bit rich for a British politician to blame globalisation for BSE and its human equivalent, new variant CJD (Creutzfeldt–Jakob disease). BSE is a disease born and bred in Britain by British farmers, taking advantage of a regulatory lapse by the British government. True, Britain – which has reported over 180,000 cases of BSE – exported some of its woes through sales of contaminated animal feed to Europe, where around 1,300 cases of BSE have been logged. But that is a failure of regulation, not a necessary consequence of trade.

Indeed, BSE is partly a product of protectionism, rather than a bane of free trade. Land in a crowded island like Britain is already expensive. Protectionism makes it even more so, because it boosts agricultural demand for land. High land prices encourage farmers to farm more intensively, so as to economise on land, just as the high cost of land in New York spurs the construction of skyscrap-ers. So rather than grazing their cattle on grass, as they do in countries like Brazil where pastureland is plentiful, farmers are tempted to feed their cows less wholesome things, like sheep's remains. Pigs have been fed sewage (shit, to be blunt); Belgian cows raised near industrial sites have been found to contain high levels of poisonous dioxins.

It is perverse to set up a choice between food trade and food safety. Freer trade and stringent safety regulation can go hand in hand: just look at the pharmaceuticals industry, where drugs are traded internationally but cannot be sold unless governments deem them safe. Globalisation in no way threatens food-safety standards. Nor does the much-maligned World Trade Organisation (WTO), which enforces the rules for global trade that governments have agreed. But critics point to the WTO's ruling against the EU's ban on hormone-treated beef as evidence that the WTO is sacrificing food safety on the altar of free trade, and they warn that the WTO could yet force Europeans to accept GM food too.

In 1985, the EU banned beef from cows treated with growth hormones that, it claims, can cause cancer. Such hormones are widely used in the US, where regulators say they are safe. In 1989, the US retaliated against what it saw as EU protectionism by imposing $100 million of sanctions on EU imports. After the WTO was set up in 1995, with new dispute procedures and new rules covering food safety and trade, the US lifted its sanctions and took its beef dispute to the WTO, which eventually ruled that the EU ban breached world-trade rules. The EU failed to lift its ban by the WTO's May 1999 deadline, so two months later the US imposed $117 million of trade sanctions on a range of European products, including Roquefort cheese – hence Mr Bové's stunt in Seattle.

The first thing to note is that the EU's ban is still in place. The WTO cannot force the EU to lift it. True, EU farmers are paying a penalty for the ban, because America has slapped 100 per cent customs duties on some of their products. But they already faced American sanctions before the WTO came into existence, so the only real difference is that the American sanctions have more legitimacy than before: they are sanctioned by a multilateral organisation, rather than imposed unilaterally. Next, note that EU governments signed up to WTO rules in 1994 and that these were subsequently ratified by national parliaments. The WTO was not trying to impose its will on the EU: it was merely acting at America's instigation to hold the EU to rules to which it had previously agreed. If the EU disagreed with the WTO's food-safety rules, it should not have signed up to them in the first place.

WTO rules say that governments have every right to set their own food-safety standards, so long as they are based on sound science; are applied only to the extent necessary to protect human, animal or plant life or health; and are neither arbitrary nor discriminatory. Each government has the right to decide what level of health risk it considers acceptable. When there is not enough scientific evidence to know whether or not something is safe, regulators are allowed to take provisional action on the basis of the information they do have in order to avoid potential risks. This is known as the precautionary principle: better safe than sorry. But regulators must seek further scientific evidence and review any provisional measures that they have taken in the light of new evidence.

Why then did the EU fall foul of WTO rules? Because it explicitly stated that its hormone ban was not a provisional measure and so did not invoke the precautionary principle as a defence. The WTO ruled against the ban because it was not based on sound science.

It is ridiculous to accuse the WTO of trying to foist dangerous food on Europeans. There is no convincing scientific evidence that growth hormones are dangerous when used responsibly, although they can be dangerous in high doses. Americans are not dropping dead in the streets, so the hormones are presumably not misused. Many products that are safe when used responsibly, such as cars, can be lethal when misused. All the same, if Europeans genuinely prefer to be safe rather than sorry, the EU should have invoked the precautionary principle in its defence. Even now, there is a way out that could satisfy the Americans and convince them to lift their sanctions. The EU could lift its ban but require that hormone-treated beef be labelled as such. America could resume its exports; Europeans who are not worried about growth hormones could eat beef treated with them, while those who are concerned could avoid it. There is no stark choice between food safety and free trade. Even free-traders prefer safe food to free trade. But tastes – and perceptions of risk – differ among individuals and countries. Rather than ban hormone-treated beef, the EU should require proper labelling.

The row over beef hormones is a light skirmish compared with a potential transatlantic war over GM foods. Many Europeans are paranoid about genetic modification; the vast majority are uneasy about it. Although GM crops may provide benefits to farmers, such as better pest resistance and improved yields, they are seen as delivering few gains to consumers. GM boosters claim that this may change once the second wave of GM crops, which offer consumers more nutritional food, hits the market. Perhaps. Meanwhile, although there is no scientific evidence that GM products currently on the market pose health risks, consumers are wary. Their fears about food safety are understandable in the wake of mad-cow disease, foot-and-mouth and dioxin poisoning. Scare-mongering by the media and environmental campaigners has made matters worse. But even if their worries are irrational, consumers have a right to choose whether or not to eat GM foods.

The problem is that European consumers' stance puts them at loggerheads with American farmers, who have embraced GM technology and for whom the economic stakes in terms of lost exports to Europe are huge. US farm exports totalled $71 billion in 2000, of which $10 billion went to the EU, down from $12 billion in 1998. Seven-tenths of the world's GM cultivation is in the US, 14 per cent in Argentina, 9 per cent in Canada, and a mere 0.03 per cent in the EU. China, South Africa, Australia and a few other countries also grow some GM crops. European farmers stopped planting GM seeds after José Bové in France and Greenpeace's Lord Melchett in Britain among others attacked fields that were being used for trials. Soybeans, which are used in all manner of processed foods, account for 53 per cent of GM crops; maize for 27 per cent, cotton for 9 per cent and oilseeds for 8 per cent. A quarter of all US corn is now GM. Europe, Japan, Taiwan and South Korea have largely switched to buying non-GM maize and soya from Brazil and China rather than the US.

The European Commission has tried to strike a balance between consumer rights and free trade. In October 1998, the European Commission imposed a moratorium on new approvals of GM plant varieties. It also required all foods containing more than 1 per cent GM ingredients to carry a label. In February 2001, it tightened the vetting rules, but EU governments blocked a lifting of the moratorium on approvals until laws were in place to ensure reliable tracing and labelling of GM organisms. In July 2001, the Commission came up with more proposals, with a view to allaying consumers' fears that they are surreptitiously being poisoned and thus, eventually, to lifting the moratorium. The proposals would do three things. First, introduce a system for tracing GM organisms from the farm to the supermarket. Food will need to be tested for the presence of GM material at each stage of the production chain, not just prior to sale. That requires a separate supply chain for GM and non-GM foods, a costly measure that few US farmers comply with. Second, all foods derived from GM ingredients will need to be labelled, even those that are so refined that they no longer contain any of the genetic material that identifies them as GM. Products such as highly refined corn and soybean oils and soy-based lecithin that contain additives or flavouring derived from GMOs will be labelled: 'This product does not contain but is derived from GM organisms.' Third, imports of food and animal feed from the US that contain up to 1 per cent of GM material that is not approved for sale in the EU will be allowed in, although they will have to be labelled. This is an important concession to US farmers, because it is hard to prevent GM and non-GM crops from mixing, either because of cross-pollination in the fields or during shipping. The EU has approved only twenty-one GM crops, the US forty. But US exporters say it is hard to detect such small concentrations reliably. The EU is not alone in requiring GM products to be labelled: Japan, Australia, New Zealand and other countries do too. Thailand, the world's biggest rice exporter, is bringing in strict laws on labelling and traceability.

Where does the WTO fit in to all this? Providing information to consumers through labels is perfectly compatible with world-trade rules, but the US may have legitimate grounds to appeal to the WTO over the EU's procedures for approving GM products. The US claims these are unnecessarily slow, complicated and unpredictable; the EU has not approved any new GM crops since October 1998. A potential European ban on GM foods would also be problematic if the EU fails to invoke the precautionary principle in its defence. Even so, the worst that could happen is huge American trade sanctions, which the US would be perfectly capable of imposing even if the WTO did not exist. The WTO cannot force Europeans to accept GM products if they don't want them.

A better alternative

The Bové–Lucas way is a blind alley. It would cost more, reduce choice and continue to penalise farmers in poor countries. It makes no sense, for instance, for Britain to try to feed itself when it could be importing cheaper, better-quality food from, say, Brazil. Stoking up fears about food safety abroad is farmers' latest tactic for protecting their subsidies. Thus Ben Gill, president of Britain's National Farmers' Union, rhetorically asked: 'Is it a coincidence that we had classical swine fever in East Anglia last year of an Asian origin, and foot-and-mouth now, also of an Asian origin? It raises questions about freer world trade.'[15] In fact, whereas imports have to comply with the most stringent European standards, European farmers get away – quite literally – with murder: some people have died from eating their tainted beef and farmers were then compensated, rather than penalised, for their shameful practices. When Ford had to recall millions of cars because of their faulty tires, it had to foot the bill. When European farmers had to cull their BSE-infected herds, European taxpayers had to cough up. Have European farmers paid compensation to victims of new variant CJD? Hell no. For European farmers, food safety is a secondary concern because government picks up the tab for their mistakes whatever happens. For foreign farmers trying to sell in Europe, reputation is all. If they slip up once, they risk losing the market for years.

Luiz Fernando Furlan knows this all too well. He runs Sadia, Brazil's biggest chicken exporter, which also sells turkey, pork and beef. His company, which employs 30,000 people, sells poultry, processed and unprocessed, in over sixty countries. In 2002, after the European Commission recently lifted its ban on Brazilian pork, it will start selling pork in the EU again for the first time in twenty-four years. You might have eaten Sadia products without realising it: McDonald's buy its chicken fillets and strips; Britain's Tesco and Iceland sell Sadia nuggets and stuffed chicken breasts under their own label; it supplies several German supermarket chains, including Metro. 'It's not true and unfair that we produce bad food,' says Mr Furlan. 'Standards are above average at Sadia. The EU and Japanese come here to inspect us. They have very high requirements. They are suspicious. We need to comply with the very highest standards. We are better than some EU producers. But there is more tolerance with local [European] producers. There is none with us. Plus our customers, especially the supermarket chains, inspect us regularly and have their own additional requirements. That is not usual for US and EU companies. US producers say: "This is my product, take it or leave it." But we come from a developing country, so we have to comply. We are flexible and we have to accept the requirements, otherwise we won't sell. We produce what customers want: special cuts, special packaging, all without subsidies. The EU's sanitary barriers were justified in the past, but not today. We have well-equipped vets and up-to-date labs. Brazil is much better than the EU in food safety: we have not had foot-and-mouth or swine fever.'

The EU conspires to keep out Sadia's food in a variety of ways. Sadia's chicken costs a third less than European poultry. But import taxes add a third to its price in Europe. In the case of frozen chicken breasts, the EU duty is 60 per cent. Worse, EU import tariffs are raised at times of the year when European farmers are bringing their meat to the market. Brazil's beef quota is only 5,000 tonnes a year: that means it can sell an average of only 13 grams of beef to every European each year. The EU also hits Sadia's sales in other parts of the world, because it gives export subsidies to European farmers that cut their costs by 20 to 30 per cent, so people in the Middle East can tuck into cut-price European chicken courtesy of European taxpayers. Food-safety requirements add a further 10 per cent to Sadia's costs. Sometimes the stipulations are ridiculous. In one food-processing plant, employees dealing with different products were required to remain separate, so Sadia had to build three cafeterias and three changing rooms. Sadia has never used GM products, few of which have been approved in Brazil. The US market is even worse: sanitary and regulatory barriers stop Sadia selling at all in America.

I asked Mr Furlan what he thought of EU farm protectionism. He replied: 'EU countries make more from tourism than from agriculture: there are only a few million farmers left. It's fine to protect some traditional producers, of *foie gras* or Roquefort, for instance. But I'm against artificially stimulating excess production that takes sales away from countries that can supply better products at a cheaper price. The CAP doesn't help small farmers much. Most of the benefits go to medium and large farmers. Chemical and fertiliser companies, silo owners, refrigeration and transport companies – they are not farmers but they all get big benefits. It would be better to pay small farmers a regular income without them having to produce rather than European farmers overproducing food, the Commission buying it up, storing and then selling it cheaply abroad. That kind of dumping, plus EU export subsidies, causes misery by driving farmers in developing countries out of business. Everybody in Europe is paying double for food and they get bad-quality food – just look at BSE. A green EU doesn't mean that it has to produce food surpluses or high-priced food or sell subsidised food abroad.'

Brazil is much better suited to producing food than Britain. It has vast open spaces that are ideal for growing crops and raising livestock. Land is plentiful, so it is cheap. That means low-cost, high-quality food can be produced without the potentially harmful practices of over-intensive agriculture. Cows mainly graze on grass; other livestock are fed natural corn and soybean meal. Crops are sprayed with fewer chemical fertilisers. Farms are often isolated – by forests, for instance – so disease spreads less easily. Unlike Britain, Brazil has not had foot-and-mouth, mad-cow disease or swine fever in recent years. Moreover, the climate is mild throughout the year, so there is no need for greenhouses, no worry about frost, no need to keep animals inside in winter.

The right way ahead for farm policy lies with free trade in food, combined with suitable regulation and subsidies to protect the environment, promote animal welfare and maintain food safety. Inevitably, that means uncompetitive farmers in Europe, Japan, South Korea and even America will go out of business. A generous safety net should be there to catch their fall – as it should be for laid-off steelworkers. If taxpayers feel that farmers deserve special help, they could be paid to stay at home (or go on holiday) and produce nothing – indeed that is already starting to happen. Not all farmers would disappear: there are still niches for speciality products like *jamón serrano* or gorgonzola. And if, as Greens claim, people are willing to pay a hefty premium for organic produce, some farmers will be able to make a living, unsubsidised, meeting that demand. The food shortfall would be met from places that are better suited to producing it. Countries like Australia, Argentina, Brazil and Thailand can produce safe, eco-friendly food at a fraction of the cost. Since most of the competitive food-producing countries happen to be poor, we would not only get cheaper and better food, we would also be giving the poor a handup.

Money could also be spent directly on helping poor rural areas, just as it should be on declining industrial regions. Better still, farmers could be paid to look after the countryside: to plant hedgerows in Britain, keep Alpine pastures pristine, watch over nature reserves in the American West. But the biggest boost to the environment would come simply from a fall in farming numbers, which would mean less marginal land under cultivation, less pesticide use and less soil erosion. A tax on harmful pesticides, and forcing farmers to pay the full price for the water they use, would provide a further boost. A carbon tax that discourages environmentally harmful trade would also be a good idea. Animal welfare could be protected by strict regulation. Food safety would best be enforced by an agency that is independent of farmers' lobbying, so that it had consumer rather than producer interests at heart. Like America's Food and Drug Administration, the EU's new food-safety authority should have broad regulatory powers, including the right to ban foods.

Pie in the sky? Not necessarily. New Zealand's reforming Labour government abolished subsidies and freed up farm trade in 1984. The upshot has been a healthy shake-up of the industry. Some farmers went bust, but many more cut costs, diversified and became more productive. Fertiliser use dropped once it was no longer subsidised. Once there was no longer an incentive to farm marginal land, it returned to native bush. New Zealand's rural character has been protected by legislation, and funds provided for river control, soil conservation and rural water supply. People in rural areas enjoy the same social safety net as those in cities.

Many developing-country governments need to clean up their act too. India's farm subsidies, which are meant to guarantee food security, have in fact caused widespread hunger. Not only have they bred waste and corruption, they keep food prices high in a country where half the children are chronically malnourished. While granaries burst with rotting stocks, people starve because the government's primary objective is to prop up prices. This obscene scheme, together with free electricity and irrigation water, eats up a seventh of the country's income.

But the onus is on rich countries to set an example. The EU made a show of helping the world's forty-nine poorest countries with an initiative, known as 'Everything but Arms', to abolish all barriers to their exports. But grubby producer pressure nullified its benefits by excluding bananas (until 2006) and sugar and rice (until 2009) from the plan – renamed 'Everything but Farms' by wags. For all the talk about solidarity with poor countries that Pascal Lamy, the EU's trade commissioner, spouts, he prefers to pander to French farmers. While European and American farmers live fat on the land, many poor farmers in poor countries starve. Not only do poor farmers find it hard to export, they also face competition at home from subsidised European and American exports. The hardest hit are often the very poorest. It is immoral and it is wrong. Tell that to José Bové (or Pascal Lamy) next time he protests his concern for the poor.

NINE

Endangered Earth?

How globalisation can be green

The Industrial Revolution left London choking and buried beneath waste. The modern economy is a fire-breathing vampire of petroleum which is slowly cooking our planet. To claim that a massive increase in global production and consumption will be good for the environment is preposterous. The audacity to make such a claim with a straight face accounts for much of the heated opposition to the World Trade Organisation.

THILO BODE, executive director, Greenpeace International[1]

In a world of globalised, deregulated commerce in which everything is tradeable and economic strength is the only determinant of power and control, resources move from the poor to the rich, and pollution moves from the rich to the poor. The result is a global environmental apartheid.

VANDANA SHIVA, *The World on the Edge*[2]

Where once there was the fertile green of the Amazon rainforest, there now lies the ugly urban sprawl of Manaus. Foreign tourists flock here to catch a glimpse of the 'meeting of the waters', where two rivers – one black, one muddy yellow – converge. They come too to see the city's famous opera house, which was inaugurated on New Year's Eve 1896. It was built with the vast fortunes of the rubber barons who tapped the area's natural wealth to feed the world's insatiable demand for rubber. Imagine it: a European-style opera house 1,000 miles up the Amazon, slap bang in the middle of the jungle. With its huge golden chandeliers, wrought-iron columns from Britain, crystal from Murano, hand-carved wooden chairs from France, all of them crafted by the finest European workmen, as well as a ceiling painting mimicking the view from under the Eiffel Tower, the gaudy opulence of the Teatro Amazonas is almost the only lasting testimony to the nineteenth-century rubber boom, which briefly made Manaus one of the richest cities on earth. Manaus was – after Buenos Aires, the capital of what was then the world's richest country – the second city in Latin America to get street lights. But the boom didn't last. A perfidious Briton, Henry Wickham, smuggled rubber seeds out of the Amazon, enabling the British to set up rival plantations in Ceylon and Malaysia. That, and the advent of artificial rubber, broke Brazil's monopoly and consigned Manaus to decline after around 1920.

In the late 1960s, the Brazilian government decided to encourage Manaus's development by making it a free-trade zone. Despite the obvious inconvenience of being miles away from raw materials, suppliers and customers, tax breaks have lured all sorts of companies to set up factories in the middle of the rainforest. Manaus produces televisions, videos, hi-fis, mobile phones, Gillette shavers, even Honda motorbikes – but hardly any food. As Peter Collins of *The Economist* points out, it's crazy. 'Consider the absurdity of a city in the middle of the world's biggest tropical forest having to ship in a large proportion of its fruit and vegetables.'[3] Tax breaks have also fuelled a population explosion: 1.5 million people live in Manaus, four times as many as in 1970.

Even so, local politicians claim that assembling foreign goods with taxpayers' subsidies is better than chopping down the rainforest.

Perhaps. But Manaus also has another potential selling point. It promotes itself as a gateway for foreign tourists to the unspoilt nature of the Amazon. The city itself may be an ugly mess, the countryside around it scarred by thoughtless or desperate logging, but it is still closer to Eden than other concrete jungles. For hardy travellers, it is the starting point for an exotic jungle tour deep into the Amazon. For less adventurous folk, there are jungle hotels, like the one on Silves Island, 300 kilometres east of Manaus (in the Amazon, like the empty Australian outback, 300 kilometres away counts as nearby), which is supported by the Brazilian arm of the World Wide Fund for Nature (WWF). Tourists can go on forest walks and boat rides where they come face to face with unique local wildlife, like the *japin*, which imitates other birds' singing and can even copy a child's cry, or the *maguary*, a bird that can grow as big as 1.6 metres (five feet three inches) tall. 'The income generated by the Aldeia dos Lagos hotel will go towards the conservation of fishing lakes in the region and will also help to improve the quality of life for local people,'[4] says Regina Vasquez of WWF-Brazil. The hotel, which aims to promote community-based eco-tourism, is run by a local community organisation, with technical and financial support from the WWF. This is just one example of how globalisation can be good for the environment.

The green peril

It's not hard to tell horror stories about the global environment. Here are six. One: the world uses 70 per cent more energy than thirty years ago, and energy use is projected to rise by over 2 per cent a year for the next fifteen years. Unless a big effort is made to increase energy efficiency and reduce our reliance on fossil fuels, greenhouse-gas emissions are set to rise by a half. The resulting global warming could have devastating consequences. Two: although acid rain is decreasing in rich countries thanks to tough regulations on sulphur-dioxide and nitrogen-oxide emissions, it is rising in poor ones. On current trends, sulphur-dioxide emissions in Asia will double by 2020. Three: over the past fifty years, excess nitrogen – mainly from fertilisers, human sewage and burning fossil fuels – has started to overwhelm the global nitrogen cycle, causing all sorts of problems, from less fertile soil to poisoned lakes, rivers and coastal waters. If current trends continue, the amount of biologically available nitrogen will double in twenty-five years. Four: forests are still being cut down at a rapid rate. Between 1960 and 1990, around a fifth of all tropical forests in the world were cleared. In the Amazon alone, around 20,000 square kilometres – an area the size of Israel – are cleared every year. In poor countries, subsistence farmers are cutting down trees because they need arable land, and governments are promoting the development of large-scale ranches and plantations where once there were forests. In rich countries, where most forests have already been cut down, forest cover is stable or rising, but natural forests are often unprotected. Forest clearing and pollution threaten biodiversity in many areas, as do 'exotic invaders': foreign plants introduced by humans. Forest fires in Indonesia each year produce a huge blanket of smog that envelops much of south-east Asia and keeps the tourists away. Five: three-fifths of the world's coral reefs and a third of all fish species are under threat. Most oceans are already over-fished, so fish catches are falling. Six: global water use is rising fast; some predict that competition for scarce water supplies will cause wars in the twenty-first century. One in three people live in a country with moderate or high water shortages; two in three may do so within thirty years unless serious efforts are made to conserve water.[5]

These are terrible facts. But is globalisation to blame? Only in part. Shipping goods across borders burns fuel, which pollutes the air and contributes to global warming. Increased trade also boosts economic growth, which, in the absence of proper environmental laws, can harm the environment. For instance, if forests are not properly managed, demand for wood from the world market may encourage unsustainable logging. But globalisation is by no means responsible for all, or even most, environmental degradation. The huge rise in the world's population, from 2.5 billion in 1950 to 6 billion now, is a much bigger culprit. Fragile ecosystems often cannot cope with the increased strain on their resources. Many poor Brazilians are cutting down trees in the Amazon not to sell them to foreigners, but because they need land to farm and feed themselves. Moreover many environmental problems are primarily local or domestic. The choking smog that hangs over Mexico City has little to do with trade: it is caused by too many people driving heavily polluting cars. (The old Volkswagen Beetles that cram the city's streets pollute up to fifty times as much as newer models do.)[6] The environmental crime that is the draining of the Aral Sea happened in a closed economy, the Soviet Union. Similarly, the stripping bare of all of North Korea's forests by desperately poor people in need of firewood has happened in a country that is shut off from the outside world.

The more important question is whether continued globalisation is compatible with protecting the environment. The answer is yes – so long as national environmental laws are brought up to scratch and countries act together to tackle cross-border problems like global warming. For instance, a carbon tax that forced airfreight companies to bear the full environmental cost of transporting goods across the world would ensure that only trade whose economic benefits outweighed those environmental costs took place. Over time, it would encourage greater fuel economy, especially if governments committed themselves to ratchet the tax progressively up. More modest local measures can do a world of good too. As the Aldeia dos Lagos hotel shows, globalisation can be green.

Good for trade, good for greenery

If you were looking to encourage green globalisation, a good place to start would be abolishing government subsidies that encourage overfarming, overfishing and excessive energy use. The pesticides and chemical fertilisers used by farmers poison the environment: Europe's rivers and lakes bear witness to it. A sensible government would tax pesticides so that they were used less – only when the boost to food yields exceeded the damage they do to the environment. But what does the European Union do? It subsidises pesticide use, which is bad for taxpayers and bad for our rivers. Clearly, the more European farmers produce, for export or for domestic consumers, the more pesticides they use and the more the environment is poisoned. But that's not all. As we saw in chapter eight, rich-country governments also dole out other subsidies and impose trade barriers which together push up the price of food and land. That gives farmers a further incentive to overproduce, and overuse agro-chemicals. The upshot is that farm trade is restricted and the environment suffers. Abolishing the handouts and the import duties, as well as taxing pesticide and fertiliser use, would not only boost trade – giving people a wider choice of cheaper food – but also help the environment. It's a win-win scenario.

Governments' fishing policies are even more wrong-headed. The Food and Agriculture Organisation (FAO) reckons that two-thirds of fish stocks in the oceans are overfished or on the verge of being overfished. If you own a fish farm, you will be careful to manage stocks so that they don't get depleted. The problem with the world's fish is that nobody owns them, so no country has an incentive to curb their fishermen. On the contrary: one country's restraint allows others to catch more, so everyone overfishes. Governments have started to tackle this problem by limiting fishing in their coastal waters to domestic trawlers. This makes the sea around a country a bit more like a fish farm; but fishing on the open sea, where many fish live and migrate, is still a free for all. Unfortunately, governments make matters worse by subsidising fishermen. The WWF reckons that governments worldwide spend $15 billion on subsidies to fishermen. The upshot is that the fishing industry is over twice as big as its sustainable level. People pay twice over for this folly: through higher taxes and because there will be less fish on the dinner table in the long run. Clearly, the more fishermen catch, whether for domestic dinner plates or foreign ones, the worse the problem gets. But if governments abolished subsidies, carefully controlled fishing in their territorial waters and clubbed together to manage stocks in the open seas, free trade could go hand in hand with sustainable fishing. Once stocks were allowed to recover, people would pay less tax and have more fish on their plate. Norway has slashed its fishing subsidies by 90 per cent and taken measures to manage its fish stocks better: it now has higher stocks, bigger catches and a leaner and more profitable industry. Another win-win.

Energy subsidies are worse still. Burning fossil fuels causes air pollution and contributes to global warming, so governments ought to be taxing oil and coal (or carbon more generally) to force companies to take account of the environmental damage they cause. In some cases, governments do exactly that: Europeans pay swingeing petrol taxes, for instance. But Americans pay hardly any tax on their gasoline, and some oil-producing countries, like Russia and Venezuela, subsidise petrol prices. Kerosene, the fuel that planes burn, is not taxed. Worse, governments dole out massive subsidies to the oil and coal industries. Coal is the dirtiest fuel of the lot, and yet many governments – Britain's, Germany's and Poland's, to name but three – subsidise the industry. The oil industry also gets huge handouts: Greenpeace reckons big oil companies in America get $15 billion to $35 billion a year in subsidies, although others think the figure is much smaller. Because companies do not pay the full environmental cost of burning fossil fuels, trade makes matters worse: both directly, because shipping goods across borders uses up fossil fuels, and indirectly, because it boosts economic growth, which leads to even more fossil-fuel use. But here too, globalisation could be green. If governments abolished energy handouts, trade would be freer and less damaging to the environment. If governments actually taxed carbon use appropriately, only trade whose economic benefits outweighed the environmental costs would take place. Another win-win.

Worldwatch, an American environmental think-tank, estimates that governments worldwide spend $650 billion on environmentally harmful subsidies.[7] For instance, Germany spends $7.3 billion a year propping up uncompetitive hard-coal mines. That is an astonishing $86,000 per miner. It would be cheaper – and much better for the environment – to shut down the mines and pay miners not to work. The OECD reckons that if rich-country governments imposed a carbon-based fuel tax, a tax on chemical use and eliminated harmful subsidies, they could drastically improve the environment for a very small price: less than 1 per cent of one year's GDP. Poor countries would benefit even more, since they typically waste even more money on damaging subsidies.

A fourth win-win would be to liberalise trade in environmental services – an industry that turns over $420 billion a year worldwide. Trade and investment barriers prevent modern eco-friendly technologies from spreading as fast as they could. They also make it harder for environmental consultants and suppliers of green solutions to ply their trade internationally. Freeing up trade in environmental services would be good for the economy and good for greenery.

A global view

Looking at individual environmental problems tells you part of the story, but it ignores the bigger picture. Opening up national economies to trade has five broad effects on the environment. First, industries relocate as countries specialise in areas where they have a comparative advantage. Some countries will attract more dirty industries, like steel mills or chemical factories; others will lure cleaner sectors, such as computer programming or call centres. So trade shifts pollution problems around the world. Second, globalisation spreads greener technologies. Companies that set up factories abroad often bring eco-friendly technologies with them, and force local competitors to clean up their act. Exporters often have to raise their standards to meet their customers' demands. For instance, producers of Thailand's famous *tuk-tuks* (motorised three-wheelers) are raising their safety and emission standards in order to sell in new foreign markets. Third, trade boosts economic growth. Unless production becomes cleaner and less resource-consuming at the same time, and consumers are more willing to recycle waste, this economic growth will harm the environment. Fourth, when people get richer, they eventually demand – and can afford to pay for – a cleaner environment. If governments respond with tougher environmental laws, economic growth can lead to a cleaner environment. (Richer people also tend to have fewer children, which reduces the strain on the environment from rapid population growth.) But fifth, some people – wrongly, as we shall see – claim that globalisation causes a 'race to the bottom' as governments lower their environmental standards to attract foreign investment.

The overall impact of globalisation on a country's environment depends on the balance between these five effects. Typically, economic growth initially harms the environment in poor countries. But then, as people get richer, they become willing and able to clean up the mess they have made. Just look at London. Fifty years ago, the air was thick with the smog from coal fires. Now it is much richer, but its air is cleaner, because coal fires have been banned and there is no industry in the city any more. Compare it with Delhi. Environmentalists ought to smile on Delhi: it has lots of bikes and buses, but few cars. Yet the air burns your eyes and chokes your lungs: all the vehicles spew out noxious fumes. London has more traffic, but its cars no longer use leaded petrol and it has more breathable air.

Alan Krueger and Gene Grossman of Princeton University have tried to estimate[8] how rich a country has to become before its citizens demand a cleaner environment. They reckon that the turning point happens when annual income per person reaches around $5,000. That is roughly how rich the Czech Republic is – around 10 per cent richer than Mexico or Brazil. Once annual income reaches $8,000 per person, roughly where South Korea is, they find that almost all the pollutant levels they measure – urban air pollution, as well as nitrogen, sewage and heavy-metal concentrations in river basins – have begun to fall. 'We find no evidence that environmental quality deteriorates steadily with economic growth. Rather, for most indicators, economic growth brings an initial phase of deterioration followed by a subsequent phase of improvement,' they conclude.

Clearly, there is nothing mechanical about this process. Some people may demand a cleaner environment when they are poorer; others may not mind air pollution if they rely on air conditioning in their Mercedes. Equally importantly, governments have to respond to people's demands for tougher eco-laws. Democratic ones are likely to be more susceptible to green demands than dictatorships, although even authoritarian countries can clean up their act. Many people claim that pressure for a cleaner environment in Beijing started after Zhu Rhonji, the Chinese prime minister, got ill from the choking smog in 1998 and ordered a clean up. By the Olympics in 2008, all the boilers in the city will use cleaner fuels instead of coal.

The cheering thing is that if governments do decide to clean up, increased trade can more than pay for the environmental damage it causes. Studies show that the overall economic benefits of increased trade are far greater than the environmental costs. One report[9] estimated that the freeing of world trade caused by the Uruguay Round of the GATT, which ended in 1994, raised global nitrogen-dioxide and carbon-dioxide levels by 0.5 per cent, sulphur-dioxide levels by 0.2 per cent and carbon-monoxide levels by 0.1 per cent. Yet the gains to the world from freer trade were worth some $500 billion. The study calculated that a small fraction of this gain would be more than enough to pay to clean up the environmental damage caused. It could be done, and it should be done.

But what if it isn't done? Should we limit trade instead? Only as a last resort (for instance, to help enforce international environmental agreements, as I will discuss later). Trade restrictions are generally a costly and blunt way of tackling environmental problems. Restricting farm trade might help the environment, but it would do nothing to tackle the environmental damage caused by producing food for the home market. A far better way to help the environment is to get rid of harmful agricultural subsidies. Moreover, trade barriers that aim to help the environment often do more harm than good. Take logging. If Brazil is incapable of managing its forests properly and the Amazon is being cut down to supply tropical wood to rich countries, a ban on such trade might seem like a good idea. But if loggers who can no longer export wood turn to ranching to make a living instead, they may end up clearing even more forest than before.

There is a better solution. Why not label wood that comes from sustainable forests instead? If people in rich countries are willing to pay more for furniture made with such wood, trade can give local people an incentive to manage their forests sustainably. That is exactly what the Forest Stewardship Council does. Based in Oaxaca, in southern Mexico, this international non-profit organisation is introducing an international labelling scheme for forest products, which provides a credible guarantee that the product comes from a well-managed forest. All forest products carrying their logo are independently certified as coming from forests that meet its internationally recognised standards. Another idea: if Brazilian forests are deemed to provide a service to the world by absorbing carbon dioxide that would otherwise contribute to global warming, then rich countries that produce the carbon dioxide could pay Brazil to maintain its trees.

All puff and no fire

People like Vandana Shiva, an Indian environmentalist, rage that globalisation is shifting polluting industries from rich countries to poor ones. Industries are moving to take advantage of laxer environmental laws in poor countries, she claims. This worsens pollution in poor countries and increases global emissions, since the industries that have moved are allowed to pollute more in poor countries than they were in rich ones. This 'eco-dumping' in 'pollution havens' is not only leading to an 'environmental apartheid'. It may also put pressure on rich-country governments to drive down their environmental laws, or at the very least prevent them from raising them as much as they should. Footloose companies, it is said, can hold a gun to governments' head: relax your environmental standards or we take our factories and jobs elsewhere. Fears about a 'race to the bottom' led American and Canadian greens to oppose the North American Free-Trade Agreement (NAFTA) with Mexico. They claimed it would drive North American environmental standards down to Mexican levels. When Bill Clinton was elected president in 1992, he insisted that environmental (and labour) side-agreements be tacked on to NAFTA.

One way to solve this alleged problem would be for governments to agree on global environmental standards that applied everywhere. But that would have huge costs, because local tastes and conditions vary. For instance, in a crowded country where landfill space is scarce, green-minded Germans may want their companies to recycle everything. In a country with wide open spaces where people value cheaper goods more than greener ones, Brazilians may prefer to dump their waste in holes in the ground. A common recycling standard would suit neither the Brazilians nor the Germans. A minimum standard pitched at the Brazilian level would leave Germans either drowning in rubbish or, if they chose to enforce a higher standard, with the same supposed problem as before.

Fortunately, for all Ms Shiva's inflammatory language, there is no evidence that poor countries are becoming pollution havens.

Investment patterns show that rich countries are not exporting polluting industries to poor ones. One study[10] found that only 5 per
cent of foreign investment in poor countries was in dirty industries,
whereas 24 per cent of FDI in rich ones. Another study[11] found that
investment by American companies abroad was growing fastest in
clean industries, whereas investment by foreigners in America was
growing fastest in dirty industries. The main reason companies invest
in the Third World is to take advantage of cheap labour, not lax environmental laws. Although some dirty industries have moved to poor
countries, around 75 to 80 per cent of the world's polluting industries are in rich countries – and this proportion has been remarkably
stable in recent decades. Indeed, it actually rose in the 1990s. After six
years of study, the World Bank concluded: 'pollution havens – developing countries that provide a permanent home to dirty industries –
have failed to materialise. Instead, poorer nations and communities
are acting to reduce pollution because they have decided that the
benefits of abatement outweigh the costs.'

How come? Because the cost savings of relocating dirty industries to poor countries are typically more than offset by the
advantages of staying in rich ones. Pollution controls in rich countries account for only 1 per cent of the typical company's
production costs. America's Census Bureau finds that even the
most polluting industries spend no more than 2 per cent of their
revenues on abating pollution. These costs tend to fall over time, as
the laws encourage new, leaner and cleaner technologies to be
developed, as Michael Porter of Harvard Business School has suggested. What's more, eco-friendly companies may actually be able
to charge a green premium for their products from green-minded
customers. Besides, multinational companies increasingly use standard technologies in all their factories around the world, because
it is cheaper to duplicate the technology they use at home than to
re-engineer it for each country in which they operate. These technologies are often much greener than the minimum required,
because if companies anticipate that environmental laws will get
tougher over time, it makes sense to fit state-of-the-art technology

now rather than having to spend a lot to upgrade it later. Moreover, consumer campaigns threaten to damage companies' reputations if they try to take advantage of laxer pollution laws in the Third World. There are also powerful reasons for keeping production in rich countries. If you supply steel to General Motors, it may be cheaper to have your mill near its car plant. Rich countries also have better roads, better ports and better workers. Moreover, polluting industries are very capital-intensive – think of those huge blast furnaces, vast chemical factories and massive oil refineries. Since capital is relatively abundant in rich countries (as well as in up-and-coming ones like South Korea and Poland), it is cheaper there too. So most polluting industries are still in richer countries, despite their tougher environmental laws.

Nor is there any evidence of a 'race to the bottom' in environmental regulation. Although companies bleat that pollution curbs will make them uncompetitive, this has not prevented environmental laws from generally getting tougher over the past thirty years. Air and water quality standards in rich countries are much higher than thirty years ago. In the past decade, America has slashed its emissions of sulphur dioxide, which causes acid rain. Between 1988 and 1997, mean ambient concentrations of sulphur dioxide in the US fell by 40 per cent. So did emissions of poisonous carbon monoxide. The number of annual 'bad air days' in major US cities fell by two-thirds. Since the early 1970s, inflation-adjusted spending by American government and business on the environment and natural-resource protection has doubled.[12] In Britain, chemical factories' emissions of the worst pollutants have fallen 96 per cent in a decade. Sulphur-dioxide emissions are down 56 per cent; nitrogen-dioxide emissions by 38 per cent.

Dolphins, tuna, shrimp and turtles

Fears about a 'race to the bottom' are misplaced, but g
that the environment has another enemy too: the W

its obsession with free trade prevents governments from taking measures to protect the environment.

Greens' antipathy for the WTO stems from a decision made by its predecessor, the GATT, in 1991. The US had banned Mexican tuna imports because Mexican fishermen used nets that killed dolphins. Mexico complained to the GATT that this trade ban was illegal. The GATT caused a public outcry by ruling against America. It seemed to many as if unaccountable bureaucrats were sacrificing dolphins on the altar of free trade. In fact, the GATT had no problem with America's aim of protecting dolphins. Its objection was to the use of discriminatory trade sanctions to achieve this, and it suggested the alternative of labelling dolphin-safe tuna as such.

The WTO added to environmentalists' anger in 1996 when it sided with Venezuela and Brazil after they complained that American cleaner-petrol standards discriminated against them. Greens fumed that the WTO was driving a coach and horses through America's Clean Air Act. Not at all. The US was demanding higher fuel standards of foreign petrol suppliers than it was of domestic ones. Had it required that all gasoline be equally clean, there wouldn't have been a problem.

Matters got worse in 1998 when the WTO ruled against America's ban on imports of shrimp from countries using nets that trap turtles, after complaints by India, Malaysia, Pakistan and Thailand. America's ban was incredibly unfair: it stopped all imports of Thai shrimp, for instance, even though most are farmed, not caught from the sea. Yet the WTO's appeal court showed that its rules can be interpreted to meet green concerns. It recognised America's right to protect sea turtles, so long as it did this by negotiating turtle-protection agreements, as it had done with countries in the Americas, rather than by imposing its rules unilaterally. And in 2000, the WTO proved that environmental concerns could trump free trade. It rejected a complaint from Canada that France's ban on white asbestos was an unfair trade restriction. Instead it upheld the French view that the ban was needed to protect 'le's health.

The WTO does not prevent governments from protecting the environment. Its rules, to which all its member governments have previously agreed, say that governments can take any measures necessary to protect human, animal or plant life or health, or to conserve natural resources, so long as they don't discriminate arbitrarily or unjustifiably against foreigners. They also say that countries should protect the environment in ways that do not discriminate because of the way something is produced. This is a valuable principle. The big gains from trade stem from taking advantage of countries' differing production methods; to ban such differences would create open season for all protectionists. The right way to deal with people's desire to eat turtle friendly shrimp or dolphin-friendly tuna is not to impose one country's values on another: it is to label the products appropriately. Consumers, not governments, can then choose what they eat – and trade can remain free.

There is one area where WTO law is unclear. Some international agreements to tackle cross-border and global environmental problems involve, or are enforced by, trade restrictions. Take the Montreal protocol, which aims to eliminate ozone-eating CFCs. It has been a resounding success. Since it was signed in 1987, CFC use has fallen by over 70 per cent. One reason for its success is that it requires parties to the agreement to ban CFC imports from non-signatories. Conceivably, a non-signatory could challenge the import ban at the WTO. Strictly speaking, WTO arbitration panels rule only on the basis of WTO law, so there could be a problem, although the WTO panel would also take into account other international treaties. In practice, this awkward situation has never arisen and is highly unlikely to do so: the problem is mostly hypothetical. Even so, it is worth clearing it up. WTO ministers agreed in Doha in November 2001 that the new round of world-trade talks launched there should clarify the situation.

The WTO is not the devil it is made out to be. It does not prevent governments from protecting the environment. Unfortunately, they cannot always get their act together to do so.

Global solutions

Some environmental problems call out for global solutions. One is overfishing. Another is global warming. Since the early 1800s, when people began burning lots of coal, the amount of carbon dioxide in the earth's atmosphere has risen by around a third and the average temperature around the world has risen by between 0.3 and 0.6°C. Carbon dioxide, as well as methane and nitrous oxide, is a 'greenhouse gas': it traps the sun's heat in the atmosphere just as a greenhouse does. Around half the world's greenhouse-gas emissions come from rich countries. The US is a particularly bad offender: it emits eight times more carbon dioxide per person than the typical developing country. But poor countries that are growing fast, notably China, are increasing their emissions rapidly. On current trends, scientists reckon that the world's average surface temperature could rise by between 1.4 and 5.8°C over the next hundred years.

In some parts of the world, this will do little harm, or even some good, but in others, it may cause all sorts of problems. It could play havoc with seasons and rainfall. It could cause more frequent and worse storms. It could cause sea levels to rise as the polar icecaps melt, flooding coastal areas. The Maldive islands and much of Bangladesh may disappear under the Indian Ocean. Plants and animals may have trouble adjusting to this rapid climate change. Humans in temperate climes may become exposed to nasty 'tropical' diseases like malaria. Although estimates of the costs of global warming vary, governments ought to take precautionary action now before it is too late.

The problem is that no government has an incentive to cut back on greenhouse-gas emissions independently. The benefits of doing so would be slight, since the rest of the world would continue pumping out carbon dioxide. But the costs might be large, since a country that imposes the hefty carbon tax needed to curb emissions would put its industries at a potentially crippling disadvantage. If the affected companies choose to move abroad, the country that imposes the carbon tax loses out, and greenhouse-gas emissions end up no lower than before. So there is a very strong case for governments to agree collectively to reduce their emissions. That is what the Kyoto protocol aims to do. But, as negotiating the protocol has shown, reaching an international deal is easier said than done. It raises all sorts of tricky questions. Should emissions be reduced through a carbon tax or by setting quantitative limits? How far and how fast should emissions be reduced? How should the cost of reducing emissions be shared out? Each government has an incentive to hitch a free ride on others' efforts. Developing countries argue, quite reasonably, that since they have not caused the problem, they should not have to pay for tackling it – even though if their emissions continue to rise they will offset the benefits of curbs in rich countries. The upshot is that any agreement is likely to be an unsatisfactory fudge, rather than one that a rational world government would devise. It is likely to be less ambitious and more costly to implement than the optimal solution. That is exactly what has happened. To make matters worse, the biggest emitter of greenhouse gases of all, the US, has refused to sign up to Kyoto, so the modest improvements that some countries make will be more than offset by America's misbehaviour.

Globalisation is only partly responsible for global warming, so putting a stop to trade would not reverse it. A carbon tax, or a cap on carbon-dioxide emissions combined with tradeable emissions permits, is the best way to tackle it. But trade sanctions may be necessary to enforce the Kyoto protocol. Indeed, there may be a strong case for slapping trade sanctions on the US if it refuses to listen to pressure from other countries to get its house in order. If the US feels it has a right to impose sanctions on countries that harm turtles or dolphins, the rest of the world would seem perfectly entitled to slap trade sanctions on a country that endangers the livelihood of millions of people. Don't hold your breath.

TEN

Patently Wrong

*How global patent laws harm the poor
and the sick*

It is wholly unacceptable from any perspective that millions
of people are dying and will die because trade is privileged
over their dignity as human beings and over their right to
healthcare.

JAMES ORBINSKI, Médecins Sans Frontières

Weakening intellectual property rights will . . . serve to reduce
the incentives for future research into the new medicines of
the future, including innovation for neglected issues.

Glaxo Wellcome annual report, 2000

If the . . . drugs companies . . . really mean business, they
should waive their patent rights and let developing
countries make the drugs themselves under their
supervision. Kenya already has the capacity to make most of
these drugs. It is the big five [pharmaceutical companies]
who are stopping us.

DR MOHAMMED ABDULLAH, Kenya Aids Control Council

Companies that make generic copies are like pirates on the
high seas. We don't believe in piracy. We tried to stamp it
out in the seventeenth and eighteenth centuries.
    RICHARD SYKES, non-executive chairman, GlaxoSmithKline[1]

Surely it is right that Germans should pay more for their
drugs than Greeks, and Americans more than Mexicans?
                ADRIAN TOWSE, Office of Health Economics

Nkosi Johnson achieved a lot in his brief life. Aged eleven, this
brave South African boy who was born HIV-positive made a speech
at the thirteenth International Aids Conference in Durban in July
2000 that shamed his president, his country and the world for
ignoring the plight of the nearly 5 million South Africans infected
with HIV. 'Care for us and accept us – we are all human beings, we
are normal, we have hands, we have feet, we can walk, we can talk,
we have needs just like everyone else. Don't be afraid of us – we are
all the same.' Eleven months later, Nkosi was dead.

The tragedy is that Nkosi need not have died so young. Had the
South African government provided his late mother with anti-Aids
drugs when she was pregnant, he might never have been infected.
Had it provided him with anti-Aids drugs, he might have lived to be
an adult. Had he been born rich, he would have been able to afford
those drugs. Had he been born in a rich country, he would have
received them free of charge.

Nearly 3 million people in poor countries die each year from
Aids-related illnesses.[2] Aids is the fourth-biggest killer worldwide.
In the worst-hit countries, like Botswana, average life-expectancy
will soon be seventeen years shorter that it would otherwise have
been. More than 13 million children have lost a parent or are
orphaned because of the disease. Nearly 40 million people in poor
countries are infected with HIV – nearly 3 million of them children
under fifteen. Five million were infected in 2001 alone – nearly
14,000 a day. The cocktail of patented drugs needed to keep each
of them alive and well can cost up to $15,000 a year –

twenty-four times the average annual income in Zimbabwe, where one in four adults is HIV-positive. Even in comparatively rich South Africa, where the average income is $3,000 a year, only a handful of rich people can afford such high prices.

Yet the cost of producing these life-saving drugs is a fraction of what pharmaceutical companies charge for them. Cipla, an Indian company, has offered to supply generic copies of patented anti-Aids drugs for less than a dollar a day: $350 a year. At that price, many more developing countries could afford them – and rich-country donors would be able to help many more of the poor people who still couldn't.

The catch is that overriding the drug companies' patents may be illegal under the World Trade Organisation's intellectual-property pact, known as the TRIPS (trade-related aspects of intellectual-property rights) agreement. Countries that violate the TRIPS agreement can be hauled before a WTO dispute-settlement panel and, if found guilty, hit with trade sanctions by a country whose companies' patents are not being upheld.

Critics of globalisation are right to attack the TRIPS agreement. In a world that is anything but uniform, enforcing uniform standards everywhere is generally wrong – in the case of drug patents, lethally so. Nor should the WTO, whose job is freeing trade, be restricting trade in generic drugs.

The US, home to pharmaceutical giants such as Merck, Pfizer and Eli Lilly, also has its own procedure, known as Special 301, for cracking down on countries it feels are violating US companies' patents. It has bludgeoned several countries into adopting patent laws before the TRIPS agreement required it. Equally perniciously, America has inserted even tougher patent-protection requirements into its bilateral and regional trade deals, like the one with Jordan that came into force in 2001 and another with the African countries grouped in the Common Market for Eastern and Southern Africa (COMESA). It aims to do so in the mooted Free-Trade Area of the Americas (FTAA) too.

Drug companies' defence – apart from their obvious desire to earn fatter profits – is that without the temporary monopoly that a patent provides they would never be able to recoup the huge cost of developing new drugs. Undermine our patents, they say, and we simply won't bother pouring money into new drugs. No patents, no new anti-Aids drugs – it's as simple as that.

Actually, it isn't. Hardly anyone in poor countries can afford anti-Aids drugs at $10,000 a year, so pharmaceutical companies earn hardly any of their profits on these drugs from poor countries. Yet they are still spending plenty of money on research. Clearly, the profits they earn in rich countries must be more than enough to compensate them for the millions they risk on research. (The cost of developing a new drug seems to rise each time the companies are challenged: first $300 million, then $500 million, now $1 billion, who knows how much by the time this book is on the shelves?) By breaking international patent law, poor countries are not in danger of killing the goose that lays the golden eggs.

To be fair, the drug giants have other lines of defence. First, they point to principle: they claim they own the sole right to sell the drugs they have developed; generic drugs makers who usurp their rights are 'pirates' who are 'stealing' their ideas. Second, they point to the law that entrenches that principle. The WTO's TRIPS agreement extends to developing countries twenty-year patent protection similar to that which their drugs enjoy in rich countries. Third, they fret for their future profits. Once developing countries get richer, they will be able to afford to buy more patented drugs. Conceding the market now to generic producers (such as Cipla) could make it tough to grab it back later. Fourth, they fear for their profits in rich countries. If knock-offs of their patented drugs are on sale in developing countries at a fraction of the price, it may be tough to stop rich Westerners heading south to shop for their pricey drugs. Moreover, if Westerners decide that drugs companies are fleecing them, they may put pressure on their governments to cap drug prices in rich countries too. Squeeze drug-company profits too far, and society may indeed kill the golden goose.

Yet the drug companies protest too much. Patents are an evil that society deems necessary, not a God-given right. They try to strike a balance between two important aims: the need to encourage invention and the desire to spread the benefits of inventions as widely as possible. Ideas are not like other goods: one person's use of them does not diminish other people's ability to use them; nor indeed is it easy to prevent them spreading. Whereas a piece of meat can satisfy only one of us, a piece by Mozart can satisfy all of us (except the deaf). So society is better off if everyone can listen to Mozart. But how should an inventor be rewarded for improving people's lives?

Sometimes, invention is its own reward. People who stare at the stars, fiddle about in their garage or pen poetry in bed are not typically motivated by money. When Alexander Fleming chanced upon penicillin, he was not dreaming of making millions by patenting it. Jonas Salk refused to patent the polio vaccine, because he said it would be 'like patenting the sun'. But research and development is increasingly expensive – and somebody has to foot the bill. It could be governments, pursuing the public good, as America's National Science Foundation does. It could be private benefactors, like the foundation that Bill and Melinda Gates have set up. But it is usually profit-seeking companies, who require a return on their investment. Even so, it is important to remember that there are other options: that research could be paid for in other ways.

Companies could earn a return from their research in several ways. Governments or others could offer prizes for developing useful new drugs. This could be a fixed sum, a multiple of their research costs, or an amount determined at auction. In 1839 the French government bought the patent for the daguerreotype process, an early form of photography, and made it freely available. Such schemes have a big plus: drugs could then be sold at their marginal production price and so benefit many more people.

Even if patents are granted in the traditional way, giving a company a temporary monopoly and hence the power to charge high prices, there are still ways of ensuring that poor people get access to drugs. Governments could step in and pay for them, as they do in rich countries. In poor countries where governments cannot afford to foot the bill, drug companies could charge much less than they do in rich countries. In fact, they could maximise their profits by doing so if they could ensure that drugs sold in poor countries could not be bought by people in rich ones and that the low prices they charged in poor countries did not affect rich countries' willingness to pay more. After all, making some profits in poor countries by selling their drugs cheaply – albeit still above their tiny marginal production cost – is better than making hardly any profit there as they do now. But – and it's a big but – pharmaceutical companies could do even better if they could persuade rich-country governments or charities to pay inflated prices for drugs for the poor. That, in essence, is what the big game is about. As well as safeguarding their profits in rich countries, the drug giants are trying to screw the best terms possible out of rich-country donors for providing poor people with anti-Aids drugs. The TRIPS agreement is their weapon of choice, since it makes it harder for generic drug producers to compete, but they also rely on lobbying and bullying.

The drug giants are in a position of strength, but they are under attack on several fronts. In February 2001, Oxfam, a British charity, launched an international campaign to 'Cut the Cost' of patented drugs in poor countries. In the US, a coalition known as HealthGAP (Health Global Access Project) is also on the offensive. Médecins Sans Frontières (MSF), Act Up-Paris, the Treatment Action Campaign (TAC) in South Africa, the Malaysia-based Third World Network and Brazil's Grupo de Incentivo a Vida (GIV), among others, are also involved. They have already notched up a number of victories, but the war is far from won.

The TRIPS agreement gives poor-country governments some scope to override patents in the interests of public health. But the big drugs companies and the US government have used heavy-handed intimidation whenever governments have tried to make use of this flexibility. Their aim is 'TRIPS plus': eliminating governments' get-out clauses. Since they stand little chance of convincing poor WTO members to agree to tighten the TRIPS agreement, they use strong-arm tactics instead.

In March 2001, thirty-nine pharmaceutical companies sued the South African government over a law passed in 1997 that they claimed allowed the government too much latitude to ignore patents and purchase cut-price generic drugs. After the case was adjourned for a month until April, the drug companies backed down and called it off. Oxfam and its allies had used the global media to devastating effect. The drugs companies feared they might become pariahs, like tobacco companies. The damage to their reputations and share prices from going after the government, it seems, outweighed the costs of the law. It was a Brent Spar-like moment, except that, unlike Shell, the drugs companies were genuinely in the wrong.

In June 2001, the US withdrew a complaint to the WTO, made only in January, about Brazil's patent law. At issue was a clause that lets Brazil break a patent if the owner fails to make the product there. The Brazilian government had waged a highly effective international campaign against the US and its drugs companies at the World Health Organisation (WHO) and the UN Human Rights Commission, as well as in the media. 'World opinion is on our side,' said Jose Serra, Brazil's health minister. He said the case threatened the country's highly successful anti-Aids programme, which had cut deaths by a third in three years by offering patients a free cocktail of drugs. The anti-American blitz was also a reaction against the US's ingratitude in quibbling over a clause in Brazil's patent law that the government had never threatened to use. The country's patent law itself had been introduced only in 1997, eight years earlier than the WTO required, as a result of American pressure.

As the drugs giants have retreated from their bully-boy tactics, drug prices have come tumbling down. Generic companies now pose a more effective competitive threat. In part, these price cuts are PR stunts: many companies have made eye-catching offers, but with all sorts of strings attached. But some have also made more meaningful reductions. Phil Bloomer of Oxfam says that in October 2000 the lowest price the drugs giants were offering for a year's supply of triple-combination therapy, a cocktail of anti-Aids drugs, was $10,800. When India's Cipla offered the generic equivalent for $800, the patent-holders slashed their lowest price to $931. Then Cipla cut its price to $350 in February 2001 and the lowest patent price fell to $712 in March. In August, Rambaxi, another Indian company, trumped Cipla's offer with an even lower price of $295.

The campaigners' biggest success came at the WTO's ministerial meeting – the first since Seattle – in Doha in November 2001. The assembled governments issued a joint declaration that appeared to offer poor countries greater scope to override drug patents in the interests of public health. The US was keen to launch a new push for freer trade, ostensibly as part of the fight against terrorism. 'Trade is about more than economic efficiency,' Robert Zoellick, US trade supremo, had declared. 'It promotes the values at the heart of this protracted struggle.' Brazil, India and African countries exacted a price for their consent. The declaration said that the TRIPS agreement 'does not and should not' prevent governments from taking measures to protect public health.

The key issue is how much scope a government has to bypass a patent by issuing a 'compulsory licence' that allows another company to produce a patented drug. The easier it is for a government to use this get-out clause, the more pressure there is on patent-holders to cut their prices to fend off potential competition from generic drug makers. The TRIPS agreement gives a government the right to issue a compulsory licence if a patent-holder won't offer the drug on reasonable commercial terms (so long as the government pays compensation), if it behaves anti-competitively, or in a national emergency. After just three people had died of anthrax in the aftermath of September 11th, the US government threatened to override Bayer's patent on Cipro, an antibiotic, in order to screw

better terms out of the German company. Yet the US has stead-
fastly opposed poor countries, where nearly 3 million people a year
die of Aids-related illnesses, invoking a national emergency to get a
better deal on anti-Aids drugs patented by US companies. It is worse
than hypocritical. It is sick.

The Doha declaration reaffirmed countries' right to make use of
the flexibility in the TRIPS agreement to improve poor people's
access to drugs. It confirmed governments' right to issue compulsory licences. Importantly, it explicitly defined a national
emergency, saying that: 'public-health crises, including those relating to HIV/Aids, tuberculosis, malaria and other epidemics, can
represent a national emergency'. The declaration also confirmed
countries' right to import patented drugs from countries where
they are being sold more cheaply, and it extended from 2006 to
2016 the deadline for the world's forty-nine poorest countries to
start enforcing drug patents. Developing countries have generally
had to tighten their patent laws in line with the TRIPS agreement
since 2000, but the fifty or so countries that did not provide any
patent protection for pharmaceuticals when the TRIPS agreement
came into force in 1995 have until 2005 to do so.

Don't rejoice too soon. As always with legal texts, the devil is in
the detail. Stating that the TRIPS agreement 'does not and should
not' prevent governments from taking measures to protect public
health is open to legal interpretation. Oxfam was looking for the
words 'must not and will not'. Already, the Americans are arguing
that they 'fended off' attacks on the TRIPS agreement in Doha.
MSF, Oxfam and TAC are trying to test how much flexibility countries actually have by importing generic triple-combination therapy
drugs from Brazil to South Africa. Another thorny issue that needs
resolving is how to make it easier for countries that do not produce
their own generic drugs to import them, since governments are
only allowed to issue compulsory licences to supply predominantly
for the domestic market, rather than for export.

So long as rich countries choose to fund pharmaceutical
research through the monopoly profits that patents bring, drug

companies must be allowed to earn profits somewhere. If not, new life-saving drugs will not be developed. It is surely right that they should earn their profits overwhelmingly in rich countries rather than poor ones. But some US politicians think it is 'unfair' for Mexicans or South Africans to pay less for drugs than Americans do. No, it isn't. If poor American pensioners are struggling with their prescriptions bills, the government of the richest country on earth can step in to foot the bill. If millions of South Africans face death because they can't afford anti-Aids drugs, their government cannot help. It is essential for the health of people in poor countries that patented drugs be sold cheaply there. It is equally essential for the health of people in rich countries that patented drugs be sold at higher prices here.

The bigger picture

Cheaper patented drugs are only part of the solution to poor countries' healthcare problems. For a start, even at a dollar a day, anti-Aids drugs are unaffordably expensive for the world's poorest countries, where many people have to meet all their needs on less than that. Those countries need foreign aid to buy these life-saving drugs. Moreover, most of the essential drugs that poor countries need for basic healthcare are no longer under patent protection. The problem there is a lack of cash, not patents. The same is true for more practical, preventative measures that are also needed: insecticides and anti-malaria bednets, clean water, good sanitation, healthy food, more condom use.

Yet the patent system is failing in a different way too. It does not provide sufficient incentives to develop treatments for many of the diseases that affect only poor countries. The WHO reckons that only 10 per cent of medical research worldwide targets diseases that afflict the poorest 90 per cent of the world's population. Of the 1,223 new drugs launched between 1975 and 1997, only thirteen were aimed at tropical diseases. The only reason pharmaceutical companies develop anti-Aids drugs is that there is a market for them in rich countries. But whereas developing a rival to Viagra is lucrative, looking for new drugs to combat bilharzia, a nasty worm that makes life a misery for 200 million people – almost all of them poor – is not. Very little money goes on research into a malaria – or even an Aids – vaccine either. Of the $70 billion spent in 1998 on health research, $3 billion went towards research into Aids treatment drugs; $300 million on looking for an Aids vaccine. Vaccines are cheaper and easier to administer than pallia-tive drugs, but much less profitable.

Rich countries urgently need to stump up more money both to encourage research and to guarantee a market for any drugs that are developed. The US government gives incentives for research into 'orphan drugs' to treat diseases that affect fewer than 200,000 Americans and so are not a viable market. These have led to the development of over twenty new drugs since 1983. Rich countries could do the same for tropical diseases that affect millions of poor people. Donors should also promise to buy a future malaria or Aids vaccine at a reasonable price per dose, as Jeffrey Sachs of Harvard University has proposed. As he argues, a purchase fund into which donors could contribute should be set up for this purpose.

More foreign aid is being raised to fight Aids and other diseases that afflict poor countries. The global fund to fight Aids, tubercu-losis and malaria that was finally launched in January 2002 offers some hope. Eight months earlier, Kofi Annan, the UN secretary-gen-eral, had called for the creation of a special fund to tackle those diseases, which kill 6 million people a year. But although he says the fund needs $7 billion to $10 billion a year, only $1.9 billion had been pledged by the end of January 2002. Clearly, safeguards are needed so that the money is well spent. But rich countries' stingi-ness is scandalous. Spending $10 billion a year to save millions of poor people's – and some rich tourists' – lives would cost each of the 900 million people in rich (OECD) countries just $11 a year.

In December 2001, the Commission on Macroeconomics and Health came up with an even better proposal. Set up by the WHO and headed by Jeffrey Sachs, its mandate was to come up with a plan to improve the healthcare of 2.5 billion poor people who currently do without. It says 8 million lives a year could be saved if rich countries spent another $27 billion a year on aid by 2007. That sounds huge – and it is half the $54 billion currently doled out in aid – but it still amounts to only 0.1 per cent of rich-country GDP. Most governments pay lip service to giving 0.7 per cent of GDP in aid, but few live up to their high-flown rhetoric about helping the poor. America gives a miserly 0.1 per cent of GDP. Even $27 billion a year would cost people in rich countries only $30 a year each. Importantly, the scheme also requires poor countries to spend more: $35 billion a year, or an additional 1 per cent of their GDP. This is not unreasonable: poor countries typically spend too little on health and too much on arms and presidential pomp. The economic benefit of this extra foreign and local spending would be worth $186 billion a year, the Commission reckons, three times its cost. Poverty not only causes ill health; ill health exacerbates poverty too.

A trip too far

Forcing up the price of essential medicines is just one of the TRIPS agreement's many unfortunate consequences. It raises the price of all know-how and technology in poor countries: patented rice that poor farmers plant, copyrighted textbooks that poor students learn from, patented software that poor businessmen use. This is not only a massive snatch-and-grab raid on consumers in poor countries by companies in rich ones. It is an impediment to development, because it makes it harder for companies in poor countries to copy the products and processes of those in advanced ones. In an increasingly knowledge-based economy, where ideas are crucial to business success, this is a hammer blow. In 2000; the US alone earned $38 billion in royalties and licence fees from abroad – over half the global total – of which $3 billion came from

Latin America and $4.8 billion from non-Japan Asia, Africa and New Zealand.[3] Nor do upgrading intellectual-property laws and their enforcement come cheap: Mexico spent over $30 million implementing the TRIPS agreement's requirements, even though it already had a much more developed patent system than most of the poorest countries.

More fundamentally, in a world that is anything but uniform, enforcing uniform intellectual-property standards is inappropriate. The point of patents, remember, is to strike a balance between encouraging innovation and spreading the benefits of innovation. Whereas rich countries do lots of domestic research, poor countries do hardly any: nine in ten patents are owned by rich-country companies. So patent protection should be much lower in poor countries than in rich ones.

It is also a matter of local democracy: countries should be able to set their own standards that match local tastes and conditions. As they get richer and do more of their own research, they will doubtless want to toughen their patent laws. Equally, if they feel that weak patent protection deters foreign investment or technology licensing, they may want to upgrade it. But while they are still poor, they should not have tougher laws imposed on them. For most of the nineteenth century, when Switzerland was poor, it had no patent system at all. Now that it is home to some of the world's top drug companies, like Novartis and Roche, it has stringent patent laws.

Look at it another way. The WTO is all about freeing trade. The TRIPS agreement is about restricting it. Tearing down trade barriers exposes companies to greater competition – and so means lower prices for consumers everywhere, not least poor countries. Enforcing global intellectual-property standards reduces competition in poor countries – and so raises prices for those who can least afford to pay. For that reason, not only should the TRIPS agreement not be at the WTO, it should not exist at all.

What is true for intellectual-property standards is generally true for labour and environmental standards too. Setting a uniform minimum everywhere is a bad idea when countries are so different. The balance between the costs and benefits of standards is different in rich and poor countries. When you are dirt-poor, you are better off taking a cheap, heavily polluting bus to work than going on foot. When you are rich, you can afford to pay more for a more eco-friendly car. When you are a poor farmer, your children may need to help out in the fields in order to put food on the table. When you are a rich banker, you can afford to support your children through university. Imposing on poor countries the environmental and social standards that apply in rich ones would force poor people to go on foot or starve. As countries get richer, people expect and can afford higher standards. But while they are still poor, they should not have higher standards that would make them worse off imposed on them. If people in rich countries find social standards in poor countries offensively low, they should put their money where their mouth is and send them aid.

The main exception to this general rule is for environmental problems that cut across national borders, like global warming. In such cases, governments tend to neglect the costs of environmental damage outside their borders when setting domestic regulations. A good example is fishing: individual countries may fail to limit overfishing even though all end up suffering as a result. Even if some countries did impose limits, they might not reap any benefits if others continue to overfish, so there is a strong case for an international agreement, as was discussed in chapter nine.

Critics are right to point out that it is inconsistent for the WTO to enforce minimum intellectual-property standards, but not minimum labour and environmental standards. After all, they all involve outlawing products made in ways some people disapprove of – whether it is CDs copyrighted by others, footballs made by children, or shrimp caught in ways that harm endangered sea-turtles. Yet typically the critics are themselves inconsistent in the debate over global standards. Whereas right-wingers in rich countries support uniform patent protection but oppose global social and environmental standards, left-wingers favour the reverse. In part, this is because global patent standards help rich-country companies, whereas global social and environmental standards protect workers in rich countries by raising the costs of their competitors in poor ones. People in poor countries on both sides of the political divide are generally opposed to any form of global standard that harms them.

Guido Mantega is a left-wing economics professor who advises Luiz Inacio Lula da Silva, the Workers' Party's candidate in Brazil's October 2002 presidential election. I asked him what he thought of rich-country pressure for global labour and environmental standards enforceable by trade sanctions. 'It's an opportunistic game,' he replied. 'Of course costs are lower here: we are poorer. We can't accept rich-country standards. It's a pretext to impose more restrictions. We want to improve working conditions, but we will always be cheaper than the US. Our intention is to raise wages, but within the measure of what's possible.' Ironically, if some countries were to slap trade sanctions on those that have weak labour standards, America might be among the first victims, since its workers have far fewer rights than those in Europe – or even those in many developing countries.

There is still time to prevent the rich world imposing its labour and environmental standards on the poor. But unfortunately, the TRIPS agreement looks set to stay. Probably the best we can hope for is reform, not abolition. One option is to take the teeth out of the agreement: remove the option of enforcing it with trade sanctions. Restricting trade to enforce trade restrictions is a double violation of the WTO's *raison d'être*. Another is to press for greater flexibility for poor countries to decide when, and in what sectors, they want to use patent protection. For instance, India might want to enforce patents in software, to encourage companies like Wipro, but not in pharmaceuticals, to help Cipla.

Equally importantly, developing countries should resist pressure from the US and the EU to insert tougher patent-protection requirements into their bilateral and regional deals. As we saw in chapter seven, such regional deals are generally a bad thing in any case;

these requirements only make them worse. And they should not give in to arm-twisting to enact unilaterally tighter domestic laws than the TRIPS agreement requires, or in the case of the poorest countries, sooner than it requires.

Developing countries are also pressing for protection in rich countries for geographical indicators like basmati rice. Currently, the TRIPS agreement grants this kind of protection only to wines and spirits like champagne and Scotch whisky. Many countries, notably Brazil, want it also to protect indigenous plants and medicines from Western 'bioprospectors' who scour the developing world for potentially useful crops and drugs and then patent them in the US. They want those patenting, say, a type of plant to have to declare where they got it, prove they have the consent of its native users and agree to share any profits they make from it with them. The US, unsurprisingly, is bitterly opposed.

Such reforms are, to be sure, a tall order. But thankfully, Oxfam and others are campaigning along these lines. They deserve our whole-hearted support.

ELEVEN

Financial Failings

Why global money should be caged

I sympathise, therefore, with those who would minimise rather than with those who would maximise economic entanglement between nations. Ideas, knowledge, art, hospitality, travel – these are the things which should of their nature be international. But let goods be home-spun whenever it is reasonably and conveniently possible, and above all, let finance be national.

JOHN MAYNARD KEYNES[1]

Financial markets are supposed to swing like a pendulum: they may fluctuate wildly in response to exogenous shocks, but eventually they are supposed to come to rest at an equilibrium point that is supposed to reflect the fundamentals. Instead financial markets behaved more like a wrecking ball, swinging from country to country, knocking over the weakest and transforming the fundamentals.

GEORGE SOROS, *Open Society*

Small and open economies are inherently vulnerable to the
volatility of global capital markets. The visual image of a
vast sea of liquid capital strikes me as apt – the big and
inevitable storms through which a great liner like the USA
can safely sail will surely capsize even the sturdiest South
Pacific canoes.

PAUL VOLCKER, former chairman of the US Federal Reserve

For a few weeks in October 1998, the world economy seemed on the
brink of meltdown. The financial maelstrom that started in
Thailand in July 1997 had dragged down much of Asia, engulfed
Russia, sent stockmarkets everywhere tumbling and sunk LTCM, an
American speculative fund whose huge debts threatened to bring
down the international financial system with it. The US Federal
Reserve bailed out LTCM and made emergency cuts in American
interest rates to try to calm panicky investors' nerves. The world
waited anxiously to see if the medicine would work. The fear everywhere was of recession, depression, slump. But fortunately the
storm abated. Europe and North America emerged shaken, but relatively unscathed. Soon it was back to business as usual. Grand
talk about rebuilding the world's financial architecture proved to
be hot air. All the blueprints for reform gathered dust. Investors
found new games, like punting on glorified get-rich-quick pyra-
mid schemes known as Internet start-ups.

How quickly we forget. Or was it all a dream? Perhaps, as Jean
Baudrillard, a French thinker, suggests: 'the realm of mobile and
speculative capital has achieved so great an autonomy that even its
cataclysms leave no traces.'[2] Tell that to Thailand's tens of thousands of small businessmen whose savings turned to dust. Tell that
to the more than 1 million South Koreans who lost their jobs in
1998. Tell that to the 220 million Indonesians who have seen their
country racked by riots and fighting. American multi-millionaires
like LTCM's John Meriwether were bailed out. Ordinary Americans
and Europeans were saved by interest-rate cuts. People in poor
countries bore the brunt of the financial storm.

Game, set and match to the anti-globalisers? Not at all. Critics of globalisation tend to use the flaws of free capital flows – and the misguided policies of the IMF – to tar free trade by association. But the case for free trade in goods and services is separate to that for free trade in money. Goods markets are not inherently unstable: unlike foreign borrowing, buying foreign cars does not run the risk of wreaking havoc with the economy. Whereas the evidence that free capital flows boost developing countries' economies is paltry or non-existent, the evidence that free trade makes poor countries richer is overwhelming. Globalisation is not an all-or-nothing choice. All the benefits of free trade can be had without the costs of free capital flows, but the danger is that unless we fix international finance, countries will eventually throw the free-trade baby out with the free-capital bathwater.

Financial fundamentals

Financial markets are unlike other markets. They are inherently unstable. They are prone to *Manias, Panics, and Crashes*, the title of a classic history of financial crises by Charles Kindleberger. Why? Because they involve bets on an unknown and unknowable future. Who knows what a share in Shell's future profits is worth? Who knows what price to put on a promise of interest payments from the Russian government? Who knows how many euros a dollar should buy? It depends. It depends on a whole set of assumptions and guesses, not only about what a financial asset might actually be worth, but also on what you think other people think it might be worth, as well as on what they think you think they think it might be worth, and so on. Since everyone is making guesses about what other people are guessing, financial investors tend to move in herds. If many people think share prices are on the up, others follow to profit from the rise; if some start to doubt the story, others rush to sell before prices tumble.

This inherent instability is exacerbated by government

regulations that encourage banks to gamble. Big banks know that the central bank is likely to bail them out if they get into trouble, because letting them go bust would bring down other banks and companies with them, thus endangering the country's financial system and its economy. That gives banks a big incentive to lend recklessly. If they win big, they make hefty profits; if they lose big, taxpayers are likely to pick up the tab. The US savings and loan (S&L) scandal, for instance, cost American taxpayers hundreds of billions of dollars.

The bets that people make about the future can actually influence the future they are making guesses about. If investors decide that Internet shares are a sure-fire winner and pour money into them to profit from their rosy prospects, Internet share prices will rocket. If investors then change their minds and pull their money out, prices slump. If banks decide that London house prices are on the up and so are willing to lend larger sums to people who want to buy their own place, more money is available to spend on housing and this bids up house prices. But if banks get cold feet and decide to pare back their loans, prices fall back. If speculators decide that the dollar can only strengthen against the euro and so sell euros for dollars, it becomes a self-fulfilling prophecy. If eventually their ardour for the greenback cools and they cash in their US currency for European money, the dollar weakens. And so on.

If it were all just a game played by gamblers in London, New York and Tokyo, it would scarcely matter. To quote John Maynard Keynes, it would simply be 'a game of snap, of Old Maid, of Musical Chairs – a pastime in which he is victor who says Snap neither too soon nor too late, who passes the Old Maid to his neighbour before the game is over, who secures a chair for himself when the music stops. These games can be played with zest and enjoyment, though all the players know that it is the Old Maid which is circulating, or that when the music stops some of the players will find themselves unseated.'[3] But the financial game has real consequences for people's jobs and savings, companies' prospects and the economy as a whole.

One day, investors may think an investment looks attractive. The next, they may change their minds. Such financial mood swings can devastate an economy because people and companies cannot adjust as quickly as the electronic flickers on traders' screens. When Internet shares are perceived to be hot, people divert money that could have been better used elsewhere – investing in oil companies, say, building new roads or paying off credit-card bills – into investments that turn out to be duds. This is a vast waste of economic resources. If everyone in the economy is placing similarly over-optimistic bets on Internet share prices continuing to rise and borrowing furiously to do so, an almighty boom is likely to turn into an almighty bust when people find their debts are much greater than their depreciated assets. People lose their jobs, their retirement savings and their houses. The same applies to London house prices, as borrowers who over-extended themselves in the go-go years at the end of the 1980s know all too well. Not only did they suffer personally, but the economy as a whole took several years to shake off the burden of all the extra debt. As for the bubbly dollar, it lures money into America that could have been invested more productively elsewhere; it drives countries like Argentina, which hitched their fortunes to the US currency and could not live with the consequences, into recession; and it hurts American companies like Bethlehem Steel that might otherwise be more competitive. In Europe, the languishing euro raises the cost of imports – and perhaps inflation in general – and undermines confidence in the euro economy.

The costs of financial markets' mishaps are huge. The worst recessions in history – including the Great Depression in the 1930s, Japan's decade-long stagnation and East Asia's collapse in 1997–8 – have all followed financial crises. That is why financial markets have often been kept caged, both within countries and globally. Yet they can bring huge benefits too. For a start, they funnel savers' money to companies that need to invest and to borrowers who want to live temporarily beyond their means. Older people's savings finance young people's house-buying; the interest young people pay provides for the old's retirement. Rich people's nest eggs fund the growth of companies that give jobs to poorer people. In essence, financial markets link the present and the future: they allow savers to convert their current income into future spending; and vice versa for borrowers. They also make it possible to finance bigger investments than any individual ever could. A family-run firm that relied entirely on its owner's savings would not be able to make big investments. Today's big companies need to raise finance from millions of individual savers. And financial markets create 'liquidity': whereas the owner of a factory cannot easily get his investment out, someone who has bought shares in a traded company can simply sell them if they need their money back. Moreover, they allow investors to diversify and thus reduce their total risk. Rather than putting all their eggs in one basket, they can spread them among several. They also transfer, share and pool risks. People can insure against the risks of interest rates going up by taking out a fixed-rate mortgage; companies can hedge against the risk of an adverse currency movement by buying a futures contract that fixes the future rate at which currencies are exchanged. When they work well, financial markets channel savings to their most productive uses. Everyone is better off: savers earn higher returns on their money; companies reap the benefits of profitable investments; the economy grows faster. For all these reasons, studies show that countries with bigger banking systems and capital markets tend to enjoy faster economic growth.

The potential benefits of global financial markets are an extension of those of domestic ones. They allow a country as a whole to borrow another's savings to invest or live temporarily beyond its means. Take Japan, which has a rapidly ageing population and a sluggish economy. Its national savings exceed its investment needs. Japanese investors can earn a higher return by investing those savings abroad, in a country where there are plenty of profitable investment opportunities but few savings to finance them. Developing countries are typically in that situation. Like young people, they have few savings but many investment needs. If poor countries had to rely on their own savings, they could invest less in education, roads or factories, and so their economies would grow more slowly. Another plus is that a country that suffers a temporary recession or natural disaster can borrow abroad to cushion the blow. Individual investors benefit not only from higher returns but also from diversifying their risks. Their pensions, for instance, need not depend solely on the performance of local markets. Moreover, when global financial markets work well, they allocate capital to its most productive uses, thus boosting economic growth.

 Unfortunately, these benefits are usually not as big as one might hope. Although Portugal borrowed over 16 per cent of its annual income in 1981 to modernise its economy, it is exceptional. Countries are rarely able to borrow more than around 5 per cent of their national income before alarm bells start ringing and international investors become wary of lending more. So total investment in developing countries, typically just over 20 per cent of national income, may not get such a big boost from foreign funds.

Some forms of foreign capital are certainly good. Foreign direct investment (FDI) – long-term investment in factories, machinery, offices and so on – is generally a boon. For a start, the investment is tied down; it cannot flee at the click of a mouse. Moreover, unlike foreign debt, FDI does not need to be serviced: so if the investment turns sour, a country will not be left with crippling interest payments it cannot afford. If the investment turns out to be raging success, the country does not do as well as it would have done had it borrowed, because the profits go abroad. Even so, countries still benefit from FDI, because, as we saw in chapter two, foreign companies typically pay higher wages than local ones, and bring with them much-needed technology.

Other forms of foreign capital can be a mixed blessing. Short-term borrowing from foreign banks has caused many a developing country to come a cropper. In 1982, Latin American governments teetered on the edge of default. They had borrowed too much from Western banks that had previously been only too willing to lend, but suddenly refused to continue extending the term of their loans. Countries such as Mexico and Brazil suffered a lost decade of stagnant growth and falling wages as a result. It is not unlike credit-card companies that send you countless offers to borrow at cheap rates. If you take them up on their offers and borrow too much – or if they simply decide that they no longer want to lend you as much – you are in trouble. It can take years to work off your debts – and the banks that once beat a path to your door will now slam theirs shut in your face. Certainly, Latin American governments were partly responsible for this lost decade: they borrowed recklessly and wasted the money. But it takes two to tango – foreign banks were to blame too. As late as July 1982, a month before Mexican government officials travelled to Washington to tell their American counterparts that the country could not honour its debts, the yield on Mexican bonds was lower than on those of presumably safe borrowers like the World Bank, indicating that investors thought the risk that Mexico would not pay on time was negligible.[4]

The Latin American debt crisis was not an isolated event. Financial crises happen time and time again. Although circumstances differ, the evidence that the root of the problem lies in financial markets themselves is overwhelming.

Mexico hit the buffers again in 1994. This time, though, the government was hardly being profligate: it was running a budget surplus and building up reserves of foreign currency rather than borrowing from foreign banks. In fact, nearly everyone – journalists, businessmen, politicians – had swooned over Mexico's 'miracle'. It seemed to have broken free of the bonds of the lost decade, become a paradise for business and had hitched itself to its once-distant neighbour, the US, through NAFTA. Reassured by the Mexican peso's peg to the US dollar, investors poured vast sums into the economy: a whopping $30 billion net of outflows in 1994, or 7 per cent of its national income. And why not? If Mexico was indeed experiencing an economic miracle, all the better that foreign money was propelling it further ahead. Yet by December – at the end of a year that kicked off with the Zapatista uprising in Chiapas, was punctured by the assassination of the presidential front-runner in March and witnessed growing doubts about the sustainability of the Mexican 'miracle' – the country was forced to devalue the peso as investors took fright. Lenders jacked up the interest rates the Mexican government had to pay on its short-term debt. Worse still, because a lot of the debt was in dollars, it was even more costly to meet the repayments in devalued pesos. Mexico's economy shrank by 6 per cent in 1995 and wages plunged. But foreign borrowers were bailed out: the US government and the IMF stumped up dollars to make sure Mexico could pay its debts.

As Mexico suffered the hangover from its Tequila crisis, foreign capital sought out investment opportunities in other 'emerging markets', as the Third World had now been rechristened. It added to the money that was already pouring into Thailand and other East Asian countries that had boomed in recent decades as they exported their way to success. Foreign banks fell over themselves to dole out cash to Thai banks, who lent the money on, mainly to local finance houses. The Thais were only too happy to accept, since these foreign-currency loans were much cheaper than borrowing at local interest rates. They then made ever-bigger loans to Thai investors who poured the money first into property and then into shares. Soon, Thailand was awash in credit. The economy boomed. Crucially, because the Thai baht was linked to the US dollar, the Thai authorities could do little to prevent this financial bubble: as we saw in chapter six, countries that fix their exchange rate lose control of their money supply. The booming economy drove up wages, making exports more expensive and thus stunting their growth. Free-spending consumers splurged on imports. Thailand developed a yawning trade deficit. But no matter: foreign cash continued to pour in to finance it. If foreigners' optimism about the Thai economy's prospects was justified and the money they were shovelling in was being wisely invested, fine. But investors started to fret that, as in Mexico in 1994, they had become too bullish, and that once sentiment about Thailand swung, there would be a stampede for the door. Even so, they were reassured that they would get their money back by the fact that the finance houses they had lent to often had close links to the government. So there was a good chance that if everything went belly up, Thai taxpayers would pick up the tab. There was also the hope that if things turned really nasty, the IMF would bail them out. It looked like a risk-free bet, and this encouraged foreigners to keep the money flowing.

In 1996 and early 1997, the game started to turn against Thailand. Partly, this was because the country's economic prospects dimmed: a weaker Japanese yen made its exports, which were already suffering from weaker demand in some of their markets, less competitive. But mostly, it was because the financial house of cards was starting to fall down. As Paul Krugman put it: 'it was simply a matter of the house beating the gamblers, which in the long run it always does'.[5] As some of the loans turned bad, some of the Thai finance houses and speculators who had fed off them went bust. Foreign lenders were less willing to fork out more cash. This rapidly becomes a vicious circle. Without the oxygen of new loans, bubbly property and share prices start to fall, driving local speculators out of business and further deterring fresh foreign money. As money drained out of the Thai economy, the currency came under pressure, just as the Mexican peso had in 1994. The Thai authorities spent their currency reserves trying to defend the baht. Devaluation seemed out of the question: it would be not only a huge knock to the country's prestige, but also a hammer blow to the economy, since all those foreign-currency debts would be much harder to repay. Raising interest rates might have stemmed the outflow temporarily, but only at the cost of pushing an already fragile economy into recession.

As it became more likely that the baht would eventually be devalued, locals and foreigners started to place huge bets on this happening. They borrowed vast sums in baht and bought dollar assets with them, anticipating that the baht would soon be devalued and that they could more than repay their loans with their strong dollars. This accelerated the depletion of the governments' foreign-exchange reserves, as it raced to sell dollars to buy the baht that speculators were offloading. Finally, the game was up. On 2 July 1997, the Thai baht slipped its anchor. The world's attention was focused elsewhere: amid much pomp and pageantry (and Chris Patten's tears), followed by fireworks and celebration from the local Chinese, Britain had just handed Hong Kong back to China. Soon, though, the world was forced to take notice.

The vicious circle of falling confidence, financial failure and currency collapse sent the Thai economy into a tailspin. The loss of confidence drove investors to take their money out of the country, which sent the currency plunging, which prompted the authorities to raise interest rates to try to stem the decline. A falling currency made dollar loans harder to repay; rising interest rates did the same for baht loans. Banks collapsed or stopped lending, dragging companies down with them, further undermining confidence. And so on. Thailand's economy shrank by 11 per cent in 1998 – more than Britain's did in the Great Depression of the 1930s. Mr Krugman compares this to the feedback loop in an auditorium:

> A microphone in an auditorium always generates a feedback loop: sounds picked up by the microphone are amplified by the loudspeakers; the output from the speakers is itself picked up by microphone; and so on. But as long as the room isn't too echoey and the gain isn't too high, this is a 'damped' process, and poses no problem. Turn the dial a little too far to the right, however, and the process becomes explosive: any little sound is picked up, amplified, picked up again, and suddenly there is an earsplitting screech. What matters, in other words, is not just the qualitative fact of feedback, but its quantitative strength; what caught everyone by surprise was the discovery that the dial was in fact turned up so high.[6]

Worse was to come. Within months, Malaysia, Indonesia, the

Philippines and even South Korea had been sucked into the financial whirlpool. This came as a huge shock. After all, the direct economic links between these economies were slight. They didn't trade much with each other; and although they sometimes competed for the same export markets, the super-cheap baht was hardly a problem for South Korean companies, which made more sophisticated products than the Thais. The financial ties were somewhat greater: not that Thais invested much in Indonesia, but outside investors lumped the two together and started to pull their money out of Indonesia just to be safe. Suddenly, investors' panic became a self-fulfilling prophecy. Even people who thought Indonesia or South Korea still had sound economic prospects rushed to take their money out before others did and they were left holding worthless investments. Speculative 'hedge funds', which had borrowed heavily to finance their gambling, made matters worse, because they were forced to cash in investments elsewhere to cover their losses as they occurred. As money seeped out of the economies, the vicious circle that had gripped Thailand kicked in. Their currency pegs came under pressure, and eventually gave way. As their currencies plunged, foreign-currency debts became unpayable. Banks, and then companies, went bust. Their economies fell off a cliff. The typical recession in America or Britain involves a fall in output of 1 per cent. A fall of 2 per cent is considered huge. Indonesia's economy, which expanded by 8 per cent in 1996 and 5 per cent in 1997, contracted by 13 per cent in 1998. South Korea's, which had grown by 7 per cent and 5 per cent in the two previous years, shrank by 7 per cent in 1998. Unemployment soared and wages slumped – in countries with basically no social safety nets except the family and the farm.

Pundits can point to economic events that helped to precipitate the fall. China devalued in 1994. The Japanese yen slumped between 1995 and 1997. Demand for electronics and semiconductors dived. All of these dented East Asian exports and hence prospects for the economy at large. But East Asia had shrugged off much bigger blows before: it grew rapidly through the early 1990s recession in many rich countries. Malaysia's prime minister, Mahathir Mohamad, blamed a conspiracy by foreign speculators, like George Soros, acting on behalf of a US government that felt Asians were getting too big for their boots. But that implies design and order where in fact there was chaos. The Asian crisis took (nearly) everyone by surprise. Some Westerners pinned the blame squarely on Asia itself. The crisis was their just deserts for the incestuous links between government, banks and business that they dubbed 'crony capitalism'. But that won't wash either. Undoubtedly, those ties were a problem – local companies had borrowed excessively and invested poorly – but they were nothing new and had not previously provoked such a crisis. What was new was that, under pressure from the US government and the IMF, East Asian countries had opened their financial markets to foreigners in the early 1990s – and borrowed liberally in foreign currency from the foreign banks that came running to their doors. As George Soros, a billionaire who knows a thing or two about financial markets, says: 'it is hard to escape the conclusion that the international financial system itself constituted the main ingredient in the meltdown'.[7] Paul Volcker, a former chairman of the US Federal Reserve, agrees. He says the blame lies 'more in the financial arena than in the structural flaws that have been at the centre of so much attention'.[8] The circuit-breakers were gone. Suddenly, developing countries were vulnerable to a run on their economies.

Poisonous medicine

In an ideal world, economic policymakers would like to be able to do three things: keep control of interest rates so that they can fight recessions and curb inflation; have stable exchange rates so as to avoid the currency roller-coaster ride that plays havoc with companies' best-laid plans; and have open financial markets so that people can freely move their money in and out and the economy can benefit from foreign investment. Unfortunately, they cannot have all three at once. When financial markets are open, policy-makers must either relinquish power over interest rates in the interests of exchange-rate stability – as Britain did when it was in Europe's exchange-rate mechanism (ERM) and as the twelve countries in the euro have done – or allow the currency to bob up and down freely in order to keep control over interest rates (as Britain does now). That is one reason why, until the early 1990s, Asian countries opted to keep controls on capital movements. It allowed them to combine currency stability with wiggle room to smooth the economic cycle. They also had the fallback of devaluation if the exchange rate became uncompetitive.

Whatever you give up, there is a cost. These costs are different for different countries, so the least-bad option for them varies too. For a huge continental economy like the United States, where trade with foreigners accounts for only a small share of economic activity and the financial sector is vast, the costs of a flexible exchange rate seem smallest – although even the US occasionally feels the need to massage its currency: in 1985 for instance, when it sought other countries' help to lower the dollar through the Plaza accord, and in 1987 when the Louvre accord tried to prop it up again. The twelve European countries that now share the euro reckon that giving up national control of their interest rates is preferable: that the costs of a one-size-fits-all monetary policy are outweighed by the havoc wreaked by the currency crises of old – like the one that ejected sterling and the Italian lira from the ERM in 1992 and caused its break-up in 1993.

Some developing countries reason in a similar way to the small European countries that have opted to join the euro. They choose to hitch their currency to that of a big rich country through a 'currency board' like the one that Hong Kong has run since 1983 – or that Argentina had until December 2001. In 1991 Argentina fixed the peso to the US dollar – supposedly forever – and bound itself by law not to print more pesos than it had dollars in its reserves. That way it could guarantee the peso's convertibility into dollars.

The advantage of a currency board is that speculators cannot force a devaluation by pulling their money out, which is what happened in Thailand, so a self-fulfilling currency crisis can be avoided. The problem is that a loss of investor confidence manifests itself in a different way. If people lose faith in the peso and convert them into dollars, the supply of pesos shrinks. This drives up interest rates, which pushes the economy into recession. The central bank cannot stimulate the economy because it is not allowed to print money – which also means it cannot bail out banks that get into trouble. Nor can it devalue to get the economy out of a tight squeeze, because its exchange rate is fixed. The government can boost spending for a while, but it risks running up huge debts if it continues to do so. So a country with a currency board can end up locked in a recession with a credit crisis. That is what has happened to Argentina. And, as Argentina's example shows, when a government finally finds the pain unbearable and abandons the currency board, its credibility end up in shreds – as does the economy.

Other developing countries have warmed to floating exchange rates. When they know that the currency can move up and down freely, local borrowers are less likely to be lulled into a false sense of security and borrow too much from abroad. Foreign lenders are also aware of this potential risk and so may be less likely to lend too much. Even so, the costs of floating exchange rates – their volatility and their propensity to move out of step with the needs of the domestic economy – are huge. Nor do they prevent currency crises: according to the World Bank, countries with flexible exchange rates have suffered more crises than those with fixed rates over the past thirty years, although these were typically less severe.

China chooses to sacrifice capital mobility instead. This restricts its citizens' freedom, but such curbs do not weigh too heavily on authoritarian rulers' minds. Nor do the costs to the economy – corruption, the extra bureaucracy needed to stop controls being evaded, the unwanted loss of 'good' foreign investment as well as nasty speculative flows – seem excessive compared with the ship-wreck neighbouring economies have suffered. Even though China has bad banks and dodgy loans aplenty, it was insulated from the self-fulfilling crisis that other Asian countries suffered because Chinese currency cannot legally be exchanged for dollars without a government licence. People cannot easily speculate on a Chinese devaluation and by doing so provoke one. Money leaks out of China, but it does not pour out. Thanks to capital controls, the authorities are free to print money to stimulate the economy, as well as to lend to banks in distress, thus preventing self-fulfilling bank runs. They can also spend liberally to keep the economy going. The Chinese government reasons that its financial sector is still too fragile to withstand international liberalisation and that it needs time to fix the flaws that precipitated the panics in Thailand and South Korea. Whether it chooses to use that breathing space actually to reform the financial system is another matter; many would argue that in the absence of foreign pressure it may drag its feet forever. But it is far from obvious that the cumulative cost of delayed reform is greater than the big bang – and bust – that Thailand and South Korea suffered. China's economy continues to grow at around 7 per cent a year (although actual growth may be somewhat less than official figures). Even so, the sooner China clears up its financial mess the better.

The conventional wisdom, peddled by the IMF and the US Treasury in the early 1990s, was that the benefits of free-capital mobility for developing countries (or at least for the Western investors that could profit from lending to them) were so great that they should throw caution to the wind and open up their financial markets. Underlying this advice was the belief that markets didn't fail, governments did. If only the government would get out of the way, the private sector would work its magic. But Asian countries already had very high savings rates: they scarcely needed more investment funds. Moreover, and this is to put it mildly, the money that poured in to Asian countries was hardly invested well. Worse, when it poured out again, it provoked a crisis – and governments were unable to rescue people from the mess that financial markets had created.

When financial mayhem threatens the US or European economy, the authorities step in to save the day. Central banks rush to cut interest rates to prop up demand. That is what the US Federal Reserve did in 1987, after Wall Street tanked on Black Tuesday; what it did again in 1998 to keep the US economy afloat; and what it did eleven times in 2001 to cushion the blow of the technology bubble bursting. Governments may also boost their spending or cut taxes to support the economy. In part, this happens automatically, because tax revenues fall in a recession and spending on social benefits rises. But governments often add their bit for good measure: the Bush administration slashed taxes and boosted spending in 2001; Gordon Brown is fortuitously increasing social spending in Britain. Contrary to what left-wingers fear and conservatives hope, Keynesianism is alive and well – in rich countries.

It is looking less healthy in poor countries. Certainly, in Asia the authorities compounded the misery. They jacked up interest rates, raised taxes and slashed spending. Not because they were stupid or masochists. But because they felt had to – to pacify speculators, and because they were under orders from the IMF and the US government, which largely dictates the Fund's policies. Whereas markets generally give rich-country governments the benefit of the doubt, they have less confidence in those of developing countries. As Paul Krugman points out, this market-enforced double standard is self-fulfilling. If markets lose confidence in a government's policies – however sound they may actually be economically – they become a problem simply because markets have decided they are one. Presto, markets provoke a crisis that validates their previous prejudice. Government policy becomes not a matter of sound economics but amateur psychology, which caters to what government officials (or the IMF) hope will be the perceptions of the markets. Unfortunately, economic policies still have an impact on the economy: high interest rates and government spending cuts cause recessions. Mr Krugman is spot on: 'What remedy does Washington offer? None. The perceived need to play the confidence game supersedes the normal concerns of economic policy. It sounds pretty crazy, and it is.'[9]

To be fair, Asian governments did choose to place their fate in the IMF's hands: they appealed for its emergency loans as a desperate last resort. But that does not excuse the Fund's mistakes and misplaced priorities. If the bailiffs are at your door and banks refuse to lend you money so you turn in despair to your parents for a loan, they should not insist that you stop wearing an earring, divorce 'that wife of yours' and force your kids to make do with only one meal a day as conditions for helping you.

Why, then, did the IMF insist on such painful medicine? Because its priority is not to cushion the blow of a country's financial crisis, but to protect the stability of the financial system. That is code for protecting the interests of lenders – big Western banks – rather than borrowers (developing-country companies and governments). The Fund's overriding concern is to prevent a country or its companies renouncing their debts, even if that means bleeding borrowers dry. Creating a recession kills off the demand for imports, thus creating a trade surplus, which can be used to pay off creditors. The IMF insists that avoiding default is in the best long-term interests of borrowers too, because default would deter foreigners from lending again, so it encourages governments to take on the debts of its bankrupt banks and companies. But sometimes, when the alternative is a wrenching slump, default is the lesser of two evils. Even when default can, strictly speaking, be avoided, lenders ought to carry more of the can for their reckless lending – which is all the more reckless because they know that the IMF (which means Western taxpayers) is likely to bail them out if their loans turn sour.

The IMF compounded this problem with specific policy mistakes. It forced Asian countries to undertake reforms that had little to do with the problem at hand. For instance, South Korea was made to lower its trade barriers unilaterally and Indonesia to privatise state-owned companies. Even though those reforms were often good for the economy, the IMF should not have trampled on Asians' right to decide for themselves. Moreover, banging on about Asia's 'crony capitalism', as if the crisis were its just deserts, hardly helped to quell the panic.

The Fund also ordered Asian governments to increase taxes and cut spending to tackle a non-existent budget problem. Unlike in Latin America in the early 1980s, it was private-sector, not government, borrowing that had got Asian economies into trouble. Indonesia's budget deficit was a mere 1 per cent of GDP in 1997, as was South Korea's; Thailand's was a still small 2 per cent of national income. Asian countries did not need to get their fiscal house in order, especially since tightening policy unnecessarily deepened the economic depression. In its defence, the IMF argued that it was pre-empting a budget problem that recession would cause. But that does not stand up: budget cuts made matters worse by aggravating the recession. It also claimed that the budget measures were needed to restore investor confidence. By wearing a fiscal hairshirt and being seen to clean up their act, governments would somehow convince markets of their virtue. But funnily enough, when governments were later allowed to relax the fiscal vice, investors scarcely minded. The IMF wrongly applied a medicine for the ills of the 1980s to the different disease of the 1990s.

Worse, the IMF made the Asian authorities hike interest rates sky-high. The aim was to try to persuade investors to keep their money in place and stop currencies falling too far. Its reasoning was that currencies would otherwise collapse, driving those with foreign-currency debts into bankruptcy and the economy into depression. Yet ludicrously high interest rates did a pretty good job of bankrupting companies and killing off the economy in any case. It is far from obvious that currencies would have fallen as far as the IMF feared had interest rates not been raised. After all, one of the factors driving currencies down was precisely the economic pain that high interest rates were inflicting. Moreover, had currencies been left to fall freely – as Jeffrey Sachs of Harvard

University, for one, suggested at the time – they would eventually have bounced back once investors thought they were cheap, and thus depression might have been avoided. Brazil's experience when it was forced to let the *real* float in January 1999 certainly suggests as much. Contrary to what the IMF feared, the *real* quickly recovered its poise after its initial fall – although the Fund then imposed its monetary quackery nonetheless.

The IMF also refused to countenance countries reimposing capital controls. Mr Krugman proposed doing so at the time, although he disassociated himself from Malaysia's decision to do so in September 1998. Some critics objected that investors' right to move their money in and out of a country was sacrosanct. 'But just as the right to free speech does not necessarily include the right to shout "Fire" in a crowded theatre, the principle of free markets does not necessarily mean that investors must be allowed to trample each other in a stampede,'[10] Mr Krugman replied. Investors might even benefit from emergency controls; and even if they do not, their interests should not always be paramount. Other critics claimed that capital controls would never work. Some said they would be ineffectual: speculators would find ways around Mr Mahathir's barricades. Others said they would be all too effective: that the economy would grind to a halt without foreign money. Often, the same people put forward both objections. A more potent criticism was that Malaysia was closing the stable door after the horse had bolted. Since it imposed controls a year after the crisis broke, money had already fled the country, so the priority was getting it back, not preventing it from leaving. Events have proved the critics wrong. True, it would have been better had Malaysia never jettisoned its capital controls in the first place. It is also true that they would have saved more pain had they been reimposed earlier. But Malaysia's capital controls were effective – and its economy did not collapse as the pundits predicted. On the contrary: unlike in Thailand, the government was able to use Keynesian methods to revive the economy. Unfortunately, Malaysia has not used the breathing space it gained to clean up its financial system as vigorously as it should have. Even so, in a crisis, capital controls are sometimes the least-bad option.

Preventing future crises

When the global financial system seemed on the brink of collapse, there was a flurry of proposals to redesign the 'world financial architecture' in order to prevent future crises. Some, like George Soros, advocated[11] turning the IMF into an international central bank that could help prevent crises and bail out countries in distress. Others, whom Mr Soros dubs 'market fundamentalists', thought the IMF should be scrapped in order to discourage banks from lending recklessly. Still others proposed a global financial regulator that would set and enforce tougher standards for banks and other participants in capital markets, notably speculative 'hedge funds' like LTCM.

Scrapping the IMF might discourage banks from taking some risks, but the flaws in financial markets run deeper than that. Money markets are inherently unstable, so crises would still happen – and when they did, they would be even more painful. There are better ways to discourage excessive lending – like forcing lenders to bear more of the cost of bail-outs. Even better is Jeffrey Sachs' proposal for a world bankruptcy court. This would not only ensure that creditors took a hit. It would also provide debtors with a framework within which they could gain access to new credit, and obviate the perverse need for higher interest rates in a crisis to try to keep investors sweet. That it would encourage borrowers to take greater risks is true; but so does domestic bankruptcy law, and yet we consider it preferable to having no means of working out debts in an orderly fashion. Anne Krueger, the number two at the IMF, suggested in December 2001 that bankruptcy procedures for governments could be a good idea. Argentina's default crisis underscores the need for them. One day, hopefully, they will become a reality. But such a change would require the co-operation of rich-country governments, so it is unlikely to happen any time soon.

An international regulator and an international central bank would also make sense: they would replicate at a global level the safeguards that exist at a national level in the US. Today's capital markets are international, but they are supervised and regulated largely on a national basis, so banks can all too easily escape proper supervision, especially in developing countries. Moreover, the IMF is not a genuine lender of last resort for countries in distress because it does not have enough funds to lend freely. It relies on others, notably the US government, when the going gets really tough. Unfortunately, though, once the storm had passed in rich countries, such radical reforms were quickly shelved. The existing system suits Western banks just fine – and Western regulators jealously guard their turf.

At least until the next big crisis, there is no prospect of root-and-branch reform. The left likes to bang on about putting 'sand in the wheels' of international finance through a so-called Tobin tax on cross-border capital flows (named after the economist who first proposed it, James Tobin), but it is a political non-starter. The guardians of orthodoxy in Washington propose only to tinker with the existing system. The Basle rules that regulate how much capital Western banks need to hold against their loans are to be reformed – by 2006. Developing countries are being encouraged to be more open about their true financial situation, so that investors aren't lulled into a false sense of security. They are advised to manage their economies more prudently and regulate their banks more effectively, so that potential crises are nipped in the bud. They are also told to let foreign banks buy local ones, to reduce the risk of banking panic and spur local rivals to improve.

These are good ideas, but they are not enough. Better bank regulation will not eliminate crises. Even if developing countries got their houses in order, they would still be vulnerable to the bubbles, mood swings and panics to which financial markets are inherently prone. To quote Joseph Stiglitz, a Nobel-prize-winning economist and former chief economist of the World Bank, 'small open economies are like rowing boats on an open sea. Although one cannot predict when it might happen, the chances of their being broadsided by a wave are significant no matter how well they are steered. Bad steering, though, increases the chances of disaster and a leaky boat makes it inevitable.'[12] As Paul Volcker has pointed out, the entire banking systems of Indonesia or Thailand or Malaysia are comparable to one decent-sized regional bank in the US.

Since developing countries cannot rely on rich countries to make the reforms needed to protect them, they have to take matters into their own hands. They should welcome stable, long-term foreign direct investment. Companies that set up factories in developing countries provide good jobs and valuable foreign know-how. But governments should impose taxes or controls on volatile short-term capital inflows, as Chile did with some success. If countries can prevent too much hot money from flowing into the country, they can stave off many a crisis before it starts. They should also stop domestic banks and companies borrowing recklessly in foreign currencies. Both these measures will reduce – but not eliminate – crises. So countries should also keep (or reimpose) some controls on money flowing out of the economy to give them a breathing space to work out their problems in difficult times. Financial mayhem is not going to go away – it is intrinsic to the system – but we can still mitigate the harm it does by creating financial firewalls.

TWELVE

Culture Clash

Individual freedom, not Coke, rules OK

I believe you can reduce the world's economies today to
basically five different gas stations . . . What is going on
today, in the very broadest sense, is that through the process
of globalisation everyone is being forced toward America's
gas station. If you are not an American and don't know how
to pump your own gas, I suggest you learn. With the end of
the Cold War, globalisation is globalising Anglo-American-
style capitalism and the Golden Straitjacket. It is globalising
American culture and American cultural icons. It is
globalising the best of America and the worst of America. It
is globalising the American Revolution and it is globalising
the American gas station.

THOMAS FRIEDMAN, *The Lexus and the Olive Tree*

Today the buzzword in global marketing isn't selling
America to the world, but bringing a kind of market masala
to everyone in the world . . . Nationality, language, ethnicity,
religion and politics are all reduced to their most colourful,

exotic accessories . . . Despite the embrace of polyethnic imagery, market-driven globalisation doesn't want diversity; quite the opposite. Its enemies are national habits, local brands and distinctive regional tastes.

NAOMI KLEIN, *No Logo*

There is no contrast of opposites in a world where the cultural hegemony of Walt Disney, Rupert Murdoch and Coca-Cola is only matched by its vapidity.

LARRY ELLIOTT and DAN ATKINSON, *The Age of Insecurity*

It is not pages from Shakespeare or scores of Mozart that litter steppe and savannah but some marketing man's logo from last year's useless, meretricious product, or a snatch of that maddening theme tune from *Titanic* . . . Globalisation is by and large the spread of American culture, ideas, products, entertainments and politics. If you view America primarily as a place of vulgarity and avarice, coarsened sensibility and rampant global ambition, you will shudder for the fate of the world . . . Western cultural imperialism reaches right into the hearts and souls, the sexual behaviour, the spirit, the religion, politics and the nationhood of the entire world. It happens haphazardly with no master-plan or empire-building blueprint, but with a vague and casual insouciance that drives its detractors to despair.

POLLY TOYNBEE, 'Who's Afraid of Global Culture?'[1]

It is five, maybe six in the morning. The sun is streaming through the glass roof of Amnesia, one of the huge nightclubs on the Mediterranean party island of Ibiza. Down below, clubbers from around the world, most of them high on ecstasy or other drugs, are moving in time to the repetitive beats of house music. They grin, they cheer, they wave in unison. It is a scene repeated in less glamorous clubs every weekend in cities around the globe.

One world united under a groove? Or a drugged global conformity?

Fears that globalisation is imposing a deadening cultural uniformity are as ubiquitous as Coca-Cola, McDonald's, Mickey Mouse – and house music. Europeans and Latin Americans, left and right, rich and poor – all of them dread that local cultures and national identities are dissolving into a crass all-American consumerism. This cultural imperialism is said to impose American values as well as products, promote the commercial at the expense of the authentic, substitute shallow gratification for deeper satisfaction.

Yet the true picture is rather different. Certainly, the commercial clutter of American capitalism seems to corrode even the most ironclad of barriers. One by one, the countries that once resisted it are succumbing. When I visited Moscow in October 1991, in the aftermath of the failed August putsch that briefly ousted Mikhail Gorbachev and accelerated Boris Yeltsin's rise to power, the queue for the recently opened McDonald's stretched as far as my eyes could see. Ten years later, in still officially communist China, the wait for Big Macs in Shanghai was rather shorter, although the punters were just as keen. But the push of the corporate giants that peddle these icons of Americana is more than matched by the pull of consumer demand. Coca-Cola aims to be 'within an arm's reach of desire', but it has yet to fit drips to everybody at birth. People still have to desire to reach for a can of Coke. Clearly, they often prefer it to the local alternative.

Revolutionary refreshment

Havana is stifling in the midday heat. I glance at the Memorial Granma, which displays in a glass case the boat with which Fidel Castro landed in Cuba in 1956 to launch the revolution, surrounded by examples of the planes, tanks and weapons used to overthrow President Batista and defend the revolution against the

American incursion at the Bay of Pigs. Then I struggle around the Museo de la Revolución, the former presidential palace where the revolutionary government announced its first new laws in 1959 and which now exhaustively chronicles plucky Cuba's increasingly solitary stand against the toxic waste of Yanqui capitalism. Not quite solitary: the US government assists Castro in his defiance of all things American by banning US companies from doing business with Cuba. Parched and tired after so many rooms of revolutionary propaganda, I make my way to the gift shop for some refreshment. And there, amid T-shirts of Che Guevara and books by Fidel Castro, they are: those oh-so-familiar red cans of Coca-Cola. Is nothing sacred? At least ordinary Cubans are safe from this American rot-gut: it is prohibitively priced out of their reach. They have to make do with 'tuKola', a local rip-off of Atlanta's most famous brew. 'It's cheaper,' explains the saleslady, 'but not as good.'

American cultural imperialism seems pretty benign: it means having the choice to drink Coke. Shock, horror – Coke is actually popular all over the world. This provokes apoplexy among critics of globalisation and pangs of angst among even many of its steadfast supporters. If globalisation allows people to enjoy the best the world has to offer, how come such 'trash' is so popular? Yet there is no accounting for taste. Nobody is forced to drink Coke. Nobody should be prevented from drinking it either.

If the fear is that national cultures are under threat, individual choices, not 'Coca-colonisation', are to blame. If the worry is that countries are becoming more alike, this is because people's tastes have converged, not because American companies are stamping out local competition. Yet here's a heretical thought: perhaps the world is not becoming uniformly Americanised, even by choice. Start with a simple observation: although Coke's global spread creates greater uniformity across countries, it adds diversity within them. Cubans once swigged rum or water; now they can also choose to gulp down Coke and tuKola. Next, note that, by and large, American exports do not rule supreme: pizza is more popular than burgers. Then ask yourself: by consuming American products, are Cubans and others really losing their national identities – or even their souls? I don't think so. People are not what they buy. Presumably, left-wingers ought to agree.

If critics of globalisation were less obsessed with 'Coca-colonisation', they might notice a rich feast of cultural mixing that belies fears about Americanised uniformity. Algerians in Paris practise Thai boxing; Asian rappers in London snack on Turkish pizza; Indians in New York learn salsa; Mexicans taste Pacific fusion dishes cooked by British chefs. As J. N. Pieterse remarks, the emphasis on cultural uniformity

> overlooks the countercurrents – the impact non-Western cultures have been making on the West. It downplays the ambivalence of the globalising momentum and ignores the role of local reception of Western culture – for example, the indigenisation of Western elements. It fails to see the influence that non-Western cultures have been exercising on one another. It has no room for crossover culture – as in the development of 'third cultures' such as world music. It overrates the homogeneity of Western culture and overlooks the fact that many of the standards exported by the West and its cultural industries themselves turn out to be of culturally mixed character if we examine their cultural lineages.[2]

The really profound cultural changes have nothing to do with Coca-Cola. Western ideas about liberalism and science are taking root in the most unlikely places. Immigration, mainly from developing countries, is creating multicultural societies in Europe and North America. Technology is reshaping culture: just think of the Internet. Individual choice is fragmenting the imposed uniformity of national cultures. New hybrid cultures are emerging, and regional ones re-emerging. National identity is not disappearing, but the bonds of nationality are loosening.

Not as American as all that

Rewind to house music. It was born in America, but in the black
urban ghettoes, not a marketing man's office. To this day, it
remains very much a minority taste in the States. It spread to
Europe in the 1980s and, combined with the appeal of ecstasy-
induced empathy and euphoria, proved irresistible, especially in
England. House music evolved in Britain, went off in new direc-
tions, split into many different subforms. It has gone from
underground to mainstream: tunes can now move from club to
BBC TV jingles in weeks. It has been repackaged and re-exported,
to continental Europe, to the rest of the world, and even back to
America. The world's top record-spinner[3] is a British DJ, Paul
Oakenfold. The world's biggest club brand is Britain's Ministry of
Sound. Many of the top house acts – Leftfield, Prodigy, Chemical
Brothers, Underworld, Basement Jaxx, to name but a few – are
British too. Yet in each country where house music arrives, boys
(and girls) in their bedrooms bash the beats on their computers
and come up with something new – Latin, Norwegian, even
Japanese house – which is then sent back out around the world.
So yes, house music is a global groove, and yes it originated in
the US, but its spread owes little to corporate America and it has
a peculiarly British flavour, as well as a huge variety of local
forms.

House music is not the only archetypal 'American' product that
is not as all-American as it seems. When Levi Strauss, a German
immigrant, started making his famous blue jeans in the 1860s for
the prospectors and frontiersmen of the Californian Gold Rush, he
combined denim cloth (originally known as *serge de Nîmes*, because
it was traditionally woven in the French town) with Genes, a traditional style of trousers worn by Genoese sailors.[4] So Levi's jeans
are in fact an American twist on a European model. Pizza Hut ped-
dles an Italian dish; Burger King is owned by Britain's Diageo.
Moreover, even quintessentially American exports are often tailored to local tastes. MTV in Asia devotes a fifth of its airtime to

local programming, promotes Thai and Chinese pop stars along with Western ones, and plays rock music sung in Mandarin. CNN en Español offers a Latin American take on world news. McDonald's sells beer in France, lamb in India and chilli in Mexico.

Nor is American culture by any means the only influence on the world. In some basic ways, America is an outlier, not a global leader. Most of the world has adopted the metric system born of the French Revolution; the US persists with antiquated measurements inherited from its British colonial past. Americans measure in inches, miles, pounds, gallons and Fahrenheit rather than centimetres, kilometres, kilograms, litres and Celsius. Most developed countries have become intensely secular, but many Americans burn with fundamentalist fervour – like Muslims in the Middle East. Where else in the developed world could there be a serious debate about teaching kids Bible-inspired 'creationism' instead of Darwinist evolution? According to Gallup polls, only 10 per cent of Americans say they hold a secular evolutionist view of the world, while 44 per cent believe in strict biblical creationism.[5]

America's tastes in sports are often idiosyncratic too. Its homegrown ones, like baseball and American football, have not travelled well, although basketball has fared rather better. Many of the world's most popular sports, notably football, originated in Britain. When I was in Asia, I lost count of how many times I was asked: 'You English? What team? Oh, Arsenal. Very good team. You like Bergkamp? I like him too.' One billion people watched France beat Brazil in the 1998 World Cup final; a mere 40 million tuned in for the 2001 baseball World Series final. Even in America's neighbour, Mexico, soccer rules unchallenged – and Mexican immigrants are helping to spread their passion in the States. Asian martial arts – judo, karate, kick-boxing – and pastimes like yoga have also swept the world.

People are not only guzzling hamburgers and Coca-Cola. McDonald's has opened over 1,200 burger joints since it first hit Britain in 1974. There are 1,100 Golden Arches restaurants in

Germany and 760 in France. Worldwide, McDonald's now has more than 29,000 outlets in 121 countries. Coca-Cola is drunk in nearly 200 countries; over 70 per cent of the company's revenues come from outside the US. Even so, McDonald's and Coca-Cola are small fry in global terms. Despite Coke's ambition of displacing water as the world's drink of choice, it accounts for less than 2 of the 64 fluid ounces that the typical person drinks a day. Upstarts like Red Bull, an energy drink peddled by a Thai-Austrian joint venture, are eroding its market share. Britain's favourite take-away is a curry, not a burger. There are over 7,500 Indian restaurants – six for every McDonald's – in the UK, up from just six in 1950. For all José Bové's concern about American fast food trashing France's culinary traditions, the French remain iffy about foreign food. France imported a mere $620 million of food from the US in 2000 – and exported three times more to America. Nor is plonk from America's Gallo displacing Europe's finest: Italy and France together account for three-fifths of global wine exports; the US, which still imports much more than it exports, has only a 5 per cent market share.[6] Italy is home to a mere 200 McDonald's outlets (and some 2,000 more non-Italian restaurants), but 23,000 pizzerias.[7] Worldwide, pizzas are more popular than burgers, Chinese restaurants seem to sprout up everywhere and sushi is spreading fast. By far the biggest purveyor of alcoholic drinks is Britain's Diageo, which sells the world's best-selling whisky (Johnnie Walker), gin (Gordon's), vodka (Smirnoff) and liqueur (Baileys), as well as Guinness. The next biggest spirits makers are France's Pernod-Ricard and Britain's Allied Domecq.

In fashion, the *ne plus ultra* is Italian or French. Trendy Americans wear Gucci, Armani, Versace, Chanel and Hermès. The US exports Calvin Klein and Ralph Lauren – and Gucci's top designer is an American, Tom Ford – but fashion is hardly an industry that America dominates. On the high street and in the mall, America's Gap is not the only international clothing chain: Sweden's Hennes & Mauritz (H&M) and Spain's Zara dress the global masses too. Nike shoes are given a run for their money by Germany's Adidas, Britain's Reebok and Italy's Fila.

In pop music, American crooners share the spoils with those from Britain, Ireland and a whole host of countries whose local music is now listened to worldwide. American stars like Mariah Carey and Madonna are global chart-toppers, but so are Britain's Elton John and Ireland's U2. The three artists who featured most widely in national top ten album charts in 2000 were America's Britney Spears, closely followed by Mexico's Carlos Santana, and the British Beatles.[8] Two Spaniards, Enrique Iglesias (son of Julio) and Alejandro Sanz, are taking the world by storm. Even tiny Iceland has produced a global star: Bjork. Popular opera's biggest singers are Italy's Luciano Pavarotti, Spain's José Carreras and Spanish-Mexican Placido Domingo. Latin American salsa, Brazilian lambada and African music have all carved out global niches for themselves. Moreover, in most countries, local artists still top the charts. Seven of the top ten albums on Amazon.fr were French when I wrote this paragraph. Same story in Britain on Amazon.co.uk. Six of the top ten on fnac.es were Spanish. But on Amazon.de, only one of the top ten was German. Statistics from the IFPI, the record-industry bible, confirm this impression. Between 1991 and 2000, local acts and artists signed to local music companies steadily increased their share of music sales, from a worldwide average of 58 per cent in 1991 to 68 per cent in 2000, with increases in each year in between. The trend is common to all regions except eastern Europe, the Middle East and Africa.[9] In Asia, three-quarters of the music market is locally produced.

America does not dominate global book sales either. Airport novelists like John Grisham and Tom Clancy sell well abroad, but perhaps the most famous living author is a Colombian, Gabriel García Márquez, author of *One Hundred Years of Solitude*. Paulo Coelho, another writer who has notched up tens of millions of global sales with *The Alchemist* and other books, is Brazilian. When I wrote this paragraph, two British writers, J. K. Rowling, the creator of Harry Potter, and the late J. R. R. Tolkein, who wrote *The Lord of the Rings* trilogy, were topping the charts in most countries I checked. An unscientific glance at Amazon's national sites reveals eight Brits in the top ten in the UK, six French in France and four Germans in Germany. Four Spaniards were among the bestsellers on fnac.es.

Newspapers are still overwhelmingly domestic. America's *Wall Street Journal* has global ambitions, yet its European edition had average daily sales of just 100,000 in the first six months of 2001. The Asian edition sold a paltry 84,000 copies. The *International Herald Tribune*, which is American-owned but sold abroad, does slightly better, but still sells only 235,000 copies worldwide. Britain's *Financial Times* also aims to be a global newspaper, but despite a sharp rise in its foreign sales, sells only around 200,000 copies abroad. A glance at the UN's *World Media Handbook* shows that everywhere national and local newspapers trounce their foreign and international rivals: *USA Today* sells 2 million copies in America, the *Sun* 3 million in Britain, *Bild* 4.5 million in Germany, the *Daily Yomiuri* 10 million in Japan. True, Rupert Murdoch's US-based News Corporation owns a third of Britain's newspaper market and Canada's Conrad Black owns another big chunk through The Telegraph Group. But Britain is an exception: most countries' newspapers are published by local companies.

Magazines are more international. From its base in Pleasantville, New York, *Reader's Digest* is published in forty-eight editions and nineteen languages and sold in more than sixty countries. Four in five magazines sold on news-stands in Canada are foreign, mainly American. But the biggest publisher in the English-speaking world is Germany's Bertelsmann, which gobbled up America's largest publisher, Random House, in 1998. *Newsweek International* sold 666,000 copies outside the US in 2001; *The Economist*'s global circulation was 760,000, of which 128,000 was in the UK. Britain's best-selling magazine is the terribly parochial *Radio Times*.

Local fare glues more eyeballs to TV screens than American pap.

Granted, news junkies worldwide watch America's CNN and music-mad teenagers tune in to MTV. American shows like *Friends*, *ER* and *The Simpsons* have a global following. *Baywatch* is the world's most popular TV programme. Nearly three-quarters of television drama exported worldwide comes from the US. America is capturing a big chunk of the global TV market, which is growing fast as cable and satellite channels multiply and governments relax controls on programming, yet it hardly has a monopoly. Australian fodder like *Neighbours* and *Home and Away* outdo America's finest in Britain. The French love Britain's *Absolutely Fabulous* (and, for some reason, Benny Hill). Russians are addicted to *The Rich Also Cry*, a Mexican soap. Brazilian TV is a raging success in Portugal. More importantly, most countries' favourite shows are home-grown. In Britain, *EastEnders* and *Coronation Street* attract up to ten times as many couch potatoes as *Friends* does. American shows have actually fallen in popularity since the days when soaps like *Dallas* and *Dynasty* had so many Britons in a lather. In nearly every European country, the most popular programmes are local.

Nor are Americans the only players in the global media industry. Of the seven market leaders that have their fingers in nearly every pie, four are American (AOL Time Warner, Disney, Viacom and News Corporation), one is German (Bertelsmann), one is French (Vivendi) and one is Japanese (Sony). What they distribute comes from all quarters: Bertelsmann publishes books by American writers; News Corporation broadcasts Asian news; Sony sells Brazilian music.

The evidence is overwhelming. Fears about an Americanised uniformity are overblown. American cultural products are not uniquely dominant; local ones are alive and well. With one big exception: cinema. True, India produces more films (855 in 2000)[10] than Hollywood does (762), but they are largely for a domestic audience. Japan and Hong Kong also make lots of movies, but few are seen outside Asia. France and Britain have the occasional global hit – *Amélie* or *Four Weddings and a Funeral*, for instance – but they are still basically local players. Not only does Hollywood dominate the global movie market, it swamps local products in most countries. Even in Japan, American fare accounts for over half the market. US films accounted for 63 per cent of box-office receipts in the EU in 1996, with a 53 per cent share in France and an 81 per cent share in Britain. But that was actually a sharp fall from a 72 per cent market share in 1991 – European cinema may be fighting back.

Hollywood movies rule supreme, but their hegemony is not as worrying as people think. Note first that Hollywood is less American than it seems. Ever since Charlie Chaplin crossed over from Britain, foreigners have flocked to California to try to become global stars. Penelope Cruz, Catherine Zeta-Jones, Ewan McGregor and Arnold Schwarzenegger are only a few of the many foreign actors who have made it big in Hollywood. Top directors are also often from outside America: think of Ridley Scott or the late Stanley Kubrick. Some of the studios are foreign-owned: Japan's Sony owns Columbia Pictures, France's Vivendi owns Universal. Even American-owned productions sometimes have a foreign feel. Two of AOL Time Warner's biggest recent hits, *Harry Potter and the Philosopher's Stone* and *The Lord of the Rings: The Fellowship of the Ring*, are both based on British books, have largely British casts, and in the case of *The Lord of the Rings*, a Kiwi director. To some extent, then, Hollywood is a global industry that just happens to be in America. Rather than exporting Americana, it serves up lowest-common-denominator pap – sex and violence, special effects, action-packed plots rather than elaborate character development – to appeal to a global audience.

Still, monopolies are generally a bad thing. Hollywood's dominance is in part due to economics: movies cost a lot to make and so need a big audience to be profitable; Hollywood has used America's huge and relatively uniform domestic market as a platform to expand overseas. According to *Screen Digest*, a British trade magazine, a major film release in the United States is typically shown on 1,300 screens, compared with 450 in Germany and even fewer in other rich countries.[11] There could be a case for stuffing subsidies into a rival European film industry, just as Airbus was created to challenge Boeing's near-monopoly, but France has long pumped money into its domestic industry to try to level the playing field without convincing foreign audiences to flock to its films. So perhaps Hollywood's success is in large part due to its popular appeal, not its market power. Like Coke or McDonald's, Disney is a choice, not an imposition.

To be fair, there is another American export that is conquering the globe: English. Around 380 million people speak it as their first language, and a further 250 million or so as their second. A billion are learning it, about a third of the world's population are exposed to it and by 2050, it is reckoned, half the world will be more or less proficient in it. A common global language would certainly be a big plus: for businessmen, for scientists and for tourists. As Claude Allègre, then France's minister of education, declared in 1998: 'English should no longer be considered a foreign language . . . In future it will be as basic [in France] as reading, writing and arithmetic.'[12] But a single world language would be far less desirable. Language is often at the heart of national culture: the French would scarcely be French if they spoke English (although the Belgian Walloons are not French even they though they share a language). Losing national languages would be especially sad if people had not freely chosen to abandon them. English may usurp other languages not because it is what people prefer to speak, but because, like Microsoft software, there are compelling advantages to using it if everyone else does.

Fear not. Although many languages are becoming extinct, this is rarely due to the spread of English. In general, the globalisation of languages is like the spread of Coke: there may be greater uniformity across countries but there is greater diversity within them. The US now has two main languages, not one. Thirty million Americans speak Spanish; both presidential candidates in the 2000 election campaigned in it. People are learning English as well as − not instead of − their native tongue, and often many more languages besides. Many Norwegians, for instance, speak several Scandinavian languages, plus English and German. Indeed, some languages with few speakers, such as Icelandic, are thriving, despite Bjork's choosing to sing in English. Where local languages are dying, it is typically national rivals that are stamping them out. French has all but eliminated Provençal, and German, Swabian. Although within Britain English has killed off Cornish and in the US it is replacing Native American tongues, it is not doing away with Swahili or Norwegian. Moreover, even as English becomes a global language, it takes on new words and new forms in different places. Estonians speak Baltic English, Indians Hindi English, West Indians pidgin English. New terms – spin doctor, ballpark figure, texting, house music – are forever appearing. Ironically, the biggest 'victims' of this may be the English themselves, since Americans and the world have appropriated their language.

It's all foreign to me

Nanjing Lu, the main shopping drag in Shanghai, looks quite like London's Oxford Street: big department stores, Kentucky Fried Chicken, Starbucks, posters pushing special offers, throngs of shoppers weighed down with bags. Inside the stores, though, most of the products on offer are Chinese copies of Western brands. The customers don't seem to mind. Consumerism is rampant. In the spanking new metro, salesmen even tempt passengers with credit-card offers.

Times have certainly changed. Sydney Lock, an Anglo-Chinese businessman, recalls visiting the city in 1979. 'Everyone wore a blue suit or green suit. The streets were grey, the people desperately poor. The only cars in the streets were Chinese limousines whisking Communist bigwigs around.' The businessmen he met up with in his hotel all insisted on using the exotic luxury in his bathroom: a bathtub.

As dusk falls, I take a boat trip up the Huangpu River. On the west bank, Puxi, lies the European elegance of the Bund, the waterfront street developed by the British and French when they ran Shanghai in the 1920s and 1930s. River traffic had to pay tolls at the imperious British Customs House. All manner of European architectural styles jostle for attention: Gothic, baroque, Roman, Renaissance, neo-classical and art deco. Amid this eclectic colonial heritage, huge neon signs advertise Coca-Cola, Sprite, Canon, Nikon, TDK, L'Oréal. China's red-star flag is scarcely on display. Further along, vast cranes and even vaster ships line the river banks: the source of Shanghai's new prosperity.

On the other bank lies the millenarian madness of Pudong. Fifteen years ago, it was a village surrounded by marshland. Now, towering, idiosyncratic skyscrapers, designed by the cream of the world's architects, pierce the smoggy skyline. It feels almost Blade Runnerish. The Pearl Orient TV tower is a 468-metre-tall syringe protruding through three pink globes. The eighty-eight-storey Jin Mao building, which houses the Grand Hyatt hotel on its upper floors, is a rocket poised for lift-off. These buildings are literally awesome: they demand your attention and respect.

Yet Shanghai's Westernised modernity is a veneer. The people who scuttle around in the shadow of these futuristic skyscrapers are still at heart Chinese. They look more sophisticated than their cousins in the comparatively backward hinterland, they dress in Western garb and doubtless dream of *Dallas* lifestyles, but they certainly do not think and feel like Americans. I asked various employees at my hotel, who are presumably more internationalised than most, what they aspired to. 'To be rich,' many said. 'A strong China,' said one. 'To travel to England,' said another, perhaps angling for my sympathy. I asked them if they felt they had anything in common with Americans. 'No' was the universal reply. Shanghai's Westernisation is only skin-deep. To me, it felt very alien. Nor, contrary to what some people think, is that likely to change soon: consumer-goods companies are after your cash, not your soul.

Globalisation is far from the wholesale ransacking of people's souls by American cultural commodities that it is often portrayed as. The flotsam and jetsam of American consumer culture turn up everywhere, but they are not reshaping the world in America's image. You can choose to drink Coke, eat McDonald's and watch Disney but still not be American in any meaningful sense. One newspaper photo of Taliban fighters in Afghanistan showed them toting Kalashnikovs – as well as a sports bag with Nike's trademark swoosh. People's culture – in the sense of their shared ideas, beliefs, values and knowledge; inherited traditions; and art – may scarcely be eroded by mere commercial artefacts that, despite all the furious branding, embody at best shallow and flimsy values.

Natural cultures are much stronger than people seem to think. They can embrace some foreign influences and resist others. Amartya Sen, a brilliant economist, thinker and Nobel prize-winner, is quite right when he remarks: 'the culturally fearful often take a very fragile view of each culture and tend to underestimate our ability to learn from elsewhere without being overwhelmed by that experience'.[13]

Mr Sen's native India is a good example. The sprawling city of Bangalore is a bewildering mix of old and new. St Patrick's church offers diplomas in computing. Starbucks-style Barista espresso bars jostle with traditional stalls. Indian girls in British-style uniforms emerge from Baldwin Girls high school on Richmond Road. Shacks everywhere offer phone access; billboard ads tout mobile phones: 'Break All Barriers. Speed. Pre-paid Mobile Card.' Others tempt passers-by with 0 per cent finance on white goods. 'Interest rates on consumer loans have hit rock bottom. Buy your dream house, the posh car. And soon after you marry your dream girl, go ahead and buy everything money can buy – in dirt-cheap, easy instalments. Welcome to the consumer boom in the time of gloom,' crows the *Economic Times*. But the local newspaper talks of attacks on Muslims by Hindus in the wake of September 11th. One ad promises three lucky families at the Disney Summer Fun Festival the prize of a trip to Disneyland, USA: yet the poster is hand-painted and Mickey Mouse is misshapen and off-colour. Snehaquest.com offers 'online matchmaking for the global Indian community'. The city even has a TGI Friday's diner, complete with waiters in buffoonish red-and-white shirts with badge-emblazoned bracers, which is stuffed with local militaries in uniform. ESPN is showing English football: Arsenal's 4–2 home defeat to Charlton (I saw the wretched game three times in different places). Traffic signs recall Britain's influence: 'Give Way to Right'. Yet Indian drivers press forward nonetheless, dodging oncoming cars rather than giving way. Amid all the consumer pizzazz, people live in tents by the road and work barefoot and with bare hands in open sewers. Kids trawl through rubbish. A man rides by on a horse and cart. Is Bangalore still Indian? Of course it is.

The French epitomise the paranoia about American culture. France's cuisine, wine, art, literature, thinking, you name it, are almost universally admired. Yet the French seem convinced that centuries of cultural tradition, deeply ingrained in every French person, will go up in smoke if people are allowed to watch a few more American films or use English words. It's ridiculous. Frenchness is remarkably resilient. My father, for one, has lived in perfidious Albion for thirty years and, despite a constant bombardment of Anglo-Saxon culture, remains to the core a Frenchman in his attitudes, his values, his beliefs – and his accent.

Appearances can be deceptive. Hong Kong was a British colony for 150 years, until 1997. The street names are quintessentially British: Queensway, Connaught Road, Gloucester Road. Schoolboys wear grey wool trousers, white shirts, boring ties, blue or grey cardigans, just as they would in Britain. Their parents drive on the left, with British-style licence plates. Yet taxi drivers and shopkeepers scarcely speak English. In a McDonald's I ordered a quarter-pounder with cheese in English, but the young man behind the counter didn't understand me: he asked me to point at a menu card with pictures.

Even when countries consciously try to adopt foreign ways, they often fail. Singapore is trying desperately hard to be southern

California. People line up obediently to see the latest Hollywood blockbusters, dutifully munch their popcorn, display their Nikes with pride. Life centres around shopping. The city prides itself on its inane service culture. It is part emulation, part necessity, part government diktat. A speck on the map like Singapore cannot help being globalised: almost everything is imported. But its over-weening government sticks its oar in too. It wants Singapore to be an international city. So everything is exclusively in English: the street signs, the menus, the place names. Singapore has even rebranded itself as 'Singapore – New Asia'. Peter Mandelson would be proud. But my Chinese taxi driver spent his time swearing in broken English about 'fucking Muslims and Malaysians'. Perhaps not so New Asia after all. Despite all the government's efforts, the locals have not become citizens of the world – or even fluent in English. Singapore is a cardboard America: where are the voices of discord? Even this most globalised of places, where the government does its best to impose foreign ways, does not feel anything like America.

Take an even more extreme example. Estonia suffered forty-seven years of Russian occupation. A third of its population of 1.5 million died, fled or were deported to Siberia. The Estonian language was banned and Russians were shipped in to Russify the country. Yet in 1991, Estonia became independent again, its language intact, its Western orientation preserved, its culture bruised but resilient. If tiny Estonia can survive Stalin, surely France can survive Sylvester Stallone (although Jack Lang, when he was culture minister, hon-oured him for his services to culture, while trying to keep out his films).

Clearly, though, there is a limit to how many foreign influences a culture can absorb before being swamped. Had Stalin not died so soon after the war, Estonian culture might indeed have been snuffed out. Even when a foreign influence is largely welcomed, not imposed, it can be overwhelming. Traditional cultures in the Third World that have until now evolved (or failed to evolve) in iso-lation may be particularly vulnerable.

Noreena Hertz[14] describes the supposed spiritual Eden that was the isolated Himalayan kingdom of Bhutan being defiled by such awful imports as basketball and Spice Girls T-shirts. She observes that Bhutan is desperately poor but approvingly quotes its king who says that 'Gross National Happiness is more important than Gross National Product.' Quite. I bet the king pursues happiness in the lap of luxury. Indeed, he is responsible for the terrible basketball craze, since he had tapes of NBA games sent to him from New York. Anthony Giddens, the director of the London School of Economics, has told[15] of how an anthropologist who visited a remote part of Cambodia was shocked and disappointed to find that her first night's entertainment was not traditional local pastimes but watching *Basic Instinct* on video.

But is that such a bad thing? It is odd, to put it mildly, that many on the left support multiculturalism in the West but advocate cultural purity in the Third World – an attitude they would be quick to tar as fascist if proposed for the West. Ms Hertz and the anthropologist appear to want people in the Third World preserved in unchanging – but supposedly pure – poverty. That way, intrepid Westerners can jet out, observe and photograph the locals in their isolated human zoo, then return home to the spiritual emptiness but material comfort of the West reassured that there is a 'natural state of mankind in the wild for us to reconnect with when we feel lost',[16] to quote Polly Toynbee, a British journalist. Funnily enough, the Westerners who want the Third World preserved in aspic rarely feel like settling in this supposed paradise. And surprise, surprise, most people in the Third World quite like our Western 'trash' – and those who don't can choose to live without. Unlike the spoilt Westerners, they know just what it's like to lead an 'authentic' unspoilt life of isolated poverty. That's why they often appreciate what's new and foreign.

It's a shame if ancient cultural traditions are lost. We should do our best to preserve them, and keep them alive where possible, but people cannot be made to live in a museum. We in the West are forever casting off old customs when we feel they are no longer relevant. Nobody argues that the English should ban nightclubs to force people back to morris dancing. People in poor countries have a right to change too.

Thriving cultures are not set in stone. They are forever changing from within and without. Each generation challenges the previous one; science and technology alter the way we see ourselves and the world; fashions come and go; experience and events influence our beliefs; outsiders affect us for good and ill. Cultures that close themselves off from the rest of the world stagnate. Many of the best things come from cultures mixing: Salman Rushdie's Anglo-Indian writing, Paul Gauguin painting in Polynesia, or the African rhythms in rock and roll. Behold the great British curry (which, as Mr Sen interestingly points out, comes from India but is made with chilli originally introduced to the subcontinent by the Portuguese; ancient Indian cuisine used pepper instead). Admire the many-coloured faces of France's World-Cup-winning football team, the ferment of ideas that came from eastern Europe's Jewish diaspora, and the cosmopolitan cities of London and New York. Western numbers are Arabic; zero comes most recently from India; Icelandic, French and Sanskrit come from a common root. As John Stuart Mill so rightly observed:

> The economical benefits of commerce are surpassed in importance by those of its effects which are intellectual and moral. It is hardly possible to overrate the value, for the improvement of human beings, of things which bring them into contact with persons dissimilar to themselves, and with modes of thought and action unlike those with which they are familiar . . . it is indispensable to be perpetually comparing [one's] own notions and customs with the experience and example of persons in different circumstances . . . there is no nation which does not need to borrow from others.[17]

The true picture

Behind the clutter of Coke cans, globalisation is bringing profound – and overwhelmingly positive – cultural change. Technology is opening up new opportunities. The Internet is democratising the spread of information. At the click of a mouse, you can find about almost anything, anywhere, from anyone. A Londoner can chat to a stranger in Bangkok, Baltimore or Brazil. You can read hundreds of different views on globalisation: pro-, anti- and barmy (I recommend philippelegrain.com). You can download all sorts of music from audiogalaxy.com and order foreign books from Amazon.com. Satellite and cable television are exploding traditional broadcasters' monopoly. Fed up with Silvio Berlusconi's private and public TV monopoly? Try satellite instead. Don't believe Venezuela's official TV news? Watch BBC World or CNN en Español. Want Korean-language TV in the States or Indian TV in Britain? No problem. Cheap foreign travel is making far-off places accessible to a wider audience. You don't have to be Marco Polo to go to Mongolia these days. Most Westerners can afford to go around the world on a shoestring. Europeans who dare to venture across the Atlantic may even come to like America. George Bush can pay a visit to the Grecians. And once you get home, email and cheap phone calls allow you to stay in touch with your new foreign friends.

The second big change is that immigrants, mainly from developing countries, are turning Western societies into genuinely multicultural ones. Although Europe's former colonial powers have had a huge influence on parts of the Third World – Indians drive on the left, and educated ones speak an antiquated English; West Africans learn about 'nos ancêtres, les Gaulois' ('our ancestors, the Gauls'); Spanish and Portuguese have almost entirely eliminated native languages in Latin America – the recent flow of migration has been in the opposite direction. There are Algerian suburbs in Paris, but not French ones in Algiers; Pakistani parts of London, but not British ones of Lahore; Turkish quarters in Berlin, but not German ones in Istanbul. Whereas Muslims are a growing minority in Europe, Christians are a disappearing one in the Middle East.

This new multiculturalism can cause racial tensions. But it is still overwhelmingly a positive thing. People from poor countries get the chance of a new life. The countries they come to are enriched with all they have to offer. Londoners can dine out on Vietnamese food one night, Ecuadorian the next and Afro-Caribbean the following week. Latin Americans put on salsa classes, Indians start bhangra nights, Japanese teach judo. The melding of cultures produces vibrant new forms: Hanif Kureishi's writing; French rappers like MC Solaar; Brazilian artists in New York like Jander Lacerda.

What is happening in America is particularly exciting. Come with me to San Francisco, where my Mexican friend Carlos and I are heading for the Latino barrio for a late lunch. As we drive, the billboard ads switch from English to Spanish: the beaming faces now promise 'con AT&T siempre está cerca' ('with AT&T you are always close'). With its outsize cars and green street signs, the Mission district is still recognisably American, but with a distinctly Mexican hue. The faces of passers-by are browner; many have a dis-tinctively Indian look. Some even wear sombreros. At the Chavas cantina, Carlos orders birria, a spicy goat stew, while I go for que-sadillas, cheese tacos, with pozole, a spicy pork stew. The waitress takes the order in Spanish, and although some English can be heard, most of the tables around us buzz with Spanish. The border is 500 miles away, but it feels almost like Mexico, albeit a slightly sanitised version of it.

America can appear impervious to foreign cultures. When I wrote this paragraph, all the top ten grossing movies in the US came from Hollywood. Foreign films account for a mere 2 per cent of US box-office receipts. Only one foreign interloper – a Canadian – had forced her way into the bestseller list for books on Amazon.com, although two outsiders, a British singer and an Irish band, had muscled into the music hit-parade. But although foreign cultural products have trouble making a mark in America, foreigners themselves arrive in droves – and they are changing America even as they adopt its ways. New York cab drivers come from Ethiopia, Belarus and Laos. A million or so foreigners arrive every year (700,000 legally, 300,000 illegally), most of them Asian or Latino. Since 1990, the number of foreign-born American residents has risen by 6 million to just over 25 million – the biggest immigration wave since the turn of the twentieth century. English may be all-conquering outside America, but in some parts of the US it has become a second language (behind Spanish). Some places in Texas display signs saying 'English spoken here'. Half of the 50 million new inhabitants expected in America in the next twenty-five years will be immigrants or the children of immigrants.[18]

In a sense, the many Mexican migrants who are moving north are reclaiming the lands that the US stole from Mexico in the mid-nineteenth century. To put it in a less inflammatory way, Latinos are changing America perhaps more profoundly than any previous immigrants. Why? Because they waded through a river rather than crossing seas to get there. So – notwithstanding the barbed wire, watchtowers and tighter controls since September 11th – America's southern border is blurring. Hispanics now make up half the population in Los Angeles, over a third in Dallas and over two-fifths even in Dodge City, Kansas. A new 'Amexican' culture is being born. Did someone mention Americanised uniformity?

The third important change is that Western ideas are reshaping the way people everywhere view themselves and the world. Like nationalism and socialism before it, liberalism – political ideas about individual liberty, the rule of law, democracy and universal human rights, as well as economic ones about respect for private property rights, the benefits of free markets and the importance of consumer choice – is a European philosophy that has swept the world. Hundreds of Chinese people died in and around Tiananmen Square because they believed in universal freedoms. Burma's opposition leader, Aung San Suu Kyi, lived until recently under house arrest because she demanded democracy and human rights for her people. Russian shareholders insist that managers run companies along Western lines. Even people who resist liberal ideas, in the name of religion (Islamic and Christian fundamentalists), group identity (communitarians), authoritarianism (advocates of 'Asian values') or tradition (cultural conservatives), now define themselves partly by their opposition to them.

Faith in science and technology is even more widespread. Even those who hate the West make use of its technologies. Osama Bin Laden plots terrorism on a mobile phone and crashes planes into skyscrapers. Anti-globalisation protesters organise by email and over the Internet. José Bové manipulates twenty-first-century media in his bid to return French farming to the Middle Ages. China no longer turns its nose up at Western technology: it tries to beat the West at its own game.

Western ways are not everywhere triumphant. Many people reject Western culture. (Or, more accurately, 'cultures': Europeans and Americans disagree bitterly over the death penalty, for instance; the French and the Americans hardly see eye to eye over the role of the state either.) Samuel Huntington, a professor of international politics at Harvard, even predicts a 'clash of civilisations' that will divide the twenty-first-century world. 'Western ideas of individualism, liberalism, constitutionalism, human rights, equality, liberty, the rule of law, democracy, free markets, the separation of church and state, often have little resonance in Islamic, Confucian, Japanese, Hindu, Buddhist or Orthodox cultures. Western efforts to propagate such ideas produce instead a reaction against "human-rights imperialism" and a reaffirmation of indigenous values,'[19] he claims.

Mr Huntington's ideas are much in vogue since September 11th. Yet Francis Fukuyama, a professor of international political economy at Johns Hopkins, is nearer the mark when he talks about the 'end of history'.[20] Some cultures have local appeal, but only liberalism appeals everywhere (if not to all) – although radical environmentalism may one day challenge its hegemony. Islamic fundamentalism poses a threat to our lives but not to our beliefs. Unlike communism, it is not an alternative to liberal capitalism for

Westerners or other non-Muslims. Thank goodness! We should not shy away from extolling the universal virtues of liberal values. They are our proudest export. There is not a shadow of a doubt that life in the American protectorate of Afghanistan is better than life under the Taliban.

A trickier question is what we should do to promote human rights or democracy abroad. Should we stop trading with Burma – or China – for instance? I think it depends on whether sanctions are likely to be effective. If there is a decent chance that sanctions will help bring about changes that most local people want but cannot achieve themselves, they may be a good idea: as in the case of South Africa under apartheid, for example. But if sanctions are unlikely to bring about desirable reforms, applying them only compounds the misery of local people and may close off other avenues for reform. China's regime is loathsome in many ways. But the country is so big that shunning it is unlikely to improve matters. Double standards? Certainly. But surely the point of sanctions is to help people, not ease our consciences? Western governments should still apply some pressure on China when they can. Amnesty International and others are also right to campaign for human rights there. Arguably, denying Beijing the prize of the 2008 Olympics that it so coveted would have been a suitable sanction, but perhaps not: it would doubtless have stirred up nationalistic fervour off which the communists could feed. The 1988 Seoul Olympics sped South Korea's democratic reforms. With luck, Beijing's will too. Globalisation more broadly may also help: although it does not necessarily lead to greater democracy and respect for human rights, it may eventually help to loosen the communists' grip on power. Mainly, though, pressure for change must come from within China.

Individual freedom

The upshot of all this change is that national cultures are fragmenting into a kaleidoscope of different ones. New hybrid cultures

are emerging. In 'Amexica' people speak Spanglish: *'Como se llama*
your dog?' Regional cultures are reviving. Repressed under Franco,
Catalans, Basques, Gallegos and others assert their identity in
Spain. The Scots and Welsh break with British monoculture.
Estonia is reborn from the Soviet Union. Voices that were silent
dare to speak again.

Individuals are forming new communities, linked by shared
interests and passions, that cut across national borders.
Friendships with foreigners met on holiday. Scientists sharing their
ideas over the Internet. Environmentalists campaigning together
using email. An international Arsenal supporters' group. A worldwide Ricky Martin fan club. House-music lovers swapping tracks
online. Greater individualism does not spell the end of community.
The new communities are simply chosen, unlike the coerced traditional ones that communitarians hark back to.

The beauty of globalisation is that it can free people from the
tyranny of geography. Just because someone was born in France
does not mean they can aspire to only speak French, eat French
food, read French books, holiday in France, and so on. Does that
mean national identity is dead? Hardly. People who speak the same
language, were born and live near each other, face the same problems, have a common experience and vote in the same elections
still have plenty of things in common. For all our awareness of the
world as a single place, we are not citizens of the world but citizens
of a state. But if people now wear the bonds of nationality more
loosely, is that such a bad thing? People may lament the passing of
old ways. Indeed, many of the worries about globalisation echo
age-old fears about decline, a lost golden age and so on. But by and
large, people choose the new ways because they are more relevant
to their current needs and offer new opportunities that the old
ones did not.

The truth is that we increasingly define ourselves rather than let
others define us. We demand the right to take advantage of the
best the world has to offer. We are not betraying our culture by
doing so; we are being true to ourselves. People cannot be defined

entirely as British, or French, or black, or gay, or any other type. Being British does not define who you are: it is part of who you are. You can like foreign things and still be British. As Mario Vargas Llosa, a Peruvian author, has written: 'seeking to impose a cultural identity on a people is equivalent to locking them in a prison and denying them the most precious of liberties – that of choosing what, how, and who they want to be'.[21]

THIRTEEN

A Different World

We can build a better globalisation

The twentieth century is ending with a search to find out where the modern phase of globalisation is supposed to be leading us all: a world in which the question of production is solved once and for all, and all nations share in universal peace and prosperity? Or a soulless, standardised materialism in which the greed of the favoured few and a system skewed in favour of the rich and powerful drive the planet to the brink of extinction?

LARRY ELLIOTT and DAN ATKINSON, *The Age of Insecurity*

The champions of liberal markets are in full retreat. There is only one way they can make themselves heard over the angry shouts of the protesters. They must stop making the case for globalisation – and start fighting the cause of better globalisation.[1]

PHILIP STEPHENS, *Financial Times*

Ciudad Juárez has rarely been at the centre of things. It's a dustbowl of a town in northern Mexico's bleak Chihuahua desert. Ranchers from Chihuahua used to pause there with their cattle before crossing the Rio Grande on their way to Santa Fe. When the United States grabbed Mexican lands north of the Rio Grande in the 1850s, it became a border town. It has enjoyed brief booms, first as an illegal gambling and drinking den for US soldiers during Prohibition, later as a divorce pad for desperate Americans (including Liz Taylor). But by and large, it has been ignored. Its Texan neighbours in El Paso looked to Austin or Houston instead. Juárez itself was forced to look south to far-off Mexico City. Mexico lived by the words of its former President, Porfirio Díaz: 'poor Mexico! So far away from God, so close to the United States.'

But Juárez took on a new lease of life in the late 1960s. The Mexican government, which had shuttered the country off from its northern neighbour, decided to make a virtue of its geography instead of trying to escape from it. It allowed foreign factories to set up shop along the US border. They could import all they needed duty-free provided they exported all they made. The US Congress, hoping to deter illegal immigration, did its bit too: imports from these Mexican assembly plants, known as *maquiladoras*, were exempted from customs duties on all but their Mexican value-added. Foreign companies flocked to Juárez to take advantage of its cheap labour, tax advantages and proximity to the US. The city boomed. By 2000, 3,600 *maquiladoras* employed 1.3 million people, exporting goods (mainly electrical and electronic goods, clothes, and car parts and accessories) worth $80 billion a year, $18 billion of which was value added in Mexico.[2]

Where Juárez led, the rest of Mexico eventually followed. In the late 1980s, the country began to open up more. The walls that had isolated it from the world were torn down. Mexico chose to embrace the US rather than turn its back on it. First, in 1986, it joined the WTO's predecessor, the GATT. Then, in 1994, it concluded the North American Free-Trade Agreement (NAFTA) with the US and Canada. Guillermo Güemez, a private-sector adviser to the Mexican government during the NAFTA negotiations and now a deputy governor of the Bank of Mexico, highlights how Díaz's dictum has been turned on its head. 'Our comparative advantage is that we are next to the US,' he says.

Along the way, a funny thing happened. What started off as a make-work scheme for border-region Mexicans is now transforming the country from top to bottom. In 2000, seventy-one years of one-party rule came to an end with the election of a new president, Vicente Fox. And starting in places like Juárez and its American twin, El Paso, Mexicans and Americans who had been artificially separated by history and politics are growing together.

Many of the themes of this book come together in Juárez. First, that globalisation is primarily a political choice, not an inevitable fate. Governments once divided what geography unites. Now they are allowing Mexico and the US to come together again. 'Some people in Mexico City say we are turncoats,' remarks Carlos Salas Porras, a local businessman. 'But it is natural to look north.' Second, that globalisation benefits rich countries as well as poor ones. Until the bursting of the Internet bubble plunged America into recession, the economy on both sides of the border was growing at 5 to 7 per cent a year. American cars are cheaper thanks to the parts made in Juárez. Third, that however ugly it may look on the outside – and believe you me, Juárez isn't pretty – it is better than what came before.

Ask Efrain Luna López. He was born on a small farm in the state of Durango called, of all things, Londres. He came to Juárez because there is 'more work, more money, more job prospects'. 'I have a brother in Houston. But nearly all my family is here now. Only my parents are still in Durango. They're peasants, and too old to move. They don't like city life. We send them money back. My father earns $30 a week on the ranch. Here any worker makes at least $50. There is no work in the interior. Here, in a family of five most can work; there, only one. And everyone earns more here.' Efrain works as a bodyguard, his wife as a supervisor in a furniture store. They have two kids, aged nine and fifteen. 'My wife and I earn $350 to $400 a

week. With what we earn we don't have luxuries but we live OK. I
used to earn $400 a month in Durango. I don't like the insecurity
and the crime, the pollution, the smog. But I'm going to stay here.
I won't go back. I've been here three years. I'm established now.'

Even Veronica Rosario Leyva, a twenty-eight-year-old single
mother with three kids who works for the Centro de Estudios y
Taller Laboral (CETLAC), a local centre funded by American trade
unions that advises workers on their rights, grudgingly concedes
that: 'conditions are worse elsewhere in Mexico. There is no work
in Veracruz or Chiapas.' She used to work in an electrical components factory where she started off earning 200 pesos ($22) a week,
but five years later was making 900 pesos ($100). And although the
city is a smoggy, sprawling mess of ramshackle buildings and
streets strewn with rubbish that is running out of water, the
Mexican government is finally starting to clean it up. 'We used to
be a dumping ground,' says Mr Salas Porras. 'But now polluters are
beginning to have to pay.'

Mexico also illustrates how financial turbulence can wreck the
gains from trade. The country has done well from opening up to
foreign trade and investment: exporters pay over 50 per cent higher
wages than non-exporters; over one in five Mexicans work for firms
that have received foreign investment. But the Tequila financial
crisis in 1994–5 knocked a quarter off manufacturing workers' real
wages between 1994 and 1996 and an eighth off wages in
maquiladoras.

Juárez epitomises too how globalisation involves far more than
shipping ever more widgets across national borders. Gideon
Lichfield of *The Economist* has brilliantly captured the blending of
cultures along Mexico's border with the US. 'The taxis are big
American clunkers whose drivers listen to American radio stations.
A shop sells bottles of American-made *horchata*, a traditional Mexican
rice drink – but strawberry-flavoured, the way no traditional
Mexican drinks it. Spanish melds with English: a government
official asks his assistant to *faxear* a letter to someone. Lunch is at
1pm, not 2 or 3. Appointments are kept. Cars stop for pedestrians –

sometimes.'[3] Whereas many in Mexico City did not weep on September 11th, people in Juárez shared in Americans' pain. 'Most of us have friends and relatives in the States,' says Mr Luna López. 'We all put little American flags on our cars after September 11th.'

But Juárez also underscores that borders still matter. El Paso's firemen once responded to an emergency in Juárez, only to realise that their life insurance did not cover them across the border. Mexicans can still earn much more in El Paso than they could for doing an equivalent job in Juárez. Many of the region's biggest problems – drugs, people smuggling, environmental degradation – are exacerbated by the patchiness of cross-border co-operation: most big decisions are still made separately in far-off capitals rather than together locally.

Let me be clear: by Western standards, Juárez is not a nice place. Critics of globalisation can – and do – point to all sorts of nasty things about Juárez and places like it all around the Third World. But Mexicans from all over the country are still moving there in search of a better life. Few go home. And although Juárez, like so many other places, is now feeling the brunt of America's recession, growth will undoubtedly resume once the US economy recovers. My point is simple: all sorts of things are wrong with the world, but globalisation is overwhelmingly a force for good.

Make change your friend

Yet it is not perfect. Which brings me to my second important theme: we can improve on the globalisation we have now. Everything that has been written about brands and companies running the world has contributed to a more general sense of powerlessness in the face of misunderstood, and seemingly uncontrollable, global forces. For once, Thomas Friedman has got it spot on: 'the defining anxiety in globalisation is fear of rapid change from an enemy you can't see, touch or feel – a sense that your job, community or workplace can be changed at any moment by anonymous economic and technological forces that are anything but stable'.[4]

Fear of change is nothing new, of course. Nor is a fear of foreign influences: the barbarians are always at the gates. Nor indeed is a fear of the mysterious and the misunderstood: every society has its witches. Yet there is something vast, invisible and all-embracing about globalisation that makes it especially terrifying. As you finger a ten-pound note, the mind boggles at the thought that its value is set on a market where one million million pounds flutter around the world each day. As you type away on your computer, assembled from parts made in foreign factories by people whose lives you have little conception of, it is frightening that a computer virus from who knows where could suddenly wipe your screen clear. As you tread the well-worn path to work in the morning, you sweat a little at the thought that the devaluation of an exotic currency you had never heard of could trigger a chain of events that sees you out of a job through no fault of your own. Our lives are linked to those of people all over the world as never before. It may fill you with trepidation. But it should also fill you with awe. However huge and impersonal global markets may seem, they are merely the consequence of billions of tiny, individual – and very personal – choices.

Strip away the fear and the misunderstanding and you see that most of us – rich and poor – actually have more choice than ever before. Choice about what we eat, choice about where we work, choice about where we live, choice about who our friends are, choice about what kind of future we have. Supermarkets in Bangkok sell Marmite; Sainsbury's in London sells Thai biscuits. Chuck Swearingen's son is studying computing; Van Reiner's is in Japan. I have made many friends on my round-the-world research trip for this book with whom I stay in touch by email. But most importantly, we can make all those individual choices and still continue to shape our future collectively. Just think of the millions of people who have helped victims of human-rights abuses by writing letters through Amnesty International.

Consider too what a difference the governments that we (in the democratic world) elect still make. They are pivotal in four main ways. First, they are the gatekeepers of globalisation: they have freed trade in computers but not in food. Second, they are the rule-makers: they decide what food is safe, how much we should protect the environment, whether we should enforce monopolies (drug patents) or break them (Microsoft). Third, they are either enablers or disablers. If people are to grasp the opportunities offered by globalisation, governments need to open up their economies *and* provide peace, security, good schools, decent roads, wise laws, clean justice and so on. Open markets without good government are not enough. Good government is the difference between South Korea and Zimbabwe: both were poor in 1960; both trade a lot; one is now rich, one is sinking ever further into poverty. As Amartya Sen has rightly said: 'development requires the removal of major sources of unfreedom: poverty as well as tyranny, poor economic opportunities as well as systematic social deprivation, neglect of public facilities as well as intolerance or overactivity of repressive states'.[5] This requires open markets and good government. Foreign governments have a role to play too, through debt relief, aid and other assistance. Fourth, they are, or should be, the protectors of the poor, the weak, the sick, the vulnerable – and all those who lose out from or are left behind by globalisation. Market fundamentalists claim globalisation makes governments irrelevant; left-wing radicals that it makes governments impotent. Both are plain wrong. An agenda for a better globalisation can – and indeed must – be built around governments.

Start with the gatekeeping. The World Bank reckons[6] that abolishing all trade barriers could add $2,800 billion to the world economy – $1,500 billion of which would go to poor countries – and lift 320 million people out of poverty by 2015 if coordinated actions were also taken to promote trade and reforms in developing countries. That is equivalent to adding another France and Britain to the world economy, or nearly three more Chinas. It would slash global poverty by a quarter, the equivalent of lifting all the poor in sub-Saharan Africa out of poverty. If the new round of trade talks under the aegis of the World Trade Organisation that started in January 2002 and aims to finish by 2005 achieves even half of that, it will be a remarkable step forward.

There must be no more excuses from rich countries. It is time to do away with their obscene restrictions on farm trade, their criminal curbs on clothing trade, their safeguards for the steel industry and their anti-dumping duties on imports they deem 'too cheap'. Food and clothing are poorest countries' biggest exports: Western governments are condemning the poor to continued misery by their protectionism. Talk about fighting terrorism is fine and dandy, but George Bush could do more good by opening up America's markets to T-shirts from Pakistan and other poor countries. Words – 'the state of Africa is a scar on the conscience of the world' – and tours of Africa are all very well, but if Tony Blair really wants to help Africa, he should insist that the EU lower its farm-trade barriers. Listen to Alec Erwin, South Africa's trade minister, who fought long and hard against apartheid. 'We are trying to do everything right,' he said. 'But rich countries just keep knocking us back. We desperately need better access to Western markets.' Opening our markets would be good not only for poor countries; it would be good for us too. Freeing trade is like a tax cut: imports are cheaper so your money goes further. The poorest in Europe and America would gain most of all from cheaper food and clothes. Patrick Messerlin estimates[7] that the cost of European protectionism comes to 7 per cent of EU GDP – as much as Spain's annual economic output. Support for the farming industry costs an average family of four over $1,000 a year in higher taxes and prices – and it doesn't even guarantee us safe food.

Poor countries can also do a lot to help themselves. Although rich countries have high import duties on some products, poor countries have higher trade barriers than rich ones on average. That is a needless handicap. It penalises the poor and stifles economic growth. Even if rich countries fail to open their markets, it makes sense for poor ones to open theirs. As we have seen, the countries that have embraced globalisation are catching up with Europe and North America; those that have not are falling further behind.

The biggest gains to poor countries – and to the world – could come from opening up services markets like tourism, transport, telecoms and construction. Indian software services and Cuban healthcare could become world-beaters. Services account for three-fifths of the world economy, but only a fifth of world trade. Falling import barriers in manufactures have powered world growth over the past fifty years. Falling barriers in services could do the same over the next fifty.

The WTO also needs to get a handle on regional trade agreements. They threaten to tangle the world economy up in knots and undo much of the good work achieved multilaterally. Where they involve a serious commitment to creating a single market and when they remain open to the rest of the world, they should get the WTO's blessing, especially if they are part of a broader political project. But where they are flimsy, twenty-first-century rehashes of the import-substitution model that failed India and other developing countries in the past, or where they involve rich countries carving up poor countries' markets for themselves, they should be condemned. America's misnamed African Growth and Opportunity Act, for instance, gives Africans preferential access to US textile markets – but only if they use American cloth. Its free-trade agreement with Jordan commits that country to higher levels of patent protection than the TRIPS agreement requires. The EU's countless preferential pacts give it unequal access to weaker countries' markets. South Africa, for instance, cannot freely sell its food and wine in the EU, even through European companies get privileged access to South African markets. As for the alphabet soup of African and other regional trade deals, they are harmful shams that replicate the errors of the past. Since WTO governments are nearly all complicit, they sure as hell won't blow the whistle, but its director-general and others should.

The other barriers that need lowering are those that prevent people from moving freely. Rich countries have ageing populations. They could benefit from an infusion of young people. They also lack workers to do all sorts of tasks, from the menial ones at which Europeans and Americans now turn their noses up to skilled jobs in computing and healthcare. Nearly half of London's nurses and a quarter of its doctors are foreign. As Harvard's Dani Rodrik has rightly pointed out, the huge gaps between wages for similar tasks in rich and poor countries indicate that the benefits of freeing up migration could be huge. My mother's parents fled the Soviet army invading Estonia in 1944 and eventually found refuge in the United States. They, and America, are better off for it. Others should not be denied that opportunity. As Daniel Griswold of the Cato Institute in Washington DC points out,[8] immigrants neither take 'our' jobs nor drain government finances. They contribute their labour, their taxes and their culture – and they send much-needed money back to poor countries. An immigration free-for-all is not on the cards. But we should still open our borders more to the needy, the desperate and the hard-working of the world.

While they tear down trade barriers, countries also need to build financial firewalls. Complacency pervades both governments and the financial sector. Look, they say, Turkey had to turn to the IMF for help, Argentina has defaulted, yet other developing countries, let alone rich ones, have not been affected. The Brazilian currency is getting stronger even as Argentina's plumbs the depths (though it is now falling too). Contagion is dead. The financial crisis in 1997–8 was just a bad dream. Not so. The world financial system, and the world economy that relies on it, came perilously close to meltdown in 1998. The Federal Reserve's chairman, Alan Greenspan, admits that he was holding his breath when he cut interest rates that October in a desperate bid to keep the financial system afloat. We were lucky. There is no guarantee we always will be. The tinkering that passes for reform of global finance will not do. In the meanwhile, developing countries need to take matters into their own hands. Put prudential capital controls in place while the sea is placid. Don't wait until the storm has hit and the waves are breaking over your head. An 'emerging-markets eminent-persons group' chaired by Il SaKong, a former finance minister of South Korea, put forward some sensible suggestions[9] that have the merit of coming from developing countries that bear the brunt of financial storms. Its report should be widely read, and heeded.

Next, look at rule-making. The new WTO round should do more than free up trade. In an ideal world, the TRIPS agreement would be scrapped, but, unfortunately, America will never jettison an agreement that it fought so hard for. Developing countries should instead aim to gain more flexibility in setting their intellectual-property laws. The Doha declaration was a good first step, but it doesn't go far enough. TRIPS reform is not only sound economics. It's also a humanitarian imperative. 'Patents kill' was the simple message of some people protesting at the high price of patented anti-Aids drugs. Sometimes they do.

Patent protection needs to be weakened. Environmental protection needs to be strengthened. In part, this is a job for national governments. If globalisation is to be green, domestic environmental problems need to be tackled at source: stop subsidising pesticides, fishing and fossil fuels; impose a pesticide and a carbon tax instead. But governments also need to work in concert. The Montreal protocol proves that when they apply themselves they can tackle a serious problem like the destruction of the ozone layer. The Kyoto protocol is, hopefully, only a first step towards more meaningful efforts to limit climate change. The Bush administration's position is shameful and reckless. The US too will suffer from global warming. Americans have a duty to force their government to change its mind about co-operating with others to limit greenhouse-gas emissions.

The time has also come for a World Environment Organisation (WEO). Granted, there already is one: the United Nations Environment Programme. But have you heard of it? Probably not. It's a hopelessly bureaucratic and ineffective beast – best to put it out of its misery. The case for a new global body to deal with environmental issues is simply put. Action to tackle environmental problems is haphazard, patchy and uncoordinated. A sprawl of environmental law – over 200 separate multilateral environmental agreements – is not a substitute for focused, joined-up action. The world needs an authoritative global voice on the environment to match that of the WTO on trade or the WHO on health, a body to drive research and share information, and a forum for debating environmental issues and resolving disputes. Without a WEO, the environment will suffer more, and bodies that are ill-suited to dealing with green issues, like the WTO, will be pressed into doing so, *faute de mieux*.

The International Labour Organisation already exists to deal with labour issues, so there is no need for yet more international bureaucrats. Besides, there is less need for international co-operation on labour issues, which – unlike environmental ones – rarely cut across borders. Where workers are badly treated, it is mainly for locals to sort out the problem. Even so, people in rich countries can help. Not by imposing trade sanctions, which would do nothing to help children working on local farms, for instance, and would hit people who work for good employers as well as bad ones. Why not set up a fund to pay for children's schooling in the Third World instead? Put your money where your mouth is. If all people want is guilt-free shopping, they shouldn't pretend they actually care.

What about enabling? Here too, the duty lies primarily with national governments. However much we might despair at many governments' failure to provide for their people's needs, there is little we can – or should – do about it. Imperialism is a discredited option: we have neither the right nor the means to decide for others. Yet Europe and North America can still make a difference. For a start, we need to build on the progress made towards cancelling Third World debt. True, we are letting off the hook governments that have squandered Western loans or stuffed them in private Swiss bank accounts, but the overwhelming priority is to free poor people from the burden of debts they cannot pay. Jubilee Plus is calling for the cancellation of all the foreign debts of forty-two countries defined by the World Bank and IMF as having unsustainable debts. Quite right too. Yet debt relief cannot come without strings attached. There must be binding guarantees that governments will use the resources freed up to help the poor.

At the same time, the World Bank should be turned, as the US Congress's Meltzer Commission suggested, into a World Development Agency that offers poor countries grants, not loans. But, contrary to what the commission suggests, this agency's finances should not be curtailed. Such an agency would need to take care that the money it doled out was not wasted, but that is hardly a persuasive argument for not switching from loans to grants. After all, lots of World Bank money has been wasted on governments' pet projects rather than used for schemes that actually met local needs.

Rich countries should also give more money in aid. It is an outrage that the richest country on earth, the US, gives a mere 0.1 per cent of its national income to help less fortunate foreigners – and a large part of that is military assistance to Israel and Egypt. The extra $5 billion that President Bush has promised to spend in 2004–6 is still not enough. In 1965, America gave 0.6 per cent of its GDP. EU governments do better. They give 0.33 per cent of GDP, which they have pledged to raise to 0.39 per cent. They should meet the UN target of giving 0.7 per cent of GDP; only a few, mainly Scandinavian, countries actually do. It is not beyond the wit of man to channel aid to those who need it. Charities manage it, as can governments: the EU's cohesion funds have worked wonders in poorer European countries. Some of the extra money should go to a global fund to improve healthcare in poor countries, as suggested by Jeffrey Sachs. It should also go to fund schools that give kids the chance of a better life. Giving more aid is not only the right thing to do. It can also prevent costly future crises. As George Soros points out, NATO countries spent as much as $4 billion bombing Yugoslavia, but had difficulty finding $50 million to help

Montenegro's economic reforms. The Bush administration wants to spend $379 billion on defence in fiscal 2003 but a mere $10 billion on overseas aid.

Finally, governments need to do more to protect the vulnerable. Some people in rich countries will lose out from globalisation. They will lose their jobs or have to settle for lower wages. The priority is to equip people with the skills needed to improve their lot and move easily from job to job. Government should also help to ease and speed up the transition. And it should top up the wages of people who earn little, so that all can participate in a civilised society. Adjusting to losing your job is particularly tricky in America, because workers usually lose their health insurance too. In Europe, although the state provides for people when they are ill, it often takes far too long to find another job. Flexible labour markets combined with a generous social cushion would marry the best of both systems and ease worries about globalisation.

Some people in poor countries will lose out initially too. They are far more vulnerable because they have neither savings nor a social safety net to catch them. As *Trade Liberalisation and Poverty: A Handbook*,[10] an excellent book by Alan Winters of the University of Sussex and others, suggests, freeing trade is still overwhelmingly a good thing for poor countries. But extra care needs to be taken because poor people find it harder to adjust to change than richer people. Perhaps some of the extra foreign aid should go to funding rudimentary safety nets for poor people who initially suffer from freeing trade.

Choose hope

There is no worse counsel than despair. If only critics of globalisation opened their eyes, they would realise that many of their complaints should be directed not at globalisation itself, but at a lack of globalisation or the absence of accompanying measures to make it work better. They should think again.

Once you make the crucial step and accept that we can still shape our destiny, globalisation's opportunities are all the more apparent, its threats suddenly less menacing. The future of our open world is in our hands. We are free to make the best of it – or to waste it.

Notes

Introduction

1   United Nations Development Programme, *Human Development Report*, 2001.

2   Openness is measured by the average of exports and imports of goods and services, divided by gross domestic product in current US dollars. Whereas a huge continental economy like the United States traded only 13 per cent of its GDP in 2000, middling ones like Britain traded 28.5 per cent, France 29 per cent and Germany 34 per cent, and a small one like Ireland 93 per cent.

3   John Kay, 'The Great Paradox of Globalisation', *Financial Times*, 14 November 2001.

4   Thomas Friedman, *The Lexus and the Olive Tree*, Harper Collins, 2000.

5   Ulrich Beck, *What is Globalization?*, Polity 2000, p. 11.

6   Anthony Giddens and Will Hutton, 'In Conversation'. In *On The*

Edge: Living With Global Capitalism, eds. Will Hutton and Anthony
Giddens, Jonathan Cape, 2000, pp. 1–2.

7   John Kay, 'The Great Paradox of Globalisation'.

Chapter One: Worried Workers

1   American Institute for International Steel, *Paying the Price for Big
     Steel*, Washington DC, 2000.
2   'Romancing Big Steel', *The Economist*, 14 February 2002.
3   OECD, *Employment Outlook*, 1997, Chapter 4.
4   OECD, *Employment Outlook*, 2001, Chapter 3.
5   All statistics are from America's Bureau of Labor Statistics, see
     http://www.bls.gov/fls/flslforc.pdf.
6   OECD, *Economic Outlook*, January 2001, Annex table 63.
7   OECD, *Employment Outlook*, July 1997, Chapter 4.
8   Lori Kletzer, *Job Loss from Imports: Measuring the Costs*, Institute for
     International Economics, Washington DC, 2001.
9   Dani Rodrik, 'Has Globalization Gone Too Far?', Institute for
     International Economics, Washington DC, 1997.
10   UK National Accounts, *The Blue Book*, 2001, Table 8.2.

Chapter Two: The Poor Profit

1   Jay Mazur, 'Labour's New Internationalism', *Foreign Affairs*, 79,
     2001, no. 1, January–February 2000.
2   His name has been changed to protect his identity.
3   Jeffrey Sachs and Andrew Warner, 'Economic Reform and the
     Process of Global Integration', *Brookings Papers on Economic Activity*,
     1995.
4   Jeffrey Frankel and David Romer, 'Does Trade Cause Growth?',
     American Economic Review, June 1998.
5   David Dollar and Aart Kraay, 'Growth *Is* Good for the Poor', World
     Bank, March 2000.
6   David Dollar and Aart Kraay, 'Trade, Growth and Poverty', World
     Bank, March 2001.
7   Edward Graham, 'Fighting the Wrong Enemy', Institute for

International Economics, 2000.

8   Ibid; Daniel Rosen, 'Behind the Open Door', Institute for International Economics, 1999.

9   Edward Graham, 'Fighting the Wrong Enemy'.

10 To be more precise, the measure is the mean log distribution, which is roughly equivalent to the percentage gap between median and mean.

11 Département et Laboratoire d'Economie Théorique et Appliquée of the Ecole Normale Supérieure.

12 François Bourguignon and Christian Morrisson, 'The Size Distribution of Income among World Citizens: 1820–1990', Mimeo, Delta, 1999.

13 Quoted in David Dollar, 'Globalisation, Inequality and Poverty since 1980', World Bank, November 2001.

Chapter Three: A Brief History of Globalisation

1   Marco Polo, *The Travels of Marco Polo*, Wordsworth Editions, 1997, pp. 81–2.

2   Andre Gunder Frank, *ReOrient: Global Economy in the Asian Age*, University of California Press, 1998, p. 52. In Kevin O'Rourke and Jeffrey Williamson, 'When Did Globalization Begin?', National Bureau of Economic Research working paper 7632, April 2000.

3   For instance, Adam Smith, the great Scottish philosopher and political economist, believed that 'the discovery of America and that of a passage to the East Indies by the Cape of Good Hope, are the greatest and most important events recorded in the history of mankind'. *The Wealth of Nations*, 1776, 6th edition, 1791, vol. II, ch. VII, part III, p. 139.

4   Norman Davies, *Europe: A History*, Oxford University Press, 1996, p. 511.

5   S. Castles and M. J. Miller, *The Age of Mass Migration*, Macmillan, 1993, p. 48.

6   Norman Davies, *Europe: A History*, p. 581.

7   David Landes, *The Wealth and Poverty of Nations: Why Some Are So Rich and Some So Poor*, Abacus, 1999, p. 55.

8   Ibid. pp. 94–5.

9   Ibid. p. 98.

10   Kevin O'Rourke and Jeffrey Williamson, 'After Columbus: Explaining the Global Trade Boom, 1500–1800', National Bureau of Economic Research working paper 8186, March 2001.

11   Henry Martyn, *Considerations upon the East India Trade*, A & J Churchill, 1701, quoted in Douglas Irwin, *Against the Tide: An Intellectual History of Free Trade*, Princeton University Press, 1996.

12   Adam Smith, *The Wealth of Nations*, 1776, 6th edition, 1791, vol. IV, ch. VII, part XII, quoted in ibid.

13   Ibid.

14   Ibid. vol. IV, ch. VII, pp. 48–50.

15   James Mill, Elements of Political Economy, 1821, pp. 87, 89.

16   The following section draws on Kevin O'Rourke and Jeffrey Williamson, *Globalization and History: The Evolution of a Nineteenth-Century Atlantic Economy*, MIT Press, 1999, and 'When Did Globalization Begin?' National Bureau of Economic Research working paper 7632, April 2000. Eric Hobsbawm's masterful three-part history of the nineteenth century, *The Age of Revolution*, *The Age of Capital*, and *The Age of Empire*, was also invaluable.

17   Eric Hobsbawm, *The Age of Revolution*, Weidenfeld & Nicolson, 1962.

18   Eric Hobsbawm, *The Age of Empire*, Weidenfeld & Nicolson, 1987.

19   Jonathan Freedland, *Bring Home the Revolution: The Case for a British Republic*, Fourth Estate, 1998.

20   Thomas Jefferson, first draft of the Declaration of Independence, 1775.

21   Eric Hobsbawm, *The Age of Revolution*.

22   Eric Hobsbawm, *The Age of Empire*.

23   Michael Hardt and Antonio Negri, *Empire*, Harvard University Press, 2000.

24   David Landes, *The Wealth and Poverty of Nations*, pp. 377–8.

25   Goods exports as a share of GDP.

26   Eric Hobsbawm, *Age of Extremes: The Short Twentieth Century 1914–1991*, Abacus, 1994.

27   Daniel Yergin and Joseph Stanislaw, *The Commanding Heights*, Touchstone, 1998.

28   Some of this draws from Michael Bordo, Barry Eichengreen, Douglas Irwin, 'Is Globalisation Today Really Different than Globalisation a Hundred Years Ago?', National Bureau of Economic Research working paper 7195, June 1999.

29   www.world-tourism.org (World Tourism Organisation).

30   UNDP, *World Development Report*, 2001.

31   The following statistics are taken from various sources: WTO, 'International Trade Statistics 2001'; UNCTAD, 'World Investment Report 2001'; OECD, 'Trends in International Migration 2001'; UNESCO, 'International Flows of Selected Cultural Goods 1980–1998'; 'UNDP Human Development Report 2001'; as well as my own calculations.

32   M. Obstfeld and A. M. Taylor, *Global Capital Markets: Integration, Crisis and Growth*, Cambridge University Press, 1999.

33   David D. Dossier on Globalisation. *The Courier*, 164, July–August 1997.

34   Gross purchases and sales of securities between residents and non-residents. Bank for International Settlements (BIS), 69th Annual Report, May 1999.

35   BIS, International Banking Statistics, table 6A, External positions of reporting banks vis-à-vis individual countries, table 6.

36   Average of exports and imports of goods and services, divided by gross domestic product in current US dollars.

37   Trade can exceed GDP because GDP measures the value-added in an economy, which is smaller than the total value of transactions.

38   Martin Wolf, 'Will the Nation State Survive Globalisation?', *Foreign Affairs*, January–February 2001.

39   John Maynard Keynes, *The Economic Consequences of the Peace*, Macmillan, 1919.

40   John Gray, *New Statesman*, 24 September 2001.

41   Stephen Roach, 'Back to Borders', *Financial Times*, 28 September 2001.

42   www.washingtontradereport.com.

43   http://www.unctad.org/en/press/pdfs/pr01_36.en.pdf.

44   Ibid.

Chapter Four: Brand New World?

1   Thomas Frank, 'The Big Lie', *Guardian*, 9 July 2001.
2   'The Best Global Brands', *Business Week*, 6 August 2001.
3   Quoted in 'Brands: Who's Wearing the Trousers?', *The Economist*, 6 September 2001.
4   Erik Brynjolfsson and Michael D. Smith, 'The Great Equalizer? Customer Choice Behavior at Internet Shopbots', http://e-commerce.mit.edu/papers/tge.
5   http://www.nikebiz.com/story/hist_our.shtml.
6   http://www2.coca-cola.com/ourcompany/ourbeliefs.html.
7   Howard Shultz, *Pour Your Heart Into It*, Hyperion, 1997.
8   Naomi Klein, 'The Tyranny of the Brands', *New Statesman*, 24 January 2000.
9   Naomi Klein, *No Logo*, Flamingo, 2001.
10 Coca-Cola USA press conference. Quoted in Susan Fournier, *Introducing New Coke*, Harvard Business School, Case 500–007.
11 *Newsweek*, 24 June 1985.
12 Ibid.
13 Quoted in Richard Tomkins, 'No Logo', *Financial Times*, 7 August 2001.
14 Naomi Klein, *No Logo*.

Chapter Five: Giants with Clay Feet

1   Dealogic.
2   Ibid.
3   'The Big Leap', *The Economist*, 15 January 2000.
4   United Nations Conference on Trade and Development, World Investment Report 2001.
5   Ibid. table II.3.
6   The assets of financial multinationals are not comparable with those of non-financial ones; comparable statistics are unavailable.
7   Adam Smith, *The Wealth of Nations*, vol. 1, ch. II, p. 13.
8   OECD, *Measuring Globalisation, The Role of Globalisation in OECD Economies*, 1999. I first wrote about this in an article for *The*

Economist entitled 'Foreign Friends', 8 January 2000.

9   John Plender, 'Unpopular Capitalism', *Financial Times*, 11 September 2000.

10 Paul de Grauwe and Filip Camerman, 'How Big Are The Big Multinational Companies?' January 2002, http://www.econ.kuleven.ac.be/ew/academic/intecon/degrauwe/PaulDeGrauwe.htm.

11 Bureau of Economic Analysis, National Income and Product Accounts Tables, Table 1.14.

12 http://www.steelprofiles.com/datacenter/rank_co.htm.

13 John Kay, 'Gigantic Misconceptions', *Financial Times*, 23 March 1998.

14 Paul de Grauwe and Filip Camerman, 'How Big Are the Big Multinational Companies?'.

15 Dan Roberts, 'Boom Takeovers Unwinding, Says Survey', *Financial Times*, 22 February 2002.

16 Pankaj Ghemawat and Fariborz Ghadar, 'The Dubious Logic of Global Megamergers', *Harvard Business Review*, July–August 2000.

17 John Kay, 'Gigantic misconceptions'.

18 Adam Smith, *The Wealth of Nations*, vol. I, ch. X, part II, p. 117.

19 All the tax figures are from OECD *Revenue Statistics*, 2001.

20 Edward Luttwak, *Turbo Capitalism*, HarperCollins, 1999, p. 14.

Chapter Six: The Phantom Menace

1   Federal Reserve, *Flow of Funds Accounts*, http://www.federalreserve.gov/releases/Z1/Current/z1.pdf.

2   All the tax figures are from OECD *Revenue Statistics*, 2001. They exclude non-tax revenues.

3   Vito Tanzi, 'Globalisation, Technological Developments and the Work of Fiscal Termites', IMF working paper 00/181, November 2000.

4   Adair Turner, *Just Capital*, Macmillan, 2001.

5   OECD, *Policy Competition for Foreign Direct Investment*, 2000.

6   OECD, *Trade, Employment and Labour Standards*, 1996.

7   Richard Freeman, 'Single-Peaked vs. Diversified Capitalism: The Relation Between Economic Institutions and Outcomes'. NBER working paper 7556, February 2000.

8   UNCTAD, *World Investment Report*, 2001.
9   Bureau of Economic Affairs, http://www.bea.doc.gov/bea/newsrel/intinv00.htm.
10 Pam Woodall, 'Statistical Illusions', *The Economist*, 10 November 2001.
11 Dani Rodrik, 'Has Globalisation Gone Too Far?', Institute for International Economics, Washington DC, 1997.

Chapter Seven: Global Government

1   Mike Moore, *A Brief History of the Future: Citizenship of the Millennium* (Christchurch: Shoal Boy Press, 1998).
2   Jeffrey Frankel and Andrew Rose, 'An Estimate of the Effect of Common Currencies on Trade and Income' Draft, 2001
3   Robert Keohane and Joseph Nye, 'The Club Model of Multilateral Cooperation and the World Trade Organisation: Problems of Democratic Legitimacy', paper presented at a conference at the Kennedy School of Government, Harvard, 1 June 2000.
4   Philippe Legrain, 'Dump Those Prejudices', *Guardian*, 12 July 2001.
5   George Monbiot, 'How to Rule the World', *Guardian*, 17 July 2001.
6   Patrick Buchanan, *The Great Betrayal*, Little, Brown, 1998.
7   www.uia.org (Yearbook of International Organisations).
8   Michael Edwards, 'NGO Rights and Responsibilities: A New Deal for Global Governance', Demos, 2000.
9   Zanny Minton-Beddoes, 'The Non-Governmental Order', *The Economist*, 11 December 1999.
10 http://www.unglobalcompact.org/un/gc/unweb.nsf/content/whati-tis.htm.
11 David Henderson, 'A Flawed Consensus', *World Link*, January–February 2000, based on his essay, 'Misguided Virtue: False Notions of Corporate Social Responsibility'.
12 Naomi Klein, 'The Tyranny of the Brands', *New Statesman*, 24 January 2000.
13 Ibid.
14 Quoted in 'Brands: Who's Wearing the·Trousers?', *The Economist*, 6 September 2001.

Chapter Eight: Food for Thought

1   In *On the Edge, Living with Global Capitalism*, eds. Will Hutton and Anthony Giddens.

2   Interview with José Bové by Paul Kingsnorth, 'Have-a-Go Hero', *The Ecologist*, June 2000.

3   The Tinbergen Institute estimates that agricultural liberalisation would boost poor countries by $155 billion a year. This compares with average overseas aid of $43 billion a year in 1997–8.

4   OECD, *Agricultural Policies in OECD Countries: Monitoring and Evaluation*, 2001.

5   http://www.bls.gov/fls/flslforc.pdf.

6   Tsunehiro Otsuki, John Wilson, Mirvat Sewadeh, 'Saving Two in a Billion: A Case Study to Quantify the Trade Effect of European Food Safety Standards on African Exports', World Bank 2000.

7   Franz Fischler, 'Scrap CAP? Think Twice!', *Wall Street Journal Europe*, 20 July 2000.

8   Richard Howarth, 'A Rotten Harvest', *Wall Street Journal Europe*, 15 June 2000.

9   Tony Long, 'It has Been an Environmental Disaster', *Wall Street Journal Europe*, 29 June 2000.

10 Victor Davis Hanson, 'Farmers Harvest a Bumper Crop of Subsidies', *Wall Street Journal*, 10 August 1999.

11 Interview with José Bové by Paul Kingsnorth, 'Have-a-Go Hero'.

12 Caroline Lucas and Colin Hines, 'Stopping The Great Food Swap – Relocalising Europe's Food Supply', *The Great European Free Alliance*, European Parliament, March 2001.

13 Colin Hines, *Localisation: A Global Manifesto*, Earthscan, 2000.

14 Caroline Lucas and Colin Hines, 'Stopping The Great Food Swap – Relocalising Europe's Food Supply'.

15 Ibid.

Chapter Nine: Endangered Earth?

1   Letter to *The Economist*, 10 December 1999, in response to 'Storm Over Globalisation', a pre-Seattle editorial that I wrote on 26 November 1999.

2   In *On the Edge, Living with Global Capitalism*, eds. Will Hutton and Anthony Giddens.

3   'Bungle in the Jungle', *The Economist*, 17 February 2000.

4   http://www.panda.org/news/features/archive/06-98/story3.htm.

5   World Resources 1998–99: A Guide to the Global Environment. A collaborative report by the World Resource Institute, the United Nations Environmental Programme, the United Nations Development Programme, and the World Bank, 1998.

6   'The Right to Drive or the Right to Breathe?', *The Economist*, 7 March 2002.

7   Worldwatch, 'The Natural Wealth of Nations', 1998.

8   Gene M. Grossman and Alan B. Krueger, 'Economic Growth and the Environment', National Bureau of Economic Research, NBER working paper W4634, February 1994.

9   M. A. Cole, A. I. Rayner, J. M. Bates, 'Trade Liberalisation and the Environment: The Case of the Uruguay Round', *World Economy*, vol. 21(3), May 1998, pp. 337–47.

10   R. Repetto, 'Jobs, Competitiveness and Environmental Regulation: What Are the Real Issues?', World Resources Institute, May 1995.

11   J. Albrecht, 'Environmental Policy and Inward Investment Position of US Dirty Industries', *Intereconomics*, July/August 1998 pp. 186–94.

12   *The President's Council on Environmental Quality, Environmental Quality: 1997 Report*, Government Printing Office, 1998.

Chapter Ten: Patently Wrong

1   Quoted in David Pilling, 'Patents and Patients', *Financial Times*, 17 February 2001.

2   UN AIDS, 'Aids Epidemic Update', December 2001, http://www.unaids.org/epidemic_update/report_dec01/index.html.

3   www.bea.doc.gov (Bureau of Economic Analysis, US International Transactions Accounts Data).

Chapter Eleven: Financial Failings

1   Dublin lecture, April 1933.
2   Jean Baudrillard, *The Transparency of Evil*, Verso, 1993.
3   John Maynard Keynes, *The General Theory of Employment, Interest and Money*, Royal Economic Society, 1936.
4   Paul Krugman, *The Return of Depression Economics*, Penguin, 1999, p. 41.
5   Ibid. p. 89.
6   Ibid. p. 95.
7   George Soros, *Open Society, Reforming Global Capitalism*, Public Affairs, 2000.
8   Paul Volcker, 'The Sea of Global Finance', in *On The Edge: Living with Global Capital*, eds. Will Hutton and Anthony Giddens.
9   Paul Krugman, *The Return of Depression Economics*, Penguin, 1999, p. 41.
10 Ibid. p. 114.
11 George Soros, 'To Avert the Next Crisis', *Financial Times*, 4 January 1999.
12 Joseph Stiglitz, 'Boats, Planes and Capital Flows', *Financial Times*, 25 March 1998.

Chapter Twelve: Culture Clash

1   In *On the Edge: Living with Global Capitalism*, eds Will Hutton and Anthony Giddens.
2   J. N. Pieterse, 'Globalisation as Hybridisation', in M. Featherstone, S. Lash and R. Robertson eds, *Global Modernities*, Sage Publications.
3   In 2000, the *Guinness Book of Records* anointed him the world's most successful DJ.
4   Norman Davies, *Europe: A History*.
5   'Evolutionary Wriggling', *The Economist*, 2 September 1999.
6   http://www.fas.usda.gov/htp/horticulture/wine/winex.pdf.
7   http://www.fas.usda.gov/info/agexporter/1999/italy.html.
8   IFPI, Recording Industry Numbers in 2001, http://www.ifpi.org/site-content/press/20010906.html.

9   Ibid. http://www.ifpi.org/site-content/library/page09riin.pdf.

10   *Screen Digest.* www.screendigest.com

11   'A World View', *The Economist*, 27 November 1997.

12   Quoted in 'A World Empire by Other Means', *The Economist*, 20 December 2001.

13   Amartya Sen, *Development As Freedom*, Oxford University Press, 1999, p. 243.

14   Noreena Hertz, *The Silent Takeover*, William Heinemann, 2001.

15   Anthony Giddens, Reith Lectures, 1999.

16   Polly Toynbee, 'Who's Afraid of Global Culture?'. In *On the Edge: Living with Global Capitalism*, eds. Will Hutton and Anthony Giddens.

17   John Stuart Mill, *Principles of Political Economy*, 1848, pp. 581-2, in ibid.

18   John Micklethwait, 'Survey on the United States', *The Economist*, 9 March 2000.

19   Samuel Huntington, 'The Clash of Civilisations?', *Foreign Affairs*, vol. 72, 1993. The arguments were explored at greater length in *The Clash of Civilisations and the Remaking of World Order*, Simon & Schuster, 1996.

20   Francis Fukuyama, *The End of History and the Last Man*, Penguin, 1992.

21   Mario Vargas Llosa, 'The Culture of Liberty', *Foreign Policy*, February 2000.

Chapter Thirteen: A Different World

1   Philip Stephens, 'A Poor Case for Globalisation', *Financial Times*, 17 August 2001.

2   www.twinplantnews.com (Twin Plant News).

3   'Between Here and There', *The Economist*, 5 July 2001.

4   Thomas Friedman, *The Lexus and the Olive Tree*.

5   Amartya Sen, *Development as Freedom*.

6   World Bank, *Global Economic Prospects*, 2001.

7   Patrick Messerlin, 'Measuring the Costs of Protection in Europe', Institute for International Economics, 2000.

8   Daniel T. Griswold, 'No: Immigrants Have Enriched American Culture and Enhanced our Influence in the World', Cato Institute, 18 February 2002.

9   Emerging–Markets Eminent–Persons Group Report, *Rebuilding the International Financial Architecture*, October 2001.

10   Neil McCulloch, Alan Winters and Xavier Citera, *Trade Liberalisation and Poverty: A Handbook*, CEPR, 2001

Bibliography

It is impossible to list all the sources for this book. Even before I started researching it, I had read countless articles and papers about globalisation when working for *The Economist* and the World Trade Organisation, as well as at university.

Even so, among journalistic sources, I relied most on *The Economist* and the *Financial Times*, as well as, to a lesser extent, on the *Wall Street Journal Europe* and *International Herald Tribune*.

The best official sources on globalisation are the websites of the World Bank, the Organisation for Economic Cooperation and Development (OECD), the World Trade Organisation (WTO) and the International Monetary Fund (IMF). The United Nations Development Programme's (UNDP) *Human Development Report* and United Nations Conference on Trade and Development's (UNCTAD) *World Investment Report* are also very useful.

The National Bureau of Economic Research website is also invaluable, as is that of the Institute for International Economics.

Many of the academic papers I used had not been published when I received them; some may have been since.

Among the books I read were:

Barringer, William and Pierce, Kenneth. *Paying the Price for Big Steel* (Washington DC: American Institute for International Steel, 2000)

Beck, Ulrich. *What is Globalization?* (Cambridge: Polity, 2000)

Bhagwati, Jagdish and Hudec, Robert. *Fair Trade and Harmonization: Prerequisites for Free Trade?* (Cambridge, MA: MIT Press, 1996)

Buchanan, Patrick. *The Great Betrayal: How American Sovereignty and Social Justice Are Being Sacrificed to the Gods of the Global Economy* (New York: Little, Brown, 1998)

Burtless, Gary et al. *Globaphobia: Confronting Fears about Open Trade* (Washington DC: Brookings Institution Press, 1998)

Coyle, Diane. *The Weightless World: Strategies for Managing the Digital Economy* (Oxford: Capstone, 1997)

Davies, Norman. *Europe: A History* (Oxford: OUP, 1996)

Destler, M. L. *American Trade Politics* (Washington DC: Institute for International Economics, 1995)

Edwards, Michael. *NGO Rights and Responsibilities: A New Deal for Global Governance* (London: Demos, 2000)

Elliott, Larry and Atkinson, Dan. *The Age of Insecurity* (London: Verso, 1998)

Forrester, Viviane. *The Economic Horror* (Cambridge: Polity, 1999)

Freedland, Jonathan. *Bring Home The Revolution: The Case for a British Republic* (London: Fourth Estate, 1998)

Friedman, Thomas. *The Lexus and the Olive Tree* (London: HarperCollins paperback, 2000)

Fukuyama, Francis. *The End of History and the Last Man* (London: Penguin, 1992)

Gilpin, Robert. *The Challenge of Global Capitalism: The World Economy in the 21st Century* (Princeton: Princeton University Press, 2000)

Graham, Edward. *Fighting the Wrong Enemy: Antiglobal Activists and Multinational Enterprises* (Washington DC: Institute for International Economics, 2000)

Gray, John. *False Dawn: The Delusions of Global Capitalism* (London: Granta, 1998)

Hardt, Michael and Negri, Antonio. *Empire* (Cambridge, MA: Harvard University Press, 2000)

Hayek, Friedrich. *The Road to Serfdom* (London: Routledge, 1944)

Held, David et al. *Global Transformations: Politics, Economics and Culture* (Cambridge: Polity, 1999)

Henderson, David. *The MAI Affair: A Story and Its Lessons* (London: Royal Institute of International Affairs, 1999)

Hertz, Noreena. *The Silent Takeover: Global Capitalism and the Death of Democracy* (London: William Heinemann, 2001)

Hirst, Paul and Thompson, Graham. *Globalization in Question* (Cambridge: Polity, 1999)

Hobsbawm, Eric. *The Age of Revolution 1789–1848* (London: Weidenfeld & Nicolson, 1962)

—— *The Age of Capital 1848–1875* (London: Weidenfeld & Nicolson, 1975)

—— *The Age of Empire 1875–1914* (London: Weidenfeld & Nicolson, 1987)

—— *The Age of Extremes: The Short Twentieth Century 1914–1991* (London: Abacus, 1995)

Huntington, Samuel. *The Clash of Civilisations and the Remaking of World Order* (New York: Simon and Schuster, 1996)

Hutton, Will and Giddens, Anthony, eds. *On the Edge: Living with Global Capitalism* (London: Jonathan Cape, 2000)

International Labour Organisation. *Labour and Social Issues Relating to Export Processing Zones* (Geneva: ILO, 1998)

Irwin, Douglas. *Against the Tide: An Intellectual History of Free Trade* (Princeton: Princeton University Press, 1996)

Kapstein, Ethan. *Sharing the Wealth: Workers and the World Economy* (New York: W.W. Norton, 1999)

Keynes, John Maynard. *The Economic Consequences of the Peace* (London: Macmillan, 1919)

—— *The General Theory of Employment, Interest and Money* (London: Royal Economic Society, 1936)

Kindleberger, Charles. *Manias, Panics, and Crashes: A History of Financial Crises* (New York: John Wiley, 2000)

Klein, Naomi. *No Logo* (London: Flamingo, 2000)

Kletzer, Lori. *Job Loss from Imports: Measuring the Costs* (Washington DC: Institute for International Economics, 2000)

Krugman, Paul. *Rethinking International Trade* (Cambridge, MA: MIT Press, 1990)

—— *Pop Internationalism* (Cambridge, MA: MIT Press, 1996)

—— *The Return of Depression Economics* (London: Allen Lane The Penguin Press, 1999)

Landes, David. *The Wealth and Poverty of Nations: Why Some Are So Rich and Some So Poor* (London: Little, Brown, 1998)

Lim, Wonhyuk. *The Origin and Evolution of the Korean Economic System* (Seoul: Korea Development Institute, 2000)

Lloyd, John. *The Protest Ethic: How the Anti-Globalisation Movement Challenges Social Democracy* (London: Demos, 2001)

Luttwak, Edward. *Turbo-Capitalism: Winners and Losers in the Global Economy* (London: Weidenfeld & Nicolson, 1998)

Mann, Theodore. *Foreign Direct Investment and Development* (Washington DC: Institute for International Economics, 1998)

Marx, Karl and Engels, Friedrich. *The Communist Manifesto* (first published 1848)

McCulloch, Neil et al. *Trade Liberalisation and Poverty: A Handbook* (London: Centre for Economic Policy Research, 2001)

Messerlin, Patrick. *Measuring the Costs of Protection in Europe* (Washington DC: Institute for International Economics, 2000)

Micklethwait, John and Wooldridge, Adrian. *A Future Perfect: The Challenge and Hidden Promise of Globalisation* (London: Random House, 2000)

Monbiot, George. *Captive State: The Corporate Takeover of Britain* (London: Macmillan, 2000)

Moore, Mike. *A Brief History of the Future: Citizenship of the Millennium* (Christchurch: Shoal Bay Press, 1998)

O'Rourke, Kevin and Williamson, Jeffrey. *Globalization and History: The Evolution of a Nineteenth-Century Atlantic Economy* (Cambridge, MA: MIT Press, 1999)

Obstfeld, Maurice and Taylor A. M. *Global Capital Markets: Integration, Crisis and Growth* (Cambridge: Cambridge University Press, 1999)

OECD. *Trade, Employment and Labour Standards: A Study of Core Workers' Rights and International Trade* (Paris: OECD, 1996)

—— *Employment Outlook July 1997* (Paris: OECD, 1997)

—— *Open Markets Matter: The Benefits of Trade and Investment Liberalisation* (Paris: OECD, 1998)

—— *Measuring Globalisation: The Role of Multinationals in OECD Economies.* (Paris: OECD, 1999)

—— *Agricultural Policies in OECD Countries: Monitoring and Evaluation* (Paris: OECD, 2001)

—— *Trends in International Migration* (Paris: OECD, 2001)

—— *Economic Outlook June 2001* (Paris: OECD, 2001)

Ohmae, Kenichi. *The Borderless World* (New York: HarperBusiness, 1990)

—— *The End of the Nation State: The Rise of Regional Economics* (New York: Free Press, 1995)

Oman, Charles. *Policy Competition for Foreign Direct Investment: A Study of Competition among Governments to Attract FDI* (Paris: OECD, 2000)

Polanyi, Karl. *The Great Transformation: The Political and Economic Origins of Our Time.* (first published 1944)

Polo, Marco. *The Travels of Marco Polo*

Porter, Roger and Sauvé, Pierre, eds. *Seattle, the WTO, and the Future of the Multilateral Trading System* (Harvard: Harvard University Press, June 2000)

Sassen, Saskia. *Globalization and Its Discontents* (New York: The New Press, 1998)

Rodrik, Dani. *Has Globalization Gone Too Far?* (Washington DC: Institute for International Economics, 1997)

Rosen, Daniel. *Behind the Open Door* (Washington DC: Institute for International Economics, 1999)

SaKong, Il. *Korea in the World Economy* (Washington DC: Institute for International Economics, 1993)

Sen, Amartya. *Development As Freedom* (Oxford: Oxford University Press, 1999)

Smith, Adam. *The Wealth of Nations: An Inquiry into the Nature and Causes* (first published 1776)

Soros, George. *Open Society: Reforming Global Capitalism* (New York: PublicAffairs, 2000)

Tanzi, Vito and Schuknecht, Ludger. *Public Spending in the 20th Century: A Global Perspective* (Cambridge: Cambridge University Press, 2000)

Turner, Adair. *Just Capital: The Liberal Economy* (London: Macmillan, 2001)

UNCTAD. *World Investment Report* (Geneva: UNCTAD, 2001)

UNDP. *Human Development Report* 2001 (New York: Oxford University Press, 2001)

Wallach, Lori and Sforza, Michelle. *Whose Trade Organization? Corporate Globalization and the Erosion of Democracy* (Washington DC: Public Citizen, 1999)

Ward, Halina and Brack, Duncan. *Trade, Investment and the Environment*

(London: Royal Institute of International Affairs, 2000)

World Bank. *Trade Blocs* (New York: Oxford University Press, 2000)

— *World Development Report 2000/1* (New York: Oxford University Press, 2001)

— *World Development Indicators 2001* (Washington DC: World Bank, 2001)

— *Global Economic Prospects* (Washington DC: World Bank, 2001)

— *Globalization, Growth and Poverty* (Washington DC: World Bank, 2001)

WTO. *The Legal Texts: The Results of the Uruguay Round of Multilateral Trade Negotations* (Cambridge: Cambridge University Press, 1999)

WTO. *Trade and Environment* (Geneva: WTO, 1999)

— *International Trade Statistics* (Geneva: WTO, 2001)

— *Market Access: Unfinished Business* (Geneva: WTO, 2001)

Yergin, Daniel and Stanislaw, Joseph. *The Commanding Heights: The Battle Between Government and the Marketplace That Is Remaking the Modern World* (New York: Touchstone, 1999)

Among the many articles:

Bhagwati, Jagdish. 'The Miracle That Did Happen: Understanding East Asia in Comparative Perspective', unpublished, May 1996

— 'Play It Again, Sam: A New Look at Trade and Wages', unpublished, March 1997

— 'Why Free Capital Mobility May Be Hazardous to Your Health: Lessons from the Latest Financial Crisis', unpublished, November 1998

— Free Trade in the 21st Century: Managing Viruses, Phobias and Social Agendas, unpublished, April 1999

— 'Free Trade Today: Three Lectures', unpublished, November 2000

Blanchflower, David. 'Globalization and the Labor Market', unpublished, September 2000

Bordo, Michael et al. 'Is Globalization Today Really Different than Globalization a Hundred Years Ago?', National Bureau of Economic Research working paper 7195, June 1999

Bourguignon, François and Morrisson, Christian. 'The Size Distribution of Income Among World Citizens: 1820–1990', unpublished, DELTA, Paris

Brynjolfsson, Erik and Smith, Michael. 'The Great Equalizer? Customer

Choice Behavior at Internet Shopbots', unpublished, May 2000 (http://e-commerce.mit.edu/papers/tge)

Crafts, Nicholas. 'Globalization and Growth in the Twentieth Century', IMF working paper WP/00/44, March 2000

Deardorff, Alan and Stern, Robert. 'What the Public Should Know about Globalization and the World Trade Organization', Research Seminar in International Economics working paper, University of Michigan, July 2000

Dollar, David. 'Globalisation, Inequality and Poverty since 1980', World Bank, November 2001

—— and Kraay, Aart. 'Growth Is Good for the Poor', World Bank, March 2000

—— 'Trade, Growth and Poverty', World Bank, March 2001

Easterlin, Richard. 'The Worldwide Standard of Living since 1800', *Journal of Economic Perspectives*, winter 2000; vol. 14; no. 1

Edwards, Sebastian. 'Openness, Productivity and Growth: What Do We Really Know?', National Bureau of Economic Research working paper 5978, March 1997

'Efficiency, Equity and Legitimacy: The Multilateral Trading System at the Millennium', papers presented at a conference at the Kennedy School of Government, Harvard on 1 June 2000

Feldstein, Martin. 'Aspects of Global Economic Integration: Outlook for the Future', National Bureau of Economic Research working paper 7899, September 2000

Finger, J. Michael and Schuknecht, Ludger. 'Market Access Advances and Retreats: The Uruguay Round and Beyond', unpublished, September 1999

Fournier, Susan. 'Introducing New Coke', Harvard Business School case studies, 1999

Frankel, Jeffrey. 'Globalization of the Economy', National Bureau of Economic Research working paper 7858, August 2000

Frankel, Jeffrey and Romer, David. 'Does Trade Cause Growth?', *American Economic Review*, June 1998

Freeman, Richard. 'Single-Peaked vs. Diversified Capitalism: The Relation Between Economic Institutions and Outcomes', National Bureau of Economic Research working paper 7556, February 2000

Ghemawat, Pankaj and Ghadar, Fariborz. 'The Dubious Logic of Global Megamergers,' *Harvard Business Review*, July–August 2000

Gillespie, James and Low, Patrick. *'Free Trade at the Border by a Date Certain?'*, unpublished, July 1999

de Grauwe, Paul and Camerman, Filip. 'How Big Are the Big Multinational Companies?' unpublished, January 2002

Griswold, Daniel. 'Trade, Jobs, and Manufacturing: Why (Almost All) US Workers Should Welcome Imports' (Washington DC: Cato Institute, 1999)

—— 'No: Immigrants have Enriched American Culture and Enhanced our Influence in the World' (Washington DC: Cato Institute, 2002)

Grossman, Gene and Krueger, Alan. 'Economic Growth and the Environment, National Bureau of Economic Research', National Bureau of Economic Research working paper 4634, February 1994

Hoekman, Bernard et al. 'Tariff Peaks in the QUAD and Least Developed Country Exports', World Bank draft paper, January 2001

Keohane, Robert and Nye, Joseph. 'Globalization: What's New? What's Not? (And So What?)', *Foreign Policy*, spring 2000

Keohane, Robert and Nye, Joseph. 'The Club Model of Multilateral Cooperation and the World Trade Organisation: Problems of Democratic Legitimacy'. unpublished, June 2000

Knetter, Michael and Slaughter, Matthew. 'Measuring Market-Product Integration', National Bureau of Economic Research working paper 6969, February 1999

Krueger, Anne, ed. 'The WTO As an International Organization' (London: University of Chicago Press, 1998)

Krugman, Paul. 'Crises: the Price of Globalization?', unpublished, August 2000

Lindert, Peter and Williamson, Jeffrey. 'Does Globalization Make the World More Unequal?', National Bureau of Economic Research working paper 8228, April 2001

Lucas, Caroline and Hines, Colin. 'Stopping The Great Food Swap – Relocalising Europe's Food Supply' (Brussels: European Parliament, March 2001)

Lukas, Aaron. WTO Report Card III: 'Globalization and Developing Countries' (Washington DC: Cato Institute, June 2000)

Maskus, Keith. 'Regulatory Standards in the WTO: Comparing Intellectual Property Rights with Competition Policy, Environmental Protection, and Core Labour Standards', January 2000

Mazur, Jay. 'Labour's New Internationalism', *Foreign Affairs* January–February 2000, vol. 79, no. 1

Mussa, Michael. 'Factors Driving Global Economic Integration', unpublished, August 2000

O'Rourke, Kevin 'Globalization and Inequality: Historical Trends', National Bureau of Economic Research working paper 8339, June 2001

—— and Williamson, Jeffrey. 'When Did Globalization Begin?', National Bureau of Economic Research working paper 7632, April 2000

—— 'After Columbus: Explaining the Global Trade Boom, 1500–1800', National Bureau of Economic Research working paper 8186, March 2001

Obstfeld, Maurice. 'The Global Capital Market: Benefactor or Menace?', National Bureau of Economic Research working paper 6559, May 1998

OECD. 'International Trade and Core Labour Standards', September 2000

Ostry, Sylvia. 'Globalisation and the Nation State: Erosion from Above', unpublished, February 1998

—— 'Convergence and Sovereignty: Policy Scope for Compromise?', unpublished, July 1998.

—— 'The Deepening Integration of the Global Economy', unpublished, January 1999

Ostry, Sylvia. 'Globalisation and Sovereignty', unpublished, March 1999

—— 'Intellectual Property in the WTO: Major Issues in the Millennium Round', unpublished, April 1999

—— 'Globalization: What Does It Mean?', unpublished, October 1999

—— 'Regional Dominoes and the WTO: Building Blocks or Boomerang?', unpublished, November 1999

—— 'The Future of the World Trading System', unpublished, November 1999

—— 'The WTO After Seattle: Something's Happening Here, What It Is Ain't Exactly Clear', unpublished, January 2001.

—— 'Global Integration: Currents and Counter-Currents', unpublished, May 2001

—— 'The Future of the World Trade System', unpublished, October 2001

—— 'Why Has Globalization Become a Bad Word', unpublished, October 2001

Otsuki, Tsunehiro et al. 'Saving Two in a Billion: A Case Study to Quantify the Trade Effect of European Food Safety Standards on African Exports', World Bank, 2000

Oxfam, Loaded Against the Poor (Oxford: Oxfam, 1999)

Riker, David and Brainard, Lael. 'US Multinationals and Competition from Low-Wage Countries', National Bureau of Economic Research working paper 5959, March 1997

Rodriguez, Francisco and Rodrik, Dani. 'Trade Policy and Economic Growth: A Skeptic's Guide to the Cross-national Evidence', Centre for European Policy Research discussion paper 2143, May 1999

Sachs, Jeffrey and Warner, Andrew. 'Economic Reform and the Process of Global Integration', Brookings Papers on Economic Activity, 1995

Slaughter, Matthew and Swagel, Phillip. 'The Effect of Globalisation on Wages in the Advanced Economies', IMF working paper WP/97/43, April 1997

Srinivasan, T. N. amd Bhagwati, Jagdish. 'Outward Orientation and Development: Are Revisionists Right?', unpublished, September 1999

Stevens, Christopher and Kennan, Jane. 'The Impact of the EU's 'Everything But Arms' proposal; a report to Oxfam' (London: Institute for Development Studies, 2001)

Tanzi, Vito. Globalisation, 'Technological Developments and the Work of Fiscal Termites', IMF working paper 00/181, November 2000

Winters, L Alan. 'Trade Policy and Poverty: What Are The Links?', Centre for European Policy Research discussion paper 2382, February 2000

Wolf, Martin. 'Will the Nation State Survive Globalization?', Foreign Affairs, January–February 2001, vol. 80, no. 1

Index